Everyman, I will go with thee, and be thy guide,
In thy most need to go by thy side.

This is No. 451 of Everyman's Library. A list of authors and their works in this series will be found at the end of this volume. The publishers will be pleased to send freely to all applicants a separate, annotated list of the Library.

J. M. DENT & SONS LIMITED
10–13 BEDFORD STREET LONDON W.C.2

E. P. DUTTON & CO. INC.
286–302 FOURTH AVENUE
NEW YORK

EVERYMAN'S LIBRARY
EDITED BY ERNEST RHYS

REFERENCE

ATLAS OF ANCIENT AND CLASSICAL GEOGRAPHY

ATLAS OF ANCIENT AND CLASSICAL GEOGRAPHY

LONDON: J. M. DENT & SONS LTD.
NEW YORK: E. P. DUTTON & CO. INC.

Made in Great Britain
at The Temple Press Letchworth
and decorated by Eric Ravilious
for
J. M. Dent & Sons Ltd.
Aldine House Bedford St. London
First published in this edition 1907
Last reprinted 1942

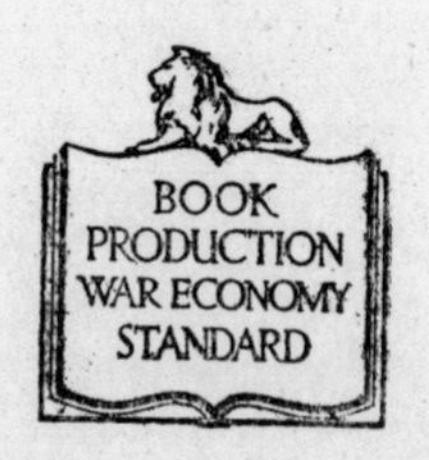

THE PAPER AND BINDING OF
THIS BOOK CONFORM TO THE
AUTHORIZED ECONOMY STANDARDS

INTRODUCTION

DR. BUTLER'S atlas, which for a time filled the place in the series taken by this volume, has only been laid aside in response to a demand for better maps, clearer in detail. The new maps are designed to lighten the search for the place-names and the landmarks they contain by a freer spacing and lettering of the towns, fortresses, harbours, rivers, and so forth, likely to be needed by readers of the classical writers and the histories of Greece and Rome. The pages too have been so arranged as to save the unfolding and refolding of each chart as it is used, while the range of subjects has been notably extended in order to show the development of the old science of geography, and to illustrate the wars and changes of frontier and rise and fall of states and empires. We begin with the voyage of the Argonauts, and the world of Homer, representing a Europe on whose outer western rim these islands lay in Cimmerian darkness, with no western hemisphere of the future Americas beyond them. The eastern survey of Herodotus, and the Eratosthenes' map which ranges from Ultima Thule in the far north to Arabia Deserta and the Indian limits, carry the record to the point where the live contact between geography and ancient history occurs. It is seen in the voyage of Nearchus who sailed as far south-east as the mouth of the Indus in 325 B.C.; and Strabo and Ptolemy bring us to the partition of the old world at the beginning of the Christian era. It was in the library of Alexandria that Eratosthenes wrote the work which began the real mapping out of the globe with the lines of latitude and longitude.

Turning to the more special maps we realize in that of Greece, as Professor Bury has shown us, how vitally its physical features affected its history and its place among the nations. We see how its ridged headland, broken by a great sea rift, and how the heights of Olympus, Ossa, and Pelion, and those of Eubœa and the island chain beyond, and how again Epirus and the Peloponnesus, gave the land its mountain barriers. But finally it was the sea decided the fate of the people; they were fairly driven to seek their outlet and their defence on its waters; and the decisive factor was the Ægean, which became in a sense the fluid axis of Greek conquest, commerce, and colonial life. In the same way, it is the map that makes us aware of the effect of position in the case of an old rival to Rome like Carthage. The line-maps of the cities include Syracuse, Thebes, Babylon, Jerusalem, Tyre, Pompeii; and among the battlefields are Marathon and Salamis, Issus and Thermopylæ.

The second half of this volume consists of an Historical Gazetteer, which is necessary to convert the map into a living document. In company with the historians, Herodotus, Thucydides, Josephus, and Arrian, with the Greek traveller, Pausanias, with the geographer, Strabo, we are able to view historic places with something approaching a contemporary feeling. This is enhanced by the work of the modern archæologists. Excavations in the last hundred years, some of the most important being in the last fifty years, have verified the ancient travel-books and enabled us to reconstruct the narrative of the historians. The results of archæological research up to the time of the historian, Grote, the celebrated archæologist, Colonel

Leake, and the German geographer, Kiepert, have been embodied in Dr. William Smith's monumental dictionaries on which the present volume has been based. But while any contribution to ancient geography must acknowledge this indebtedness, the later work of Schliemann at Mycenæ, of Sir William Ramsay in Asia Minor, of Professor Maü at Pompeii, of M. Jondet at Alexandria, of the British School at Sparta, the American School at Athens, and the German School at Olympia—to cite only a few examples—has been taken into good account.

The English spelling of Greek names presents, as always, a difficult problem. The maps, for the sake of uniformity, are compiled with indications in Latin, but in the historical section, for the benefit of those using this volume in conjunction with Greek texts, it has been thought better to keep the Greek forms as far as is conformable with English usage. In spelling Greek proper names, therefore, especially place-names, the Greek forms have been retained, except where there is an anglicized equivalent or a form, derived from the Latin, which has become so English that to dispense with it would be a pedantry. With this proviso, the Greek terminations, *os* and *on*, have been preferred, and the method of transliteration has been to use the English diphthongs *æ* and *œ* for the Greek *ai* and *oi*; *ou*, or simply *u*, for the Greek *ou*; while the diphthong *ei* has been retained, except in such names as 'Alexandria', where the single *i*, generally of doubtful quantity in English, has been consecrated by usage. In proper names also the English *c* has been used for the Greek kappa, although, in some instances, the *k* has been retained to ensure a similarity with the hard pronunciation of the Greek. In Greek words other than proper names, and this includes personifications and epithets of deities, the Greek form has been transliterated, letter for letter, this being in accordance with the practice of the Society for the Promotion of Hellenic Studies. There is a growing movement in Greek scholarship in favour of retaining the Greek forms as far as possible, but consistency in this matter is admittedly impossible. Entirely to latinize leads one into inevitable anomalies, while to transliterate all names strictly from the Greek conflicts with English literary traditions. A middle course is therefore advisable, allowing a wide latitude, but keeping, it is hoped, something of the feeling of the Greek.

We need but add that in the preparation of this Classical Atlas, the expert services of Dr. Bartholomew have been of the greatest assistance, as in the modern atlases in Everyman's Library.

Other Atlases in Everyman's Library are:

496. A Literary and Historical Atlas of Europe
553. A Literary and Historical Atlas of America
633. A Literary and Historical Atlas of Asia
662. A Literary and Historical Atlas of Africa and Australasia

CONTENTS

COLOURED MAPS

LINE MAPS

THE ATLAS
OF
ANCIENT AND CLASSICAL GEOGRAPHY

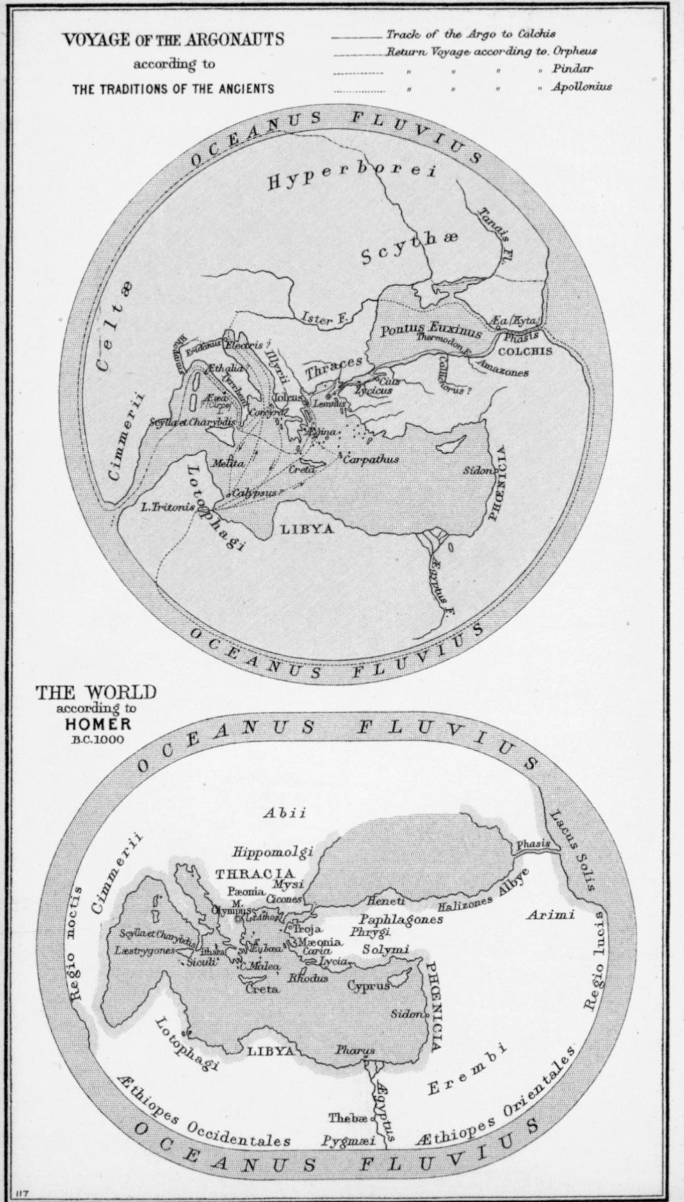

John Bartholomew & Son, Ltd. Edinburgh

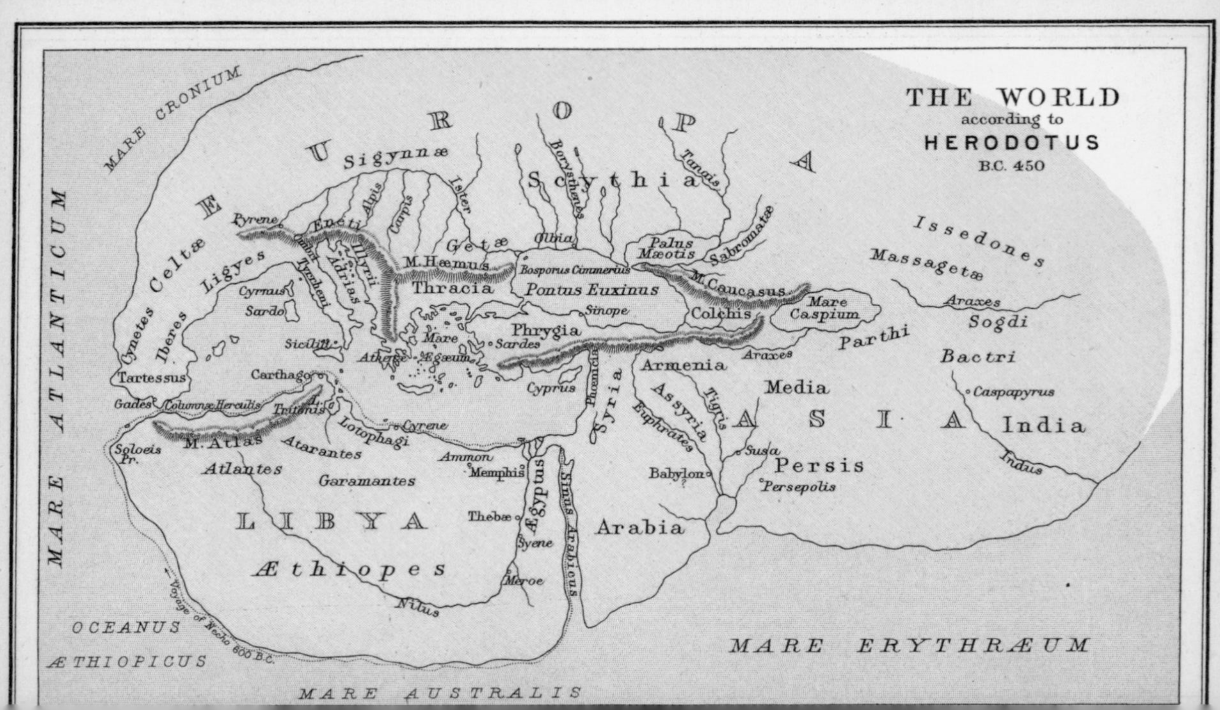
THE WORLD
according to
HERODOTUS
B.C. 450
EUROPA
ASIA
LIBYA
MARE CRONIUM
MARE ATLANTICUM
OCEANUS ÆTHIOPICUS
MARE AUSTRALIS
MARE ERYTHRÆUM
Sigynnæ
Scythia
Issedones
Massagetæ
Sogdi
Bactri
India
Caspapyrus
Indus
Araxes
Parthi
Mare Caspium
M. Caucasus
Colchis
Palus Mæotis
Sabromatæ
Tanais
Borysthenes
Olbia
Bosporus Cimmerius
Pontus Euxinus
Sinope
Phrygia
Sardes
Getæ
Ister
Carpis
Alpis
Eneti
Pyrene
Umbri
Illyrii
Adrias
Tyrrheni
M. Hæmus
Thracia
Mare Ægæum
Athenæ
Cyprus
Phœnicia
Syria
Armenia
Assyria
Tigris
Euphrates
Media
Persis
Susa
Persepolis
Babylon
Arabia
Sinus Arabicus
Ægyptus
Memphis
Thebæ
Syene
Meroe
Nilus
Ammon
Cyrene
Lotophagi
Atarantes
Garamantes
Atlantes
Æthiopes
M. Atlas
Tritonis
Carthago
Sicilia
Sardo
Cyrnus
Ligyes
Celtæ
Iberes
Cynetes
Tartessus
Gades
Columnæ Herculis
Soloeis Pr.
Voyage of Necho 600 B.C.

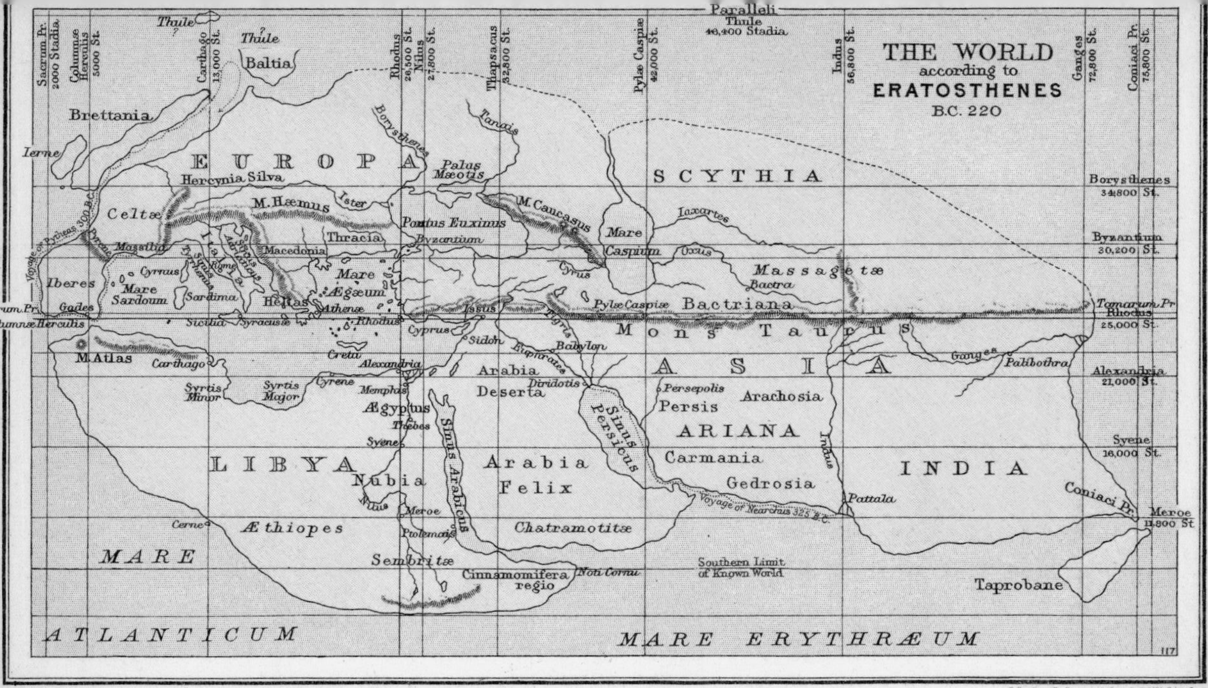

THE WORLD
according to
ERATOSTHENES
B.C. 220

3.

John Bartholomew & Son, Ltd. Edinburgh

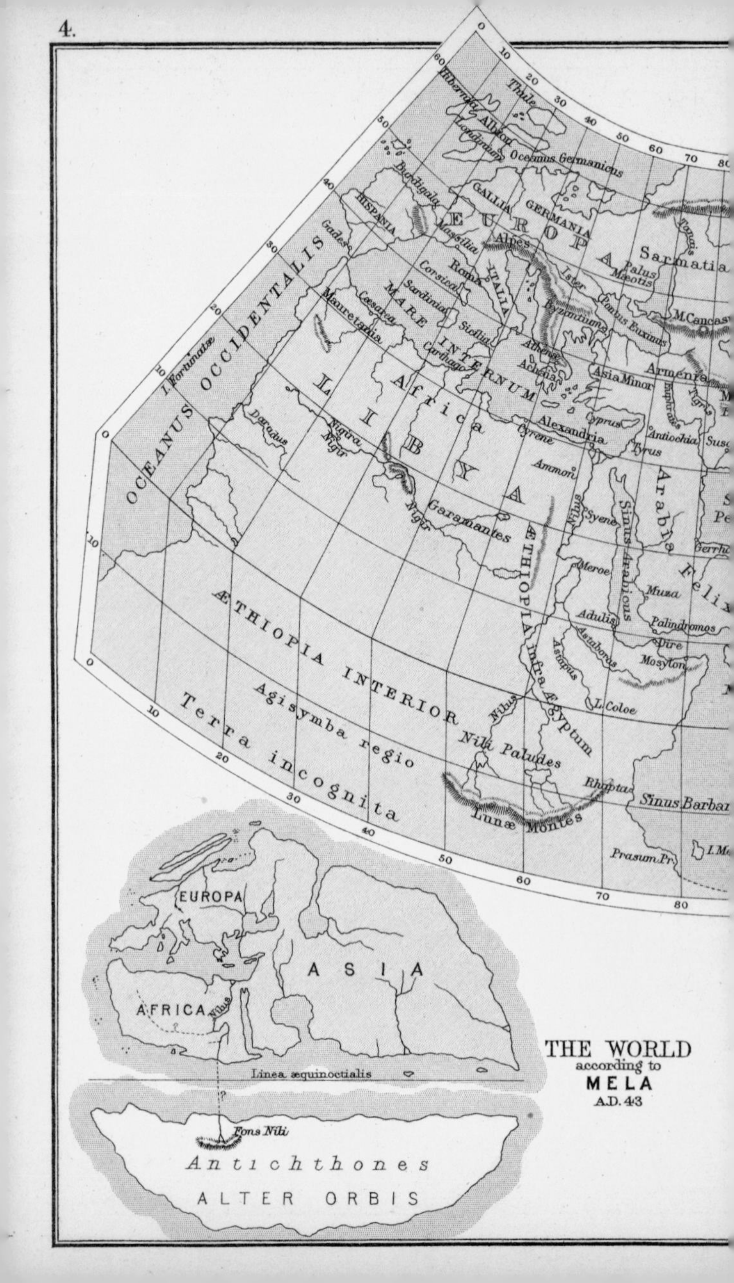

THE WORLD
according to
MELA
A.D. 43

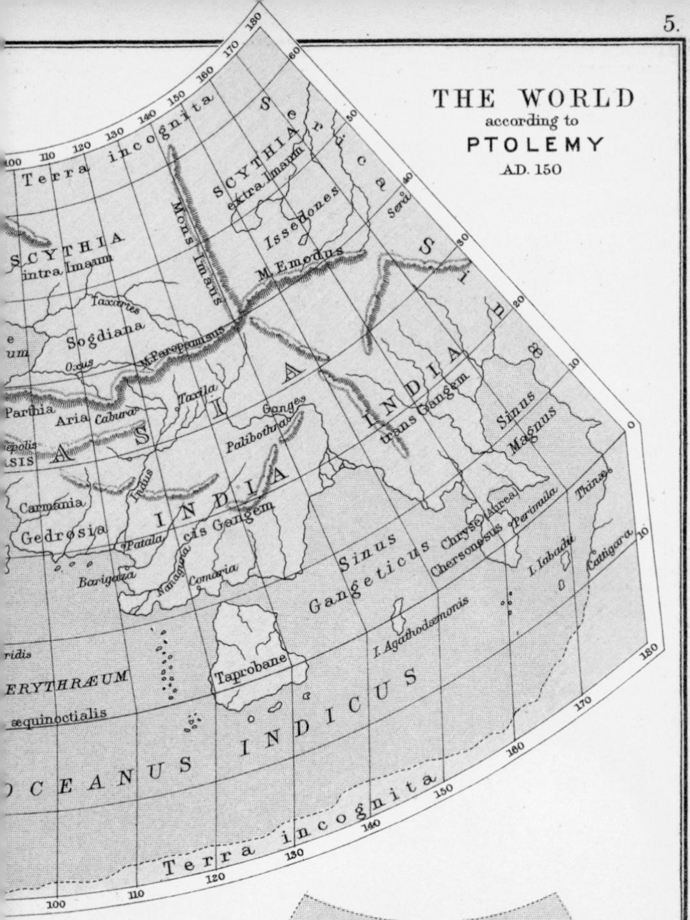

THE WORLD according to PTOLEMY A.D. 150

Terra incognita
SCYTHIA intra Imaum
SCYTHIA extra Imaum
Serica
Issedones
Sera
Mons Imaus
M. Emodus
Iaxartes
Sogdiana
Oxus
M. Paropamisus
Parthia
Aria
Cabura
Taxila
ASIA
Ganges
Palibothra
INDIA trans Gangem
Sinae
Sinus Magnus
Carmania
Gedrosia
Indus
INDIA cis Gangem
Patala
Barigaza
Nanaguna
Comaria
Sinus Gangeticus
Chryse (Aurea)
Chersonesus
Perimula
Thinae
I. Iabadii
Cattigara
I. Agathodaemonis
Taprobane
ERYTHRÆUM
æquinoctialis
OCEANUS INDICUS
Terra incognita

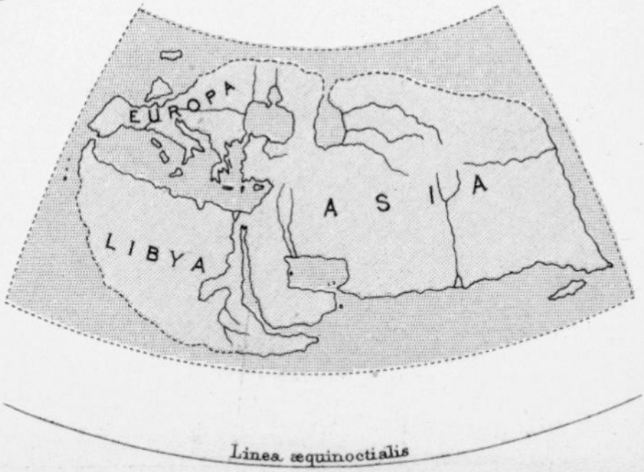

100 110 120 130 140 150 160 170 180
60 50 40 30 20 10 0 10

THE WORLD according to STRABO A.D. 18

EUROPA
ASIA
LIBYA
Linea æquinoctialis

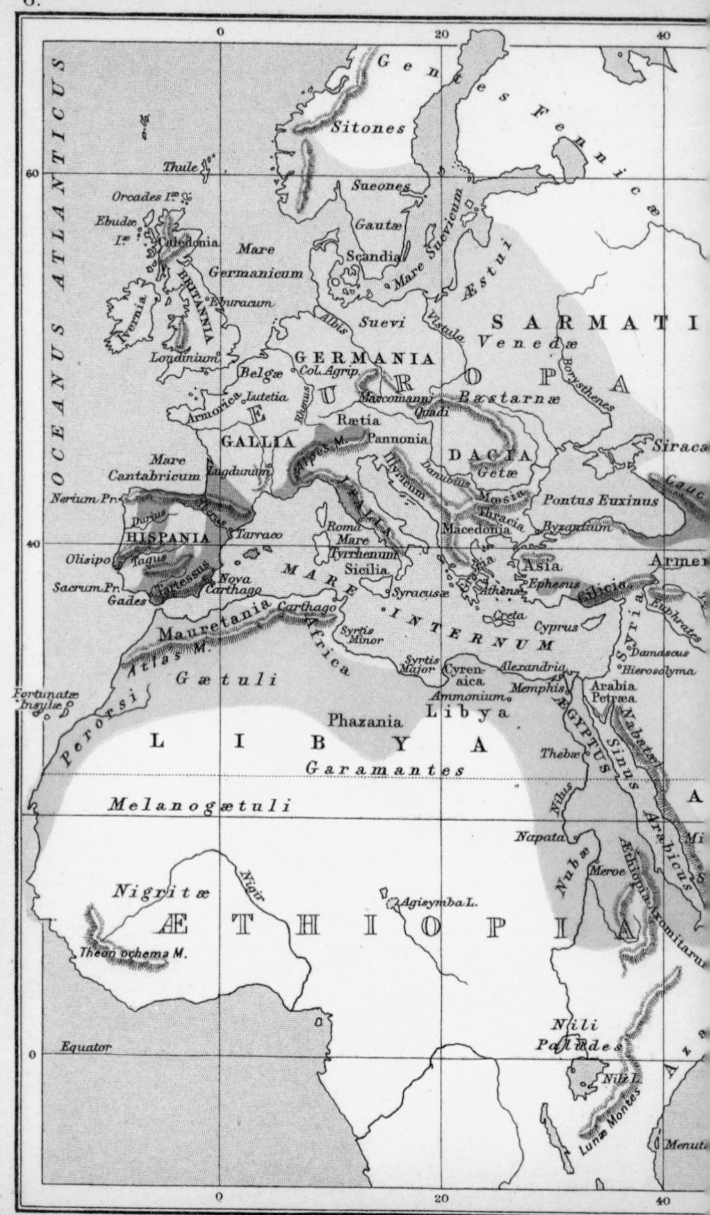
OCEANUS ATLANTICUS
Gentes Fennicæ
Sitones
Thule
Sueones
Orcades Iæ
Ebudæ Iæ
Caledonia
Gautæ
Scandia
Mare Germanicum
Mare Suevicum
Æstui
BRITANNIA
Ivernia
Eburacum
Londinium
Albis
Suevi
Vistula
SARMATI
Venedæ
GERMANIA
Col. Agrip.
Belgæ
EUROPA
Borysthenes
Marcomanni
Bastarnæ
Quadi
Armorica
Lutetia
Rhenus
Rætia
GALLIA
Alpes M.
Pannonia
DACIA
Getæ
Mare Cantabricum
Lugdunum
Illyricum
Danubius
Siraca
Cauc
Nerium Pr.
Iberus
ITALIA
Mœsia
Pontus Euxinus
Durius
Thracia
HISPANIA
Tarraco
Roma
Macedonia
Byzantium
Olisipo
Tagus
Mare Tyrrhenum
Asia
Armen
Tartessus
Sicilia
Sacrum Pr.
Nova Carthago
Syracusæ
Athenæ
Ephesus
Cilicia
Gades
MARE INTERNUM
Carthago
Creta
Cyprus
Euphrates
Mauretania
Africa
Syrtis Minor
Syria
Atlas M.
Damascus
Syrtis Major
Cyrenaica
Alexandria
Hierosolyma
Gætuli
Memphis
Arabia Petræa
Fortunatæ Insulæ
Ammonium
Libya
Perorsi
Phazania
LIBYA
ÆGYPTUS
Nabatæi
Thebæ
Sinus
Garamantes
Melanogætuli
A
Nilus
Arabicus
Napata
Nubæ
Meroe
Æthiopia Axomitarum
Nigritæ
Nigir
Agisymba L.
ÆTHIOPIA
Theon ochema M.
Nili Paludes
Equator
Nili L.
Lunæ Montes
Az
Menuth
0
20
40
60
0

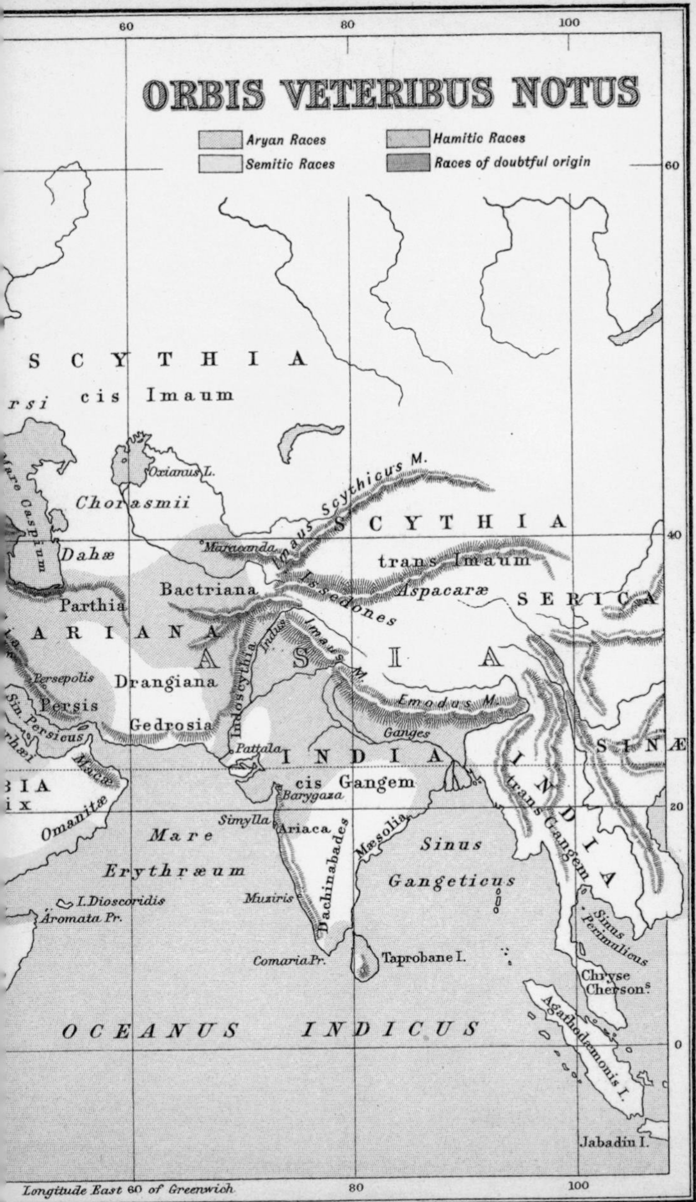

John Bartholomew & Son, Ltd. Edinburgh

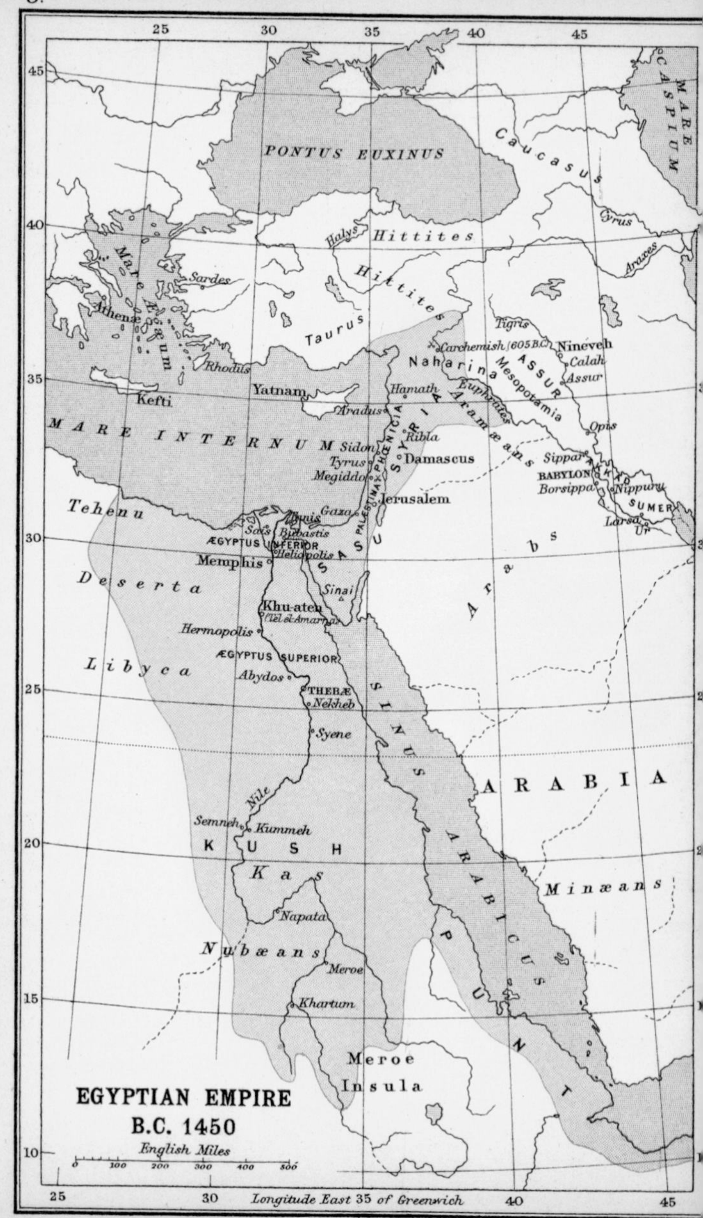
PONTUS EUXINUS
Caucasus
MARE CASPIUM
Cyrus
Araxes
Halys
Hittites
Hittites
Mare Ægæum
Sardes
Athenæ
Taurus
Tigris
Carchemish (605 B.C.)
Nineveh
Calah
Assur
ASSUR
Naharina
Mesopotamia
Rhodus
Yatnam
Kefti
Hamath
Euphrates
Aramæans
Aradus
MARE INTERNUM
Ribla
Opis
Sidon
Tyrus
Megiddo
PHOENICIA
SYRIA
Damascus
Sippar
AKKAD
BABYLON
Borsippa
Nippur
Jerusalem
SUMER
PALESTINA
Gaza
Tehenu
Tanis
Sais
Bubastis
Larsa
Ur
ÆGYPTUS INFERIOR
Heliopolis
SASU
Arabs
Memphis
Deserta
Sinai
Khu-aten
(Tel el Amarna)
Hermopolis
ÆGYPTUS SUPERIOR
Libyca
Abydos
THEBÆ
Nekheb
Syene
SINUS ARABICUS
ARABIA
Nile
Semneh
Kummeh
KUSH
Kas
Minæans
Napata
Nubæans
PUNT
Meroe
Khartum
Meroe Insula
EGYPTIAN EMPIRE
B.C. 1450
English Miles
0 100 200 300 400 500
Longitude East 35 of Greenwich
25 30 35 40 45
45 40 35 30 25 20 15 10

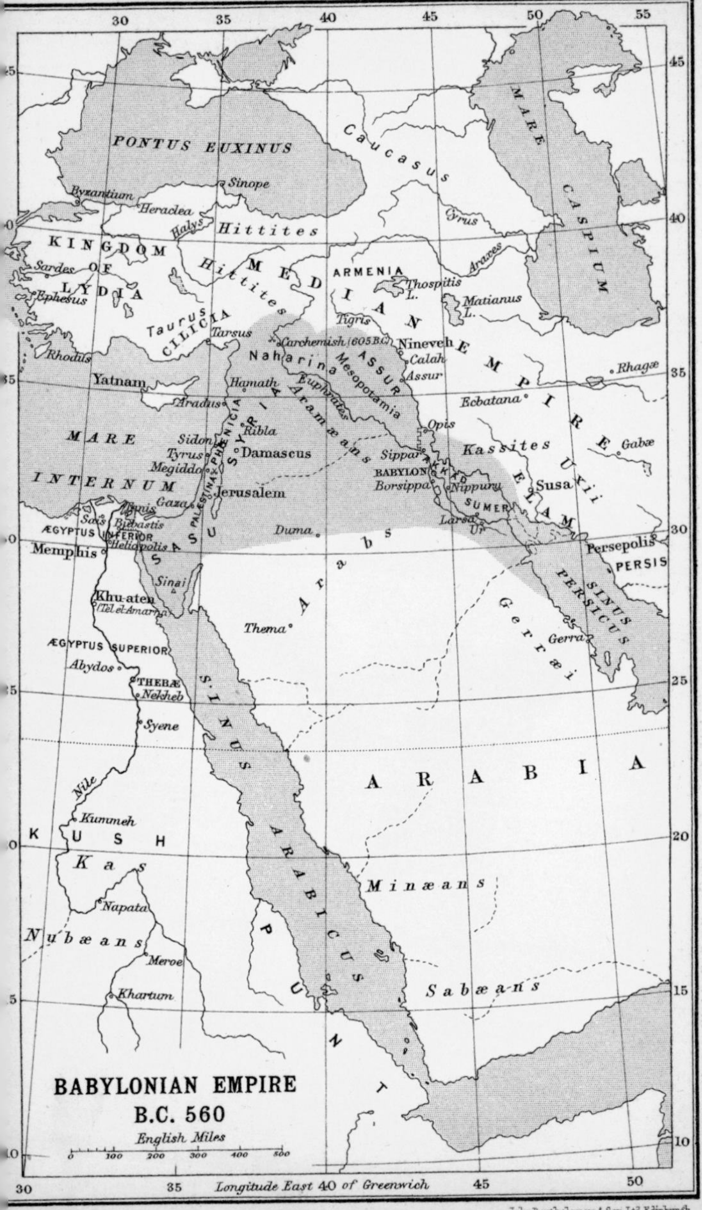

John Bartholomew & Son, Ltd, Edinburgh

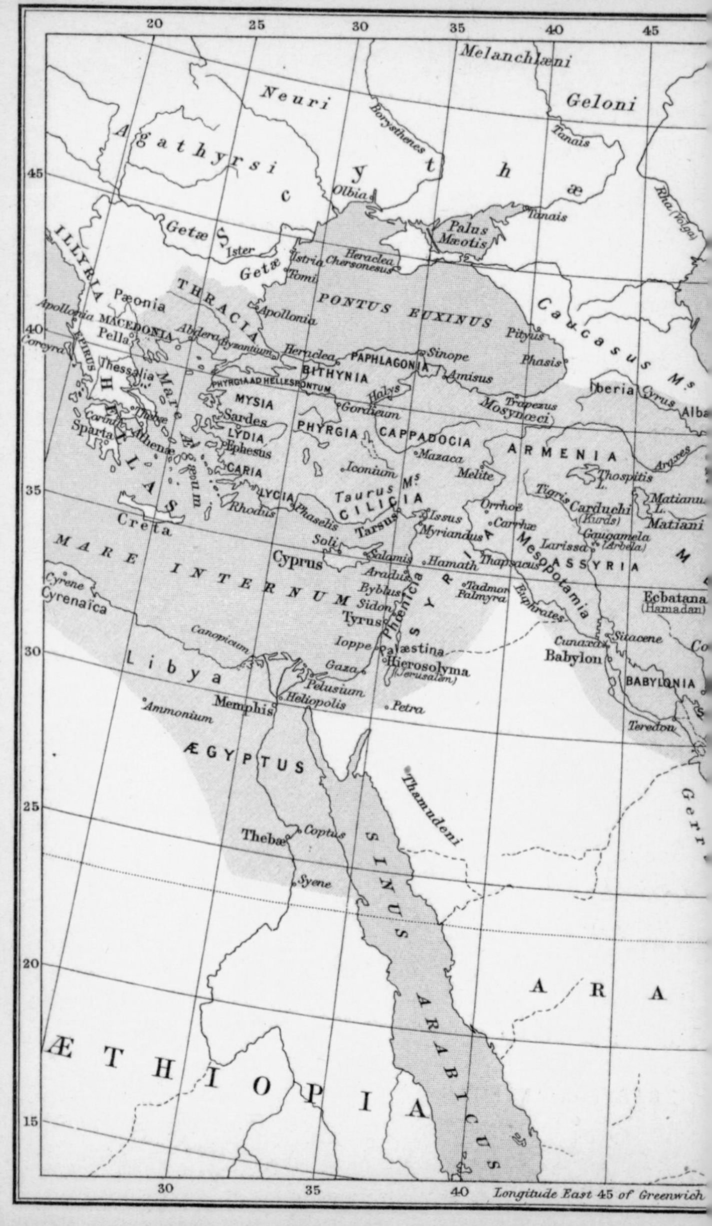
Melanchlæni
Neuri
Geloni
Agathyrsi
Scythæ
Borysthenes
Tanais
Olbia
Rha (Volga)
Getæ
Ister
Palus Mæotis
Tanais
Istria
Heraclea
Chersonesus
Tomi
ILLYRIA
THRACIA
Pæonia
Apollonia
MACEDONIA
PONTUS EUXINUS
Caucasus M.s
Pityus
Phasis
Abdera
Byzantium
Heraclea
PAPHLAGONIA
Sinope
Amisus
Pella
Corcyra
EPIRUS
Thessalia
BITHYNIA
PHRYGIA AD HELLESPONTUM
Halys
Iberia
Cyrus
Alba
MYSIA
Gordieum
Trapezus
Mosynœci
HELLAS
Mare Ægæum
Thebæ
Corinth
Sparta
Athenæ
Sardes
LYDIA
Ephesus
PHYRGIA
CAPPADOCIA
Mazaca
ARMENIA
Araxes
CARIA
Iconium
Melite
Thospitis L.
LYCIA
Rhodus
Phaselis
Taurus M.s
CILICIA
Tigris
Carduchi
(Kurds)
Matianus L.
Matiani
Orrhoe
Creta
Tarsus
Issus
Myriandus
Carrhæ
Gaugamela
(Arbela)
MARE INTERNUM
Soli
Cyprus
Salamis
Hamath
Larissa
Thapsacus
Mesopotamia
ASSYRIA
Cyrene
Cyrenaïca
Aradus
Byblus
Sidon
Tyrus
Phœnicia
SYRIA
Tadmor
Palmyra
Euphrates
Ecbatana
(Hamadan)
Canopicum
Ioppe
Palæstina
Hierosolyma
(Jerusalem)
Cunaxa
Babylon
Sitacene
Libya
Gaza
Pelusium
BABYLONIA
Memphis
Heliopolis
Ammonium
Petra
Teredon
ÆGYPTUS
Thamudeni
Thebæ
Coptus
Syene
SINUS ARABICUS
ARA
ÆTHIOPIA
20
25
30
35
40
45
15
Longitude East 45 of Greenwich

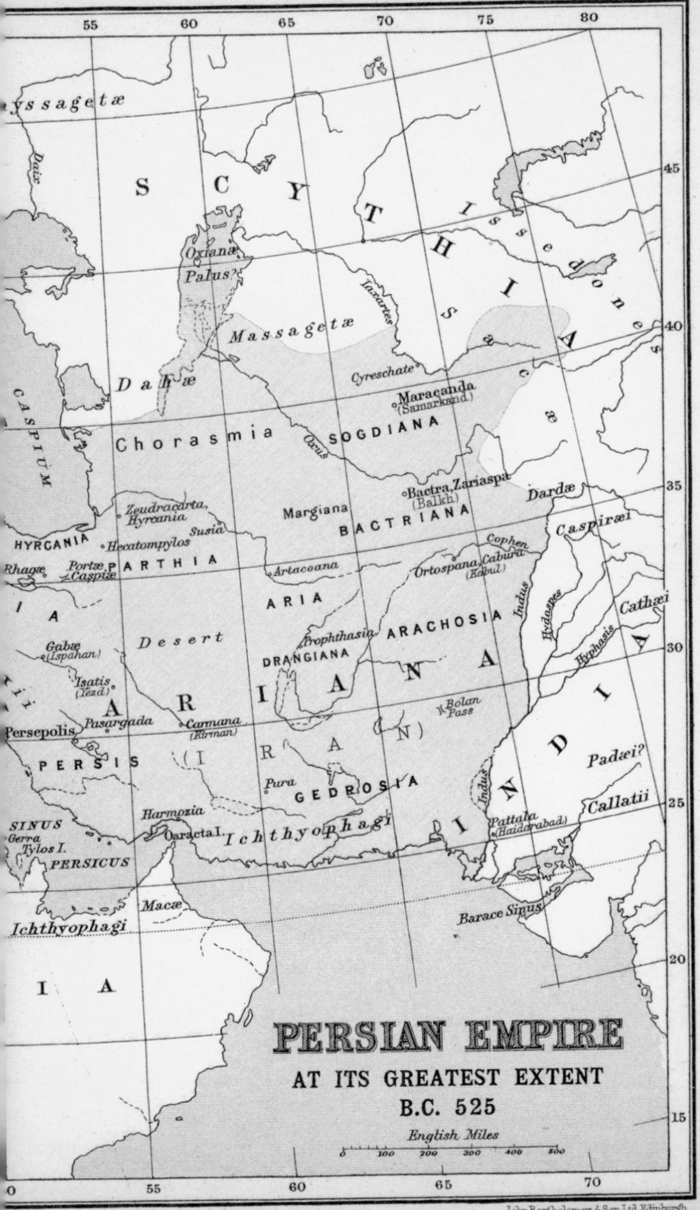
S C Y T H I A
Massagetæ
Oxiana Palus?
Issedones
Sacæ
Iaxartes
Cyreschate
Maracanda (Samarkand)
Dahæ
CASPIUM
Chorasmia
SOGDIANA
Oxus
Bactra, Zariaspa (Balkh)
Dardæ
Zeudracarta, Hyrcania
Margiana
BACTRIANA
Susia
HYRCANIA
Hecatompylos
Caspiræi
Cophen
Rhagæ
Portæ Caspiæ
PARTHIA
Artacoana
Ortospana, Cabura (Kabul)
ARIA
Indus
Hydaspes
Cathæi
Desert
Prophthasia
ARACHOSIA
Hyphasis
Gabæ (Ispahan)
DRANGIANA
ARIANA (IRAN)
Isatis (Yezd)
Bolan Pass
Persepolis
Pasargada
Carmana (Kirman)
INDIA
PERSIS
Padæi?
Pura
GEDROSIA
Harmozia
Callatii
SINUS PERSICUS
Gerra
Tylos I.
Oaracta I.
Ichthyophagi
Pattala (Haidarabad)
Macæ
Barace Sinus
Ichthyophagi
PERSIAN EMPIRE
AT ITS GREATEST EXTENT
B.C. 525
English Miles
0 100 200 300 400 500
John Bartholomew & Son, Ltd. Edinburgh

Neuri
Geloni
Agathyrsi
Scythæ
Borysthenes
Tanais
Olbia
Tanais
Rha (Volga)
Palus Mæotis
Getæ
Ister
ILLYRIA
Istria
Heraclea Chersonesus
Getæ
Tomi
THRACIA
Pæonia
PONTUS EUXINUS
Apollonia
Caucasus Ms
MACEDONIA
Pella
Abdera
Byzantium
Pityus
Corcyra
EPIRUS
Thessalia
Heraclea
Sinope
Phasis
PAPHLAGONIA
BITHYNIA
Amisus
PHRYGIA AD HELLESPONTUM
Halys
Iberia
Cyrus
Alban
MYSIA
Gordieum
Amasia
Mosynœci
Trapezus
Corinth
Thebæ
Sardes
PHYRGIA
CAPPADOCIA
Artaxarta
Sparta
Athenæ
LYDIA
Mazaca
ARMENIA
HELLAS
Mare Ægæum
Ephesus
CARIA
PISIDIA
Iconium
Cataonia
Melite
Araxes
Lycaonia
Taurus Ms
Thospitis L.
LYCIA
CILICIA
Tigris
Carduchi (Kurds)
Matianus L.
Matiani
Rhodus
Phaselis
Tarsus
Orrhoe
Issus
Carrhæ
Creta
Myriandus
Gaugamela (Arbela)
Soli
Larissa
Mesopotamia
MARE INTERNUM
Cyprus
Salamis
Hamath
Thapsacus
ASSYRIA
Cyrene
Aradus
Tadmor Palmyra
Cyrenaica
Byblus
Euphrates
Ecbatana (Hamadan)
Sidon
SYRIA
Tyrus
Phœnicia
Damascus
Parætonium
Alexandria
Canopicum
Ioppe
Palæstina
Cunaxa
Sitacene
Babylon
Libya
Gaza
Hierosolyma (Jerusalem)
Sais
Pelusium
BABYLONIA
Memphis
Heliopolis
Ammonium
Petra
Teredon
Heracleopolis
Ætana
ÆGYPTUS
Hermopolis
Thamudeni
Lycopolis
Thebæ
Coptus
SINUS ARABICUS
Apollinopolis
Syene
Berenice
Premis
ÆTHIOPIA
Longitude East 45 of Greenwich

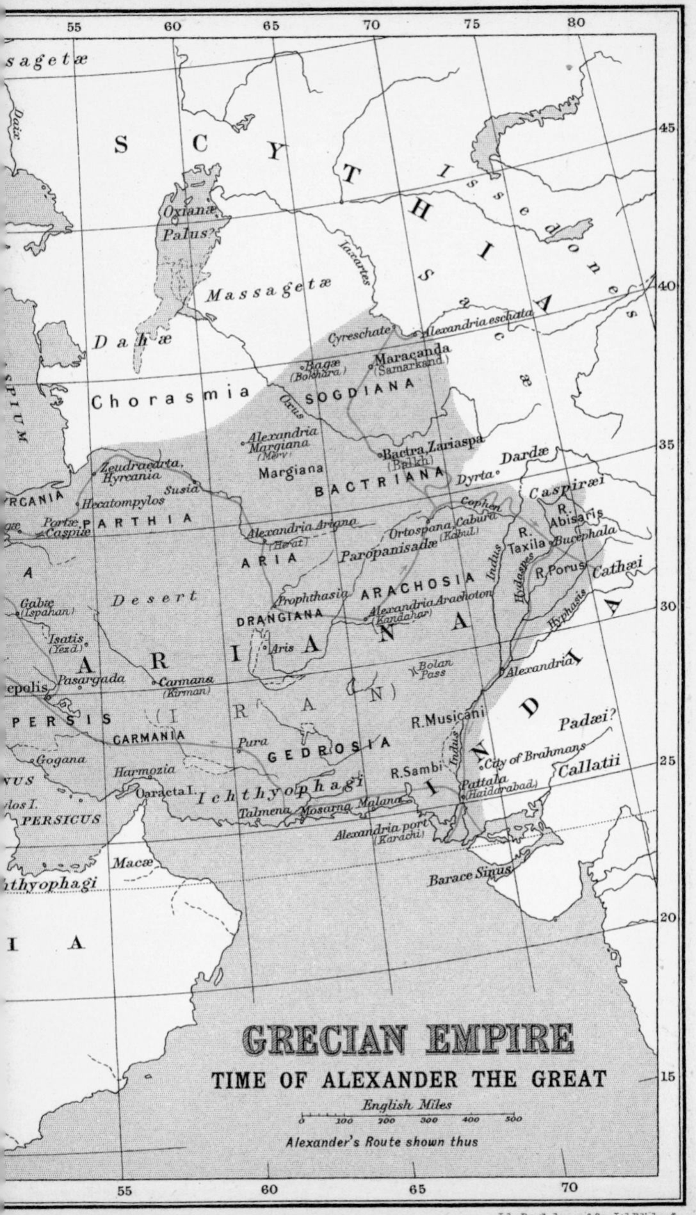

John Bartholomew & Son, Ltd. Edinburgh

ROMAN EMPIRE
AT THE DEATH OF CÆSAR
English Miles
0 100 200 400 600 800
Roman Miles
0 100 200 400 600 800
Roman Territory and Provinces
Protected States
OCEANUS ATLANTICUS
OCEANUS GERMANICUS.
Oceanus Britannicus
Oceanus Gallicus
Oceanus Cantabrius
CALEDONIA
HIBERNIA
BRITANNIA
Londinium
Eboracum
Orcades
Mare Suevic
GERMANI
GALLIA
Aquitania
Lugdunensis
Belgica
Narbo
Massilia
Burdigala
Lugdunum
VINDELICIA
NORICUM
RHÆTIA
PANNONIA
Venetia
Liguria
Mediolanum
HISPANIA
Tarraco
Baetica
Gades
Carthago Nova
Baleares Ie
Corsica
Sardinia
ROMA
Latium
Etruria
Apulia
Lucania
Neapolis
SICILIA
Syracusæ
Carthago
NUMIDIA
Tingitana
Caesariensis
Atlas M.
MEDITERRANEUM
Melita
Leptis magna
Syrtis Major
Syrtis Minor
Sabrata
Oea
AFRICA
L I B
20 15 10 5 0 5 10 15
55 50 45 40 35 30 25
0 5 10 15

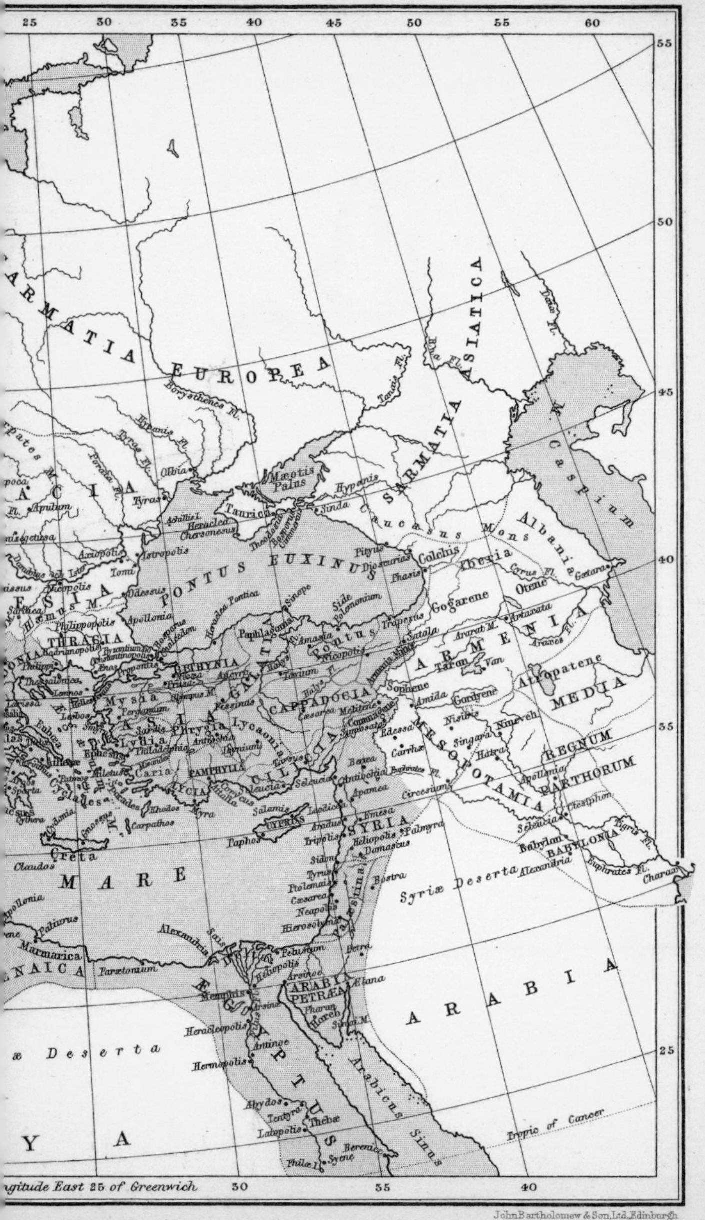

John Bartholomew & Son, Ltd. Edinburgh

ROMAN EMPIRE
AT ITS GREATEST EXTENT
THIRD CENTURY A.D.
English Miles
0 100 200 400 600 800
Roman Miles
0 100 200 400 600 800
OCEANUS ATLANTICUS
OCEANUS GERMANICUS
Oceanus Britannicus
Oceanus Gallicus
Oceanus Cantabricus
CALEDONIA
HIBERNIA
BRITANNIA
Orcades
Londinium
Eboracum
GALLIA
Lugdunensis
Belgica
Aquitania
Narbonensis
GERMANIA
HISPANIA
Tarraconensis
Lusitania
Baetica
Mare Suevicum
VINDELICIA
RHAETIA
NORICUM
PANNONIA
ITALIA
ROMA
Corsica
Sardinia
SICILIA
Baleares Is.
MEDITERRANEAN
MAURITANIA Caesariensis
Tingitana
Atlas M.
NUMIDIA
AFRICA
Carthago
Syrtis Minor
Syrtis Major
Leptis magna
Melita
Hadriaticum
ILLYRICUM
LIBYA

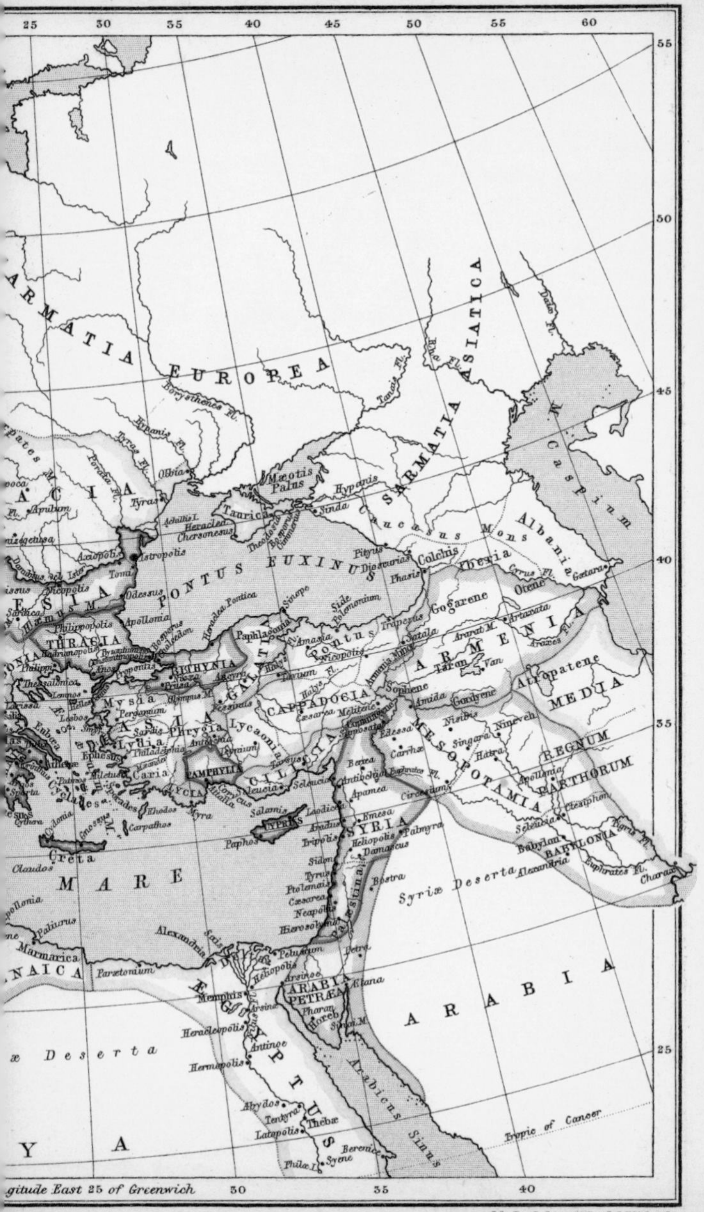

John Bartholomew & Son, Ltd. Edinburgh

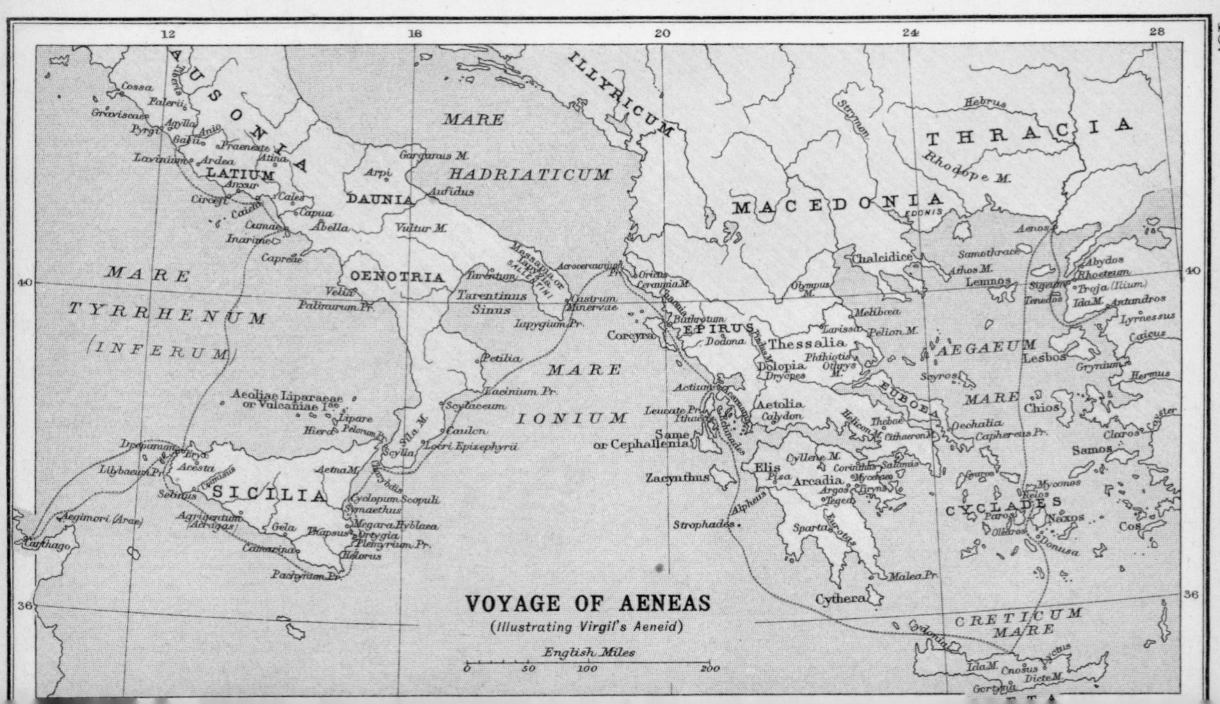
VOYAGE OF AENEAS
(Illustrating Virgil's Aeneid)
English Miles
0 50 100 200
12
16
20
24
28
40
36
AUSONIA
LATIUM
DAUNIA
OENOTRIA
SICILIA
ILLYRICUM
MACEDONIA
THRACIA
EDONIS
EPIRUS
Thessalia
Aetolia
Arcadia
Elis
EUBOEA
CYCLADES
MARE HADRIATICUM
MARE TYRRHENUM (INFERUM)
MARE IONIUM
MARE AEGAEUM
CRETICUM MARE
Cossa
Falerii
Graviscae
Pyrgi
Agylla
Gabii
Anio
Praeneste
Atina
Lavinium
Ardea
Anxur
Circeii
Caieta
Cales
Capua
Cumae
Abella
Inarime
Capreae
Velia
Palinurum Pr.
Arpi
Garganus M.
Aufidus
Vultur M.
Tarentum
Tarentinus Sinus
Iapygium Pr.
Castrum Minervae
Acroceraunium Pr.
Oricus
Ceraunia M.
Buthrotum
Dodona
Corcyra
Petilia
Lacinium Pr.
Scylaceum
Caulon
Locri Epizephyrii
Sila M.
Scylla
Charybdis
Aeoliae Liparaeae or Vulcaniae I.
Lipare
Hiera
Pelorum Pr.
Eryx
Acesta
Lilybaeum Pr.
Selinus
Aetna M.
Cyclopum Scopuli
Symaethus
Megara Hyblaea
Thapsus
Ortygia
Plemyrium Pr.
Helorus
Gela
Agrigentum (Acragas)
Camarina
Pachynum Pr.
Aegimori (Arae)
Carthago
Actium
Leucate Pr.
Ithaca
Echinades
Same or Cephallenia
Zacynthus
Strophades
Alpheus
Pisa
Cyllene M.
Corinthus
Salamis
Mycenae
Argos
Tiryns
Tegea
Sparta
Eurotas
Malea Pr.
Cythera
Calydon
Dolopia
Dryopes
Phthiotis
Othrys M.
Larissa
Pelion M.
Meliboea
Olympus M.
Chalcidice
Athos M.
Helicon M.
Thebae
Cithaeron M.
Oechalia
Caphereus Pr.
Scyros
Lemnos
Samothrace
Aenos
Hebrus
Strymon
Rhodope M.
Abydos
Rhoeteum
Sigeum
Tenedos
Troja (Ilium)
Ida M.
Antandros
Lyrnessus
Caicus
Lesbos
Grynium
Hermus
Chios
Claros
Cayster
Samos
Myconos
Delos
Paros
Oliaros
Naxos
Donusa
Cos
Gyarus
Ida M.
Cnosus
Dicte M.
Gortyna
Lyctus

John Bartholomew & Son, Ltd, Edinburgh

ITALIA
English Miles
0 10 20 30 40 50 100
Roman Miles
0 10 20 30 40 50 100
8
10
12
14
16
18
46
44
42
RHAETIA
GALLIA
ILLYRICUM
DALMATIA
LIGURIA
GALLIA CISALPINA
Transpadana
Cispadana
VENETIA
ISTRIA
ETRURIA
(TUSCIA)
UMBRIA
PICENUM
CORSICA
MARE HADRIATICUM
(SUPERUM)
Sinus Ligusticus
Apenninus Mons
Alpes Rhaeticae
Alpes Poeninae
Alpes Carnicae
Alpis Maritima
Lepontii
Insubres
Cenomani
Euganei
Salassi
Taurini
Apuani
Boii
Lingones
Senones
Frentani
Sabini
Vestini
Marsi
Aequi
Hernici
Paeligni
Mediolanum
Verona
Patavium
Aquileia
Cremona
Placentia
Parma
Mutina
Bononia
Ravenna
Ariminum
Ancona
Pisae
Luca
Florentia
Arretium
Perusia
Spoletium
Genua
Tergeste
Pola
Senia
Iader
Salonae
Delminium
Narona
Epidaurus
Ilva I.
Aleria (Alalia)
Tarquinii
Veii
ROMA
Ostia
Sipontum
Gargams Mons

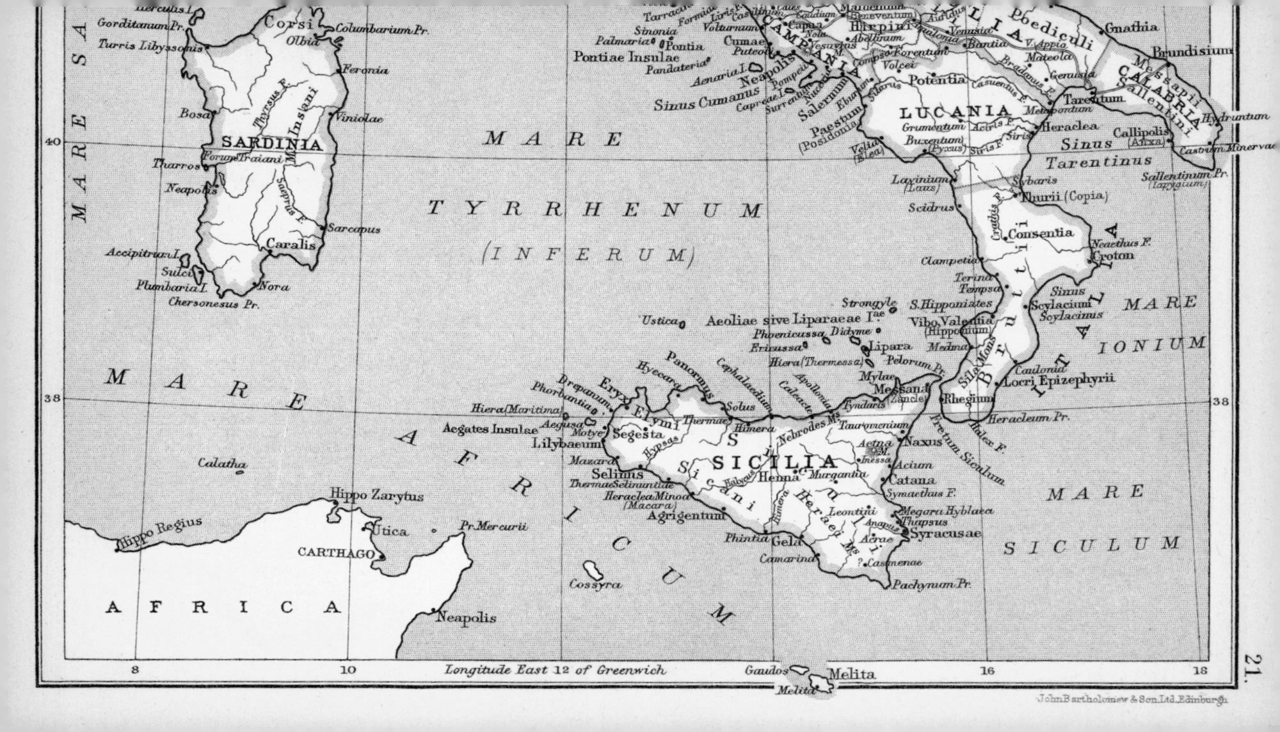
MARE TYRRHENUM (INFERUM)
MARE AFRICUM
MARE SICULUM
MARE IONIUM
MARE SA
AFRICA
SARDINIA
SICILIA
LUCANIA
CAMPANIA
CALABRIA
Bruttii
Corsi
Gorditanum Pr.
Turris Libyssonis
Columbarium Pr.
Olbia
Feronia
Thyrsus F.
Insani Ms.
Viniolae
Bosa
Forum Traiani
Tharros
Neapolis
Saeprus F.
Sarcapus
Caralis
Accipitrum I.
Sulci
Plumbaria I.
Nora
Chersonesus Pr.
Sinonia
Palmaria
Pontia
Pontiae Insulae
Pandateria
Aenaria I.
Neapolis
Sinus Cumanus
Capreae I.
Cumae
Puteoli
Volturnum
Formiae
Capua
Nola
Vesuvius M.
Pompeii
Surrentum
Salernum
Paestum (Posidonia)
Velia (Elea)
Hirpini
Beneventum
Abellinum
Compsa
Forentum
Volcei
Potentia
Venusia
Bantia
Poediculi
Gnathia
Brundisium
Messapii
Sallentini
Hydruntum
Mateola
Bradanus F.
Genusia
Tarentum
Metapontum
Heraclea
Grumentum
Aciris F.
Siris
Siris F.
Buxentum (Pyxus)
Sinus Tarentinus
Callipolis (Anxa)
Castrum Minervae
Sallentinum Pr. (Iapygium)
Laus
Sybaris
Thurii (Copia)
Scidrus
Crathis F.
Consentia
Neaethus F.
Croton
Clampetia
Terina
Tempsa
Sinus Scylacinus
Scylacium
S. Hipponiates
Vibo Valentia (Hipponium)
Medma
Sila Mons
Caulonia
Locri Epizephyrii
Rhegium
Heracleum Pr.
Halex F.
Fretum Siculum
Strongyle
Aeoliae sive Liparaeae Iae.
Ustica
Phoenicussa
Didyme
Ericussa
Lipara
Hiera (Thermessa)
Pelorum Pr.
Mylae
Messana (Zancle)
Tyndaris
Apollonia
Caleacte
Cephaloedium
Panormus
Hyccara
Eryx
Drepanum
Phorbantia
Hiera (Maritima)
Aegusa
Aegates Insulae
Motye
Lilybaeum
Segesta
Elymi
Thermae
Solus
Himera
Nebrodes Ms.
Tauromenium
Naxus
Aetna M.
Inessa
Acium
Catana
Symaethus F.
Henna
Murgantia
Sicani
Siculi
Halycus
Mazara
Selinus
Thermae Selinuntiae
Heraclea Minoa (Macara)
Agrigentum
Phintia
Gela
Camarina
Heraei Ms.
Leontini
Megara Hyblaea
Thapsus
Syracusae
Acrae
Casmenae
Pachynum Pr.
Calatha
Cossyra
Hippo Zarytus
Hippo Regius
Utica
CARTHAGO
Pr. Mercurii
Neapolis
Gaudos
Melita
8
10
Longitude East 12 of Greenwich
16
18
38
40
John Bartholomew & Son Ltd. Edinburgh

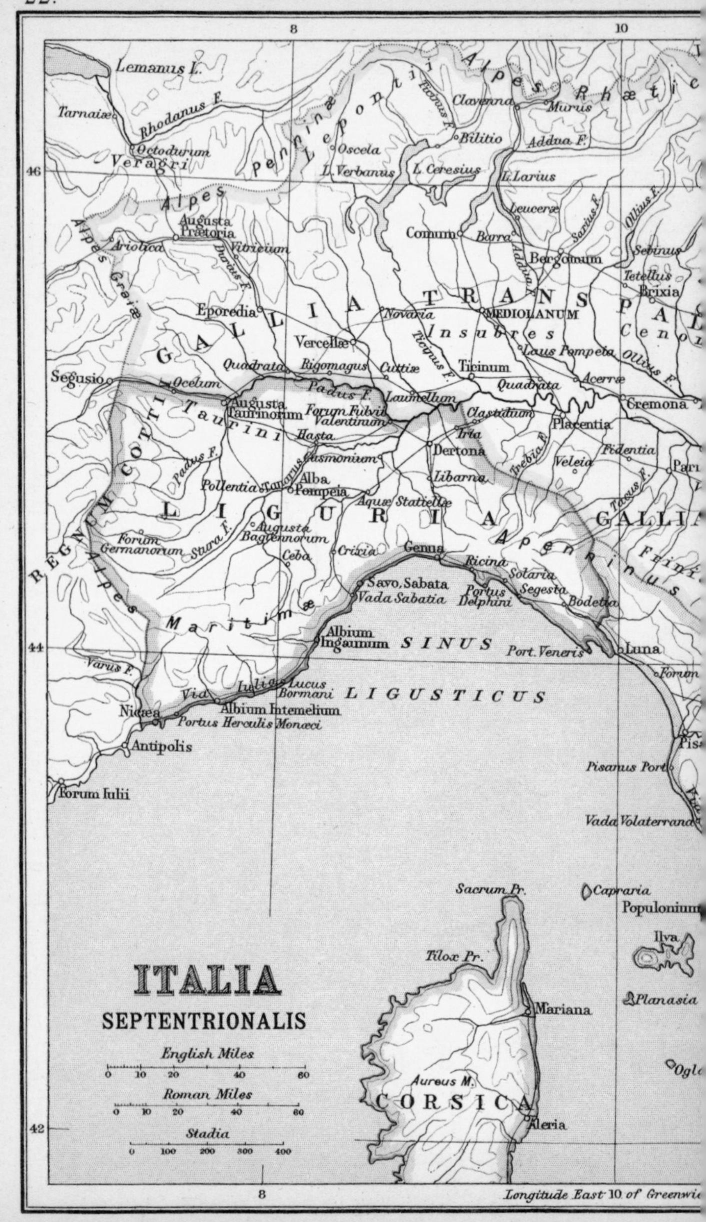
ITALIA
SEPTENTRIONALIS
English Miles
Roman Miles
Stadia
Lemanus L.
Rhodanus F.
Tarnaiæ
Octodurum
Veragri
Alpes Penninæ
Lepontii
Alpes Rhætic
Clavenna
Murus
Bilitio
Addua F.
Oscela
L. Verbanus
L. Ceresius
L. Larius
Ticinus F.
Leuceræ
Augusta Prætoria
Ariolica
Vitricium
Durius F.
Alpes Graiæ
Comum
Barra
Bergomum
Sarius F.
Ollius F.
Sebinus
Tetellus
Brixia
GALLIA TRANSPAD
Insubres
Cenom
Eporedia
Novaria
MEDIOLANUM
Vercellæ
Laus Pompeia
Quadrata
Rigomagus
Cuttiæ
Ticinum
Segusio
Ocelum
Padus F.
Laumellum
Quadrata
Acerræ
Cremona
Augusta Taurinorum
Taurini
Forum Fulvii
Valentinum
Clastidium
Placentia
Hasta
Iria
Dertona
Trebia F.
Veleia
Fidentia
Carreum
Casmonium
Parma
REGNUM COTTII
Padus F.
Pollentia
Tanarus F.
Alba Pompeia
Libarna
Aquæ Statiellæ
Tarus F.
LIGURIA
GALLIA
Augusta Bagiennorum
Forum Germanorum
Stura F.
Ceba
Crixia
Genua
Apenninus
Friniates
Ricina
Solaria
Segesta
Bodetia
Portus Delphini
Savo, Sabata
Vada Sabatia
Alpes Maritimæ
Albium Ingaunum
SINUS
Port. Veneris
Luna
LIGUSTICUS
Varus F.
Via Iulia
Lucus Bormani
Forum
Nicæa
Albium Intemelium
Portus Herculis Monæci
Antipolis
Pisæ
Pisanus Port.
Forum Iulii
Vada Volaterrana
Sacrum Pr.
Capraria
Populonium
Ilva
Tilox Pr.
Mariana
Planasia
Ogl
Aureus M.
CORSICA
Aleria
Longitude East 10 of Greenwi
46
44
42
8
10

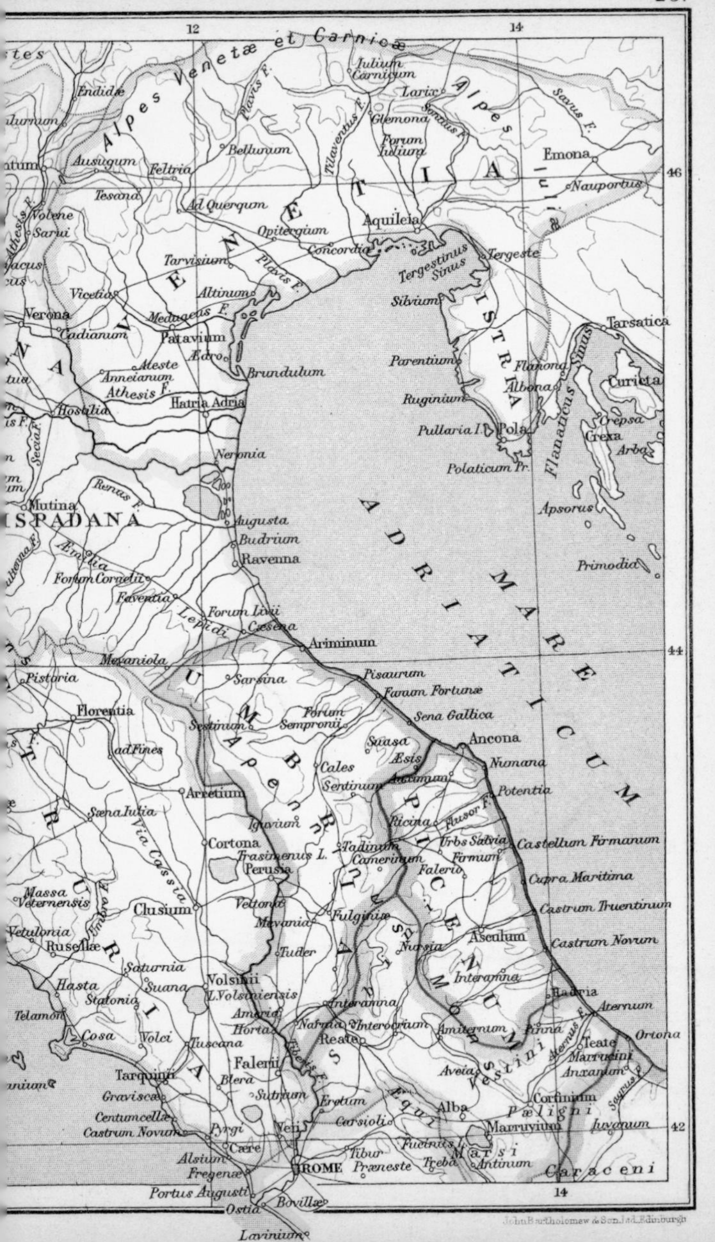

John Bartholomew & Son Ltd. Edinburgh

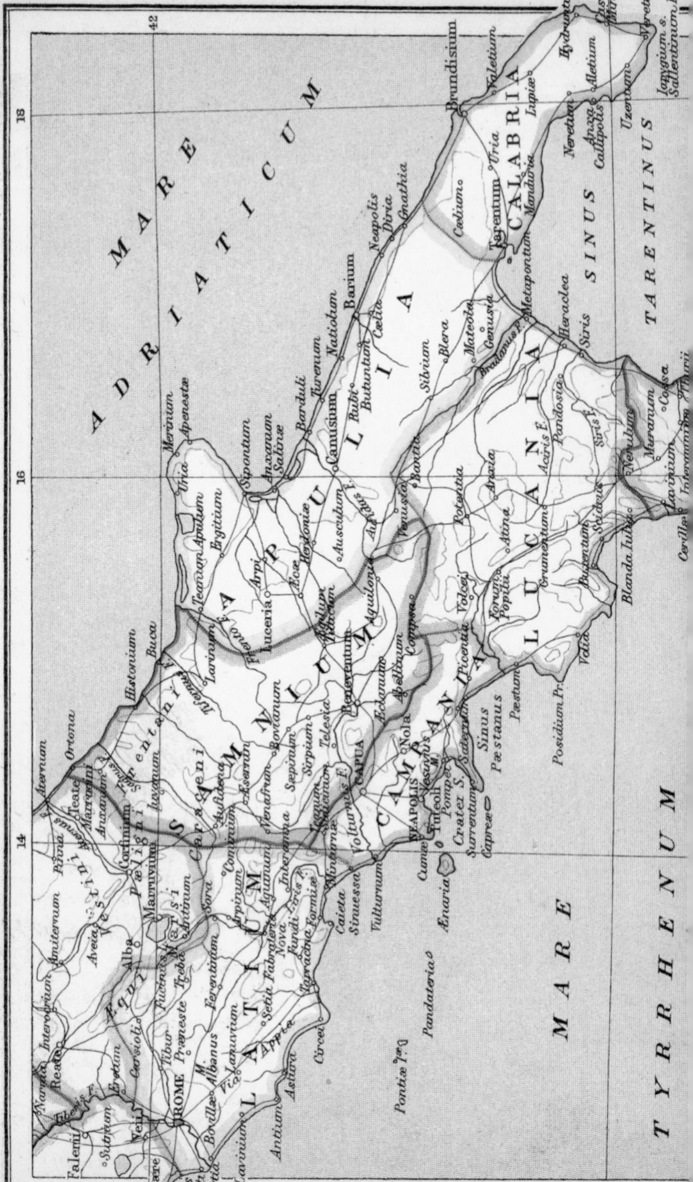

MARE ADRIATICUM

LATIUM
SAMNIUM
APULIA
CAMPANIA
LUCANIA
CALABRIA

MARE TYRRHENUM

SINUS TARENTINUS

14
16
18
42
40

Narnia
Interocrium
Reate
Amiternum
Pinna
Aternum
Falerii
Sutrium
Eretum
Veii
Cære
Teate
Ortona
Aveia
Vestini
Aternus F.
Marrucini
Anxanum
Alba
Corfinium
Peligni
Marruvium
Marsi
Frentani
Sagrus F.
Histonium
Buca
Carsioli
Æqui
Tibur
Fucinus L.
ROME
Præneste
Treba
Antinum
Iuvanum
Caraceni
Portus Augusti
Ostia
Bovillæ
M. Albanus
Ferentinum
Sora
Tifernus F.
Larinum
Teanum Apulum
Uria
Merinum
Apenestæ
Ergitium
Via Appia
Lanuvium
Lavinium
Arpinum
Cominium
Aufidena
Æsernia
Frento F.
Arpi
Luceria
Sipontum
Anxanum
Salinæ
Antium
Setia
Fabrateria
Nova
Aquinum
Venafrum
Bovianum
Astura
Fundi
Liris F.
Interamna
Sæpinum
Æcæ
Herdoniæ
Barduli
Turenum
Tarracina
Formiæ
Sirpium
Teanum Sidicinum
Telesia
Aquilonia
Ausculum
Canusium
Natiolum
Circei
Minturnæ
Caieta
Sinuessa
Volturnus F.
Beneventum
Aufidus F.
Rubi
Butuntum
Barium
Capua
Vulturnum
Æclanum
Cælia
Neapolis
Diria
Gnathia
Pontiæ I.
Nola
Abellinum
Compsa
Venusia
Bantia
Cumæ
Neapolis
Vesuvius M.
Pandateria
Puteoli
Pompei
Silvium
Blera
Ænaria
Crater S.
Salernum
Picentia
Volcei
Potentia
Mateola
Surrentum
Capreæ
Sinus Pæstanus
Cælium
Brundisium
Genusia
Forum Popilii
Atina
Anxia
Bradanus F.
Tarentum
Uria
Valetium
Pæstum
Grumentum
Aciris F.
Metapontum
Manduria
Lupiæ
Posidium Pr.
Pandosia
Heraclea
Neretum
Hydruntum
Velia
Buxentum
Scidrus
Siris F.
Siris
Anxa
Callipolis
Aletium
Castrum Minervæ
Blanda Julia
Nerulum
Uzentum
Muranum
Cossa
Veretum
Lavinium
Iapygium s. Sallentinum Pr.
Cerillæ
Interamnium
Thurii

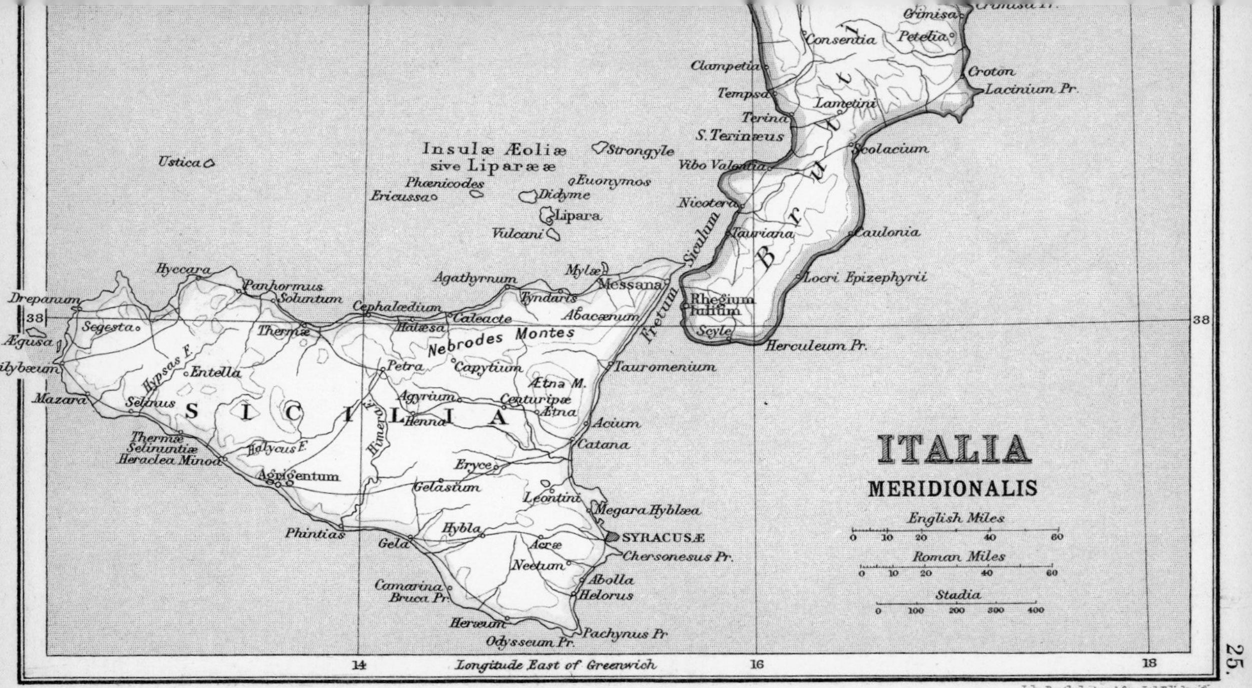

John Bartholomew & Son, Ltd. Edinburgh

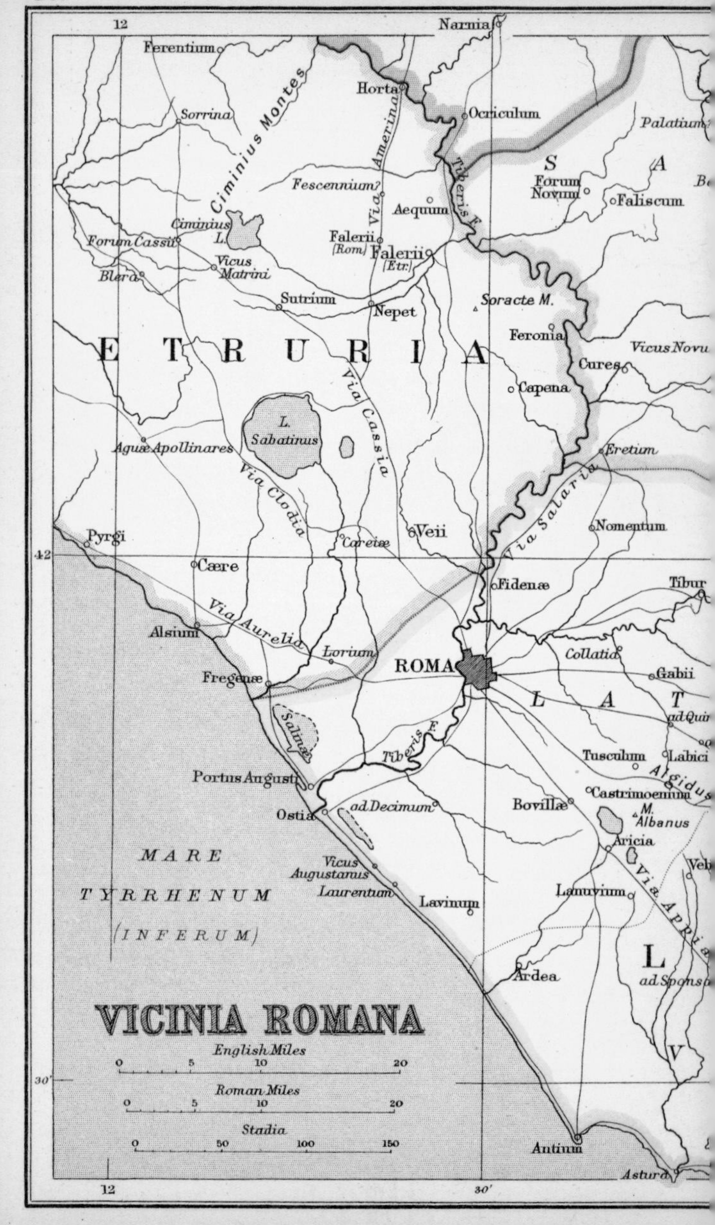
VICINIA ROMANA
English Miles
0
5
10
20
Roman Miles
0
5
10
20
Stadia
0
50
100
150
ETRURIA
MARE
TYRRHENUM
(INFERUM)
Narnia
Ferentium
Horta
Ocriculum
Sorrina
Ciminius Montes
Via Amerina
Palatium?
Fescennium?
Aequum
Tiberis F.
Forum Novum
Faliscum
Ciminius L.
Forum Cassii
Falerii (Rom)
Falerii (Etr.)
Vicus Matrini
Blera
Sutrium
Nepet
Soracte M.
Feronia
Vicus Novu
Via Cassia
Cures
Capena
L. Sabatinus
Aquæ Apollinares
Eretum
Via Clodia
Via Salaria
Nomentum
Pyrgi
Careiæ
Veii
42
Cære
Fidenæ
Tibur
Via Aurelia
Alsium
Lorium
Collatia
ROMA
Gabii
Fregenæ
L
A
T
ad Quir
Salinæ
Tiberis F.
Tusculum
Labici
Algidus
Portus Augusti
Castrimoenium
Ostia
ad Decimum
Bovillæ
M. Albanus
Aricia
Vicus Augustanus
Laurentum
Lavinum
Lanuvium
Via Appia
L
Ardea
ad Spons
V
30'
Antium
Astura
12
30'

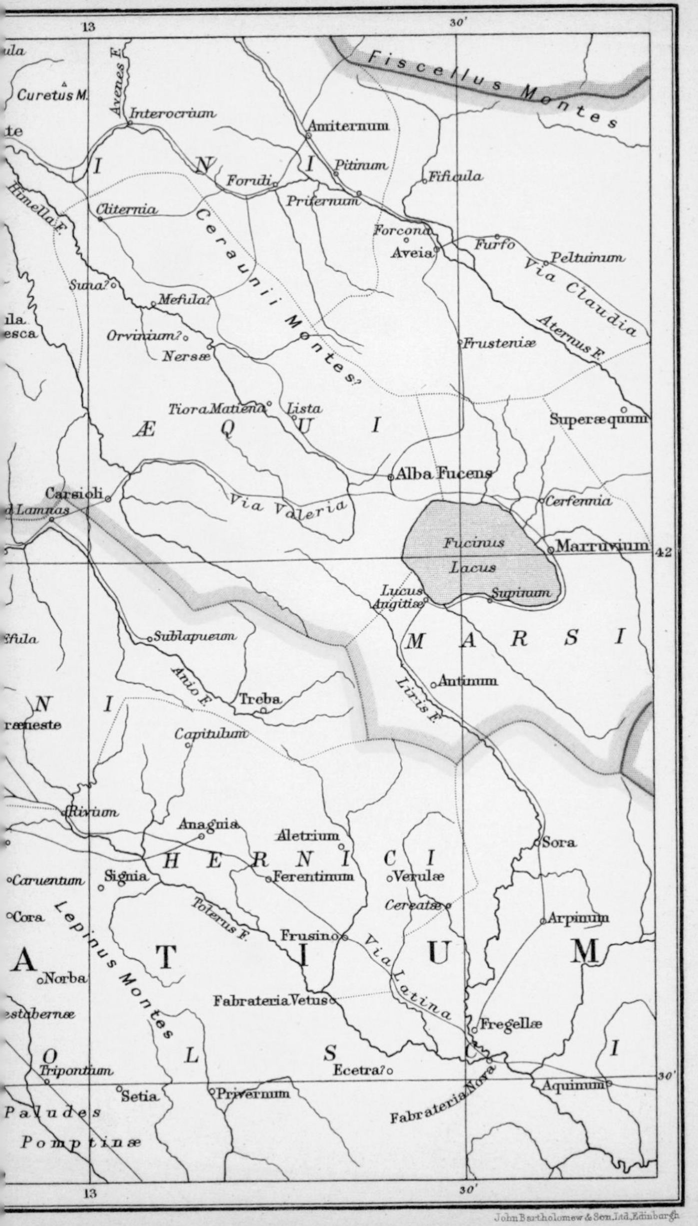

John Bartholomew & Son, Ltd, Edinburgh

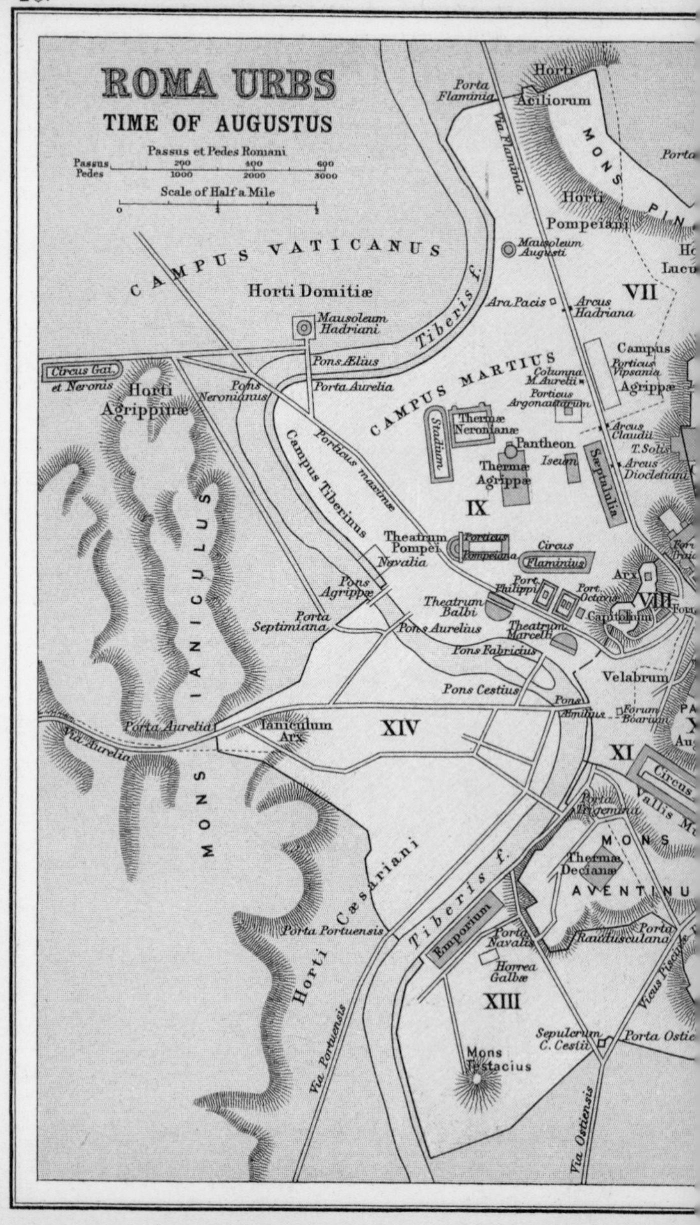
ROMA URBS
TIME OF AUGUSTUS
Passus et Pedes Romani
Passus 200 400 600
Pedes 1000 2000 3000
Scale of Half a Mile
CAMPUS VATICANUS
Horti Domitiæ
Mausoleum Hadriani
Circus Gai. et Neronis
Horti Agrippinæ
Pons Ælius
Pons Neronianus
Porta Aurelia
Tiberis f.
Porta Flaminia
Via Flaminia
Horti Aciliorum
MONS PIN
Horti Pompeiani
Mausoleum Augusti
Ara Pacis
Arcus Hadriana
VII
Campus Agrippæ
Porticus Vipsania
CAMPUS MARTIUS
Columna M. Aurelii
Porticus Argonautarum
Thermæ Neronianæ
Stadium
Pantheon
Iseum
Thermæ Agrippæ
Septa Iulia
Arcus Claudii
T. Solis
Arcus Diocletiani
IX
Porticus maximæ
Campus Tiberinus
Theatrum Pompei
Porticus Pompeiana
Circus Flaminius
Navalia
Pons Agrippæ
Arx
Port. Philippi
Port. Octaviæ
VIII
Capitolium
Theatrum Balbi
Porta Septimiana
Pons Aurelius
Theatrum Marcelli
Pons Fabricius
Velabrum
Pons Cestius
Pons Æmilius
Forum Boarium
MONS IANICULUS
Porta Aurelia
Via Aurelia
Ianiculum Arx
XIV
XI
Circus
Vallis M
Porta Trigemina
MONS AVENTINU
Thermæ Decianæ
Horti Cæsariani
Porta Portuensis
Tiberis f.
Emporium
Porta Navalis
Porta Raudusculana
Horrea Galbæ
XIII
Vicus Piscinæ
Via Portuensis
Sepulcrum C. Cestii
Porta Ostie
Mons Testacius
Via Ostiensis

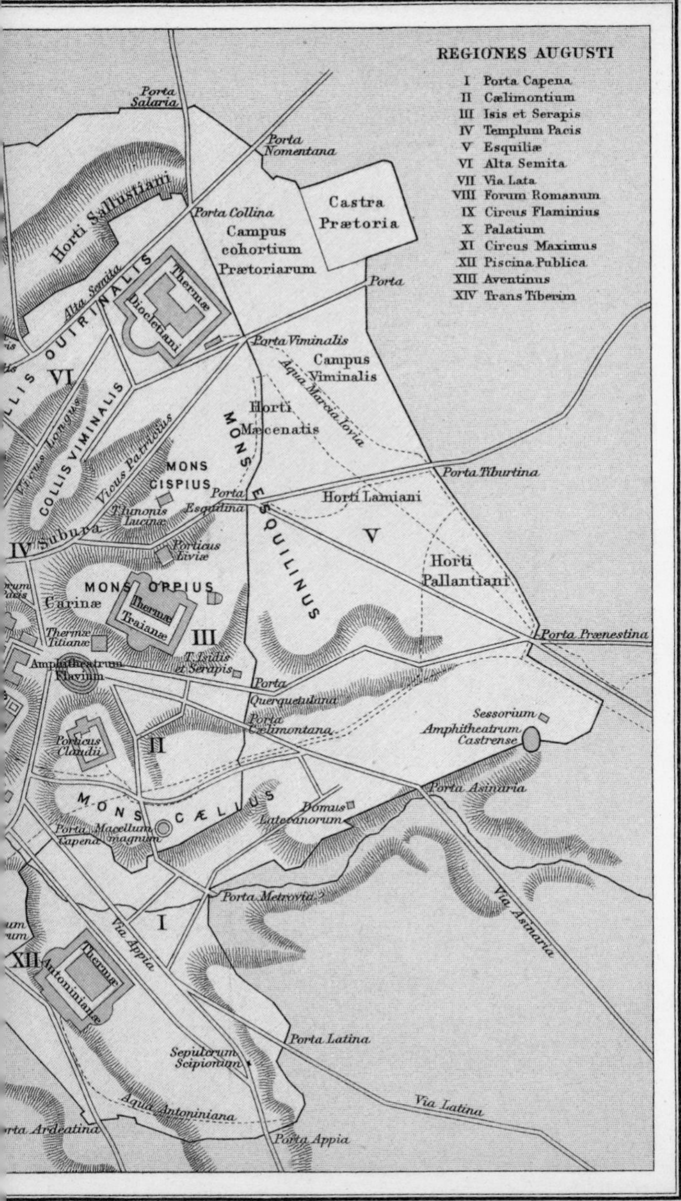
REGIONES AUGUSTI
I Porta Capena
II Cælimontium
III Isis et Serapis
IV Templum Pacis
V Esquiliæ
VI Alta Semita
VII Via Lata
VIII Forum Romanum
IX Circus Flaminius
X Palatium
XI Circus Maximus
XII Piscina Publica
XIII Aventinus
XIV Trans Tiberim
Porta Salaria
Porta Nomentana
Castra Prætoria
Horti Sallustiani
Porta Collina
Campus cohortium Prætoriarum
Porta
Thermæ Diocletiani
Alta Semita
COLLIS QUIRINALIS
Porta Viminalis
Campus Viminalis
Aqua Marcia Iovia
VI
COLLIS VIMINALIS
Vicus Longus
Vicus Patricius
Horti Mæcenatis
MONS ESQUILINUS
MONS CISPIUS
Porta Esquilina
Horti Lamiani
Porta Tiburtina
Iunonis Lucinæ
Subura
IV
Porticus Liviæ
V
Horti Pallantiani
MONS OPPIUS
Carinæ
Thermæ Traianæ
Thermæ Titianæ
III
T. Isidis et Serapis
Porta Prænestina
Amphitheatrum Flavium
Porta Querquetulana
Porta Cælimontana
Sessorium
Amphitheatrum Castrense
Porticus Claudii
II
MONS CÆLIUS
Domus Lateranorum
Porta Asinaria
Porta Capena
Macellum magnum
Porta Metrovia ?
I
Via Asinaria
Via Appia
XII
Thermæ Antoninianæ
Porta Latina
Sepulcrum Scipionum
Via Latina
Aqua Antoniniana
Porta Appia
John Bartholomew & Son, Ltd. Edinburgh

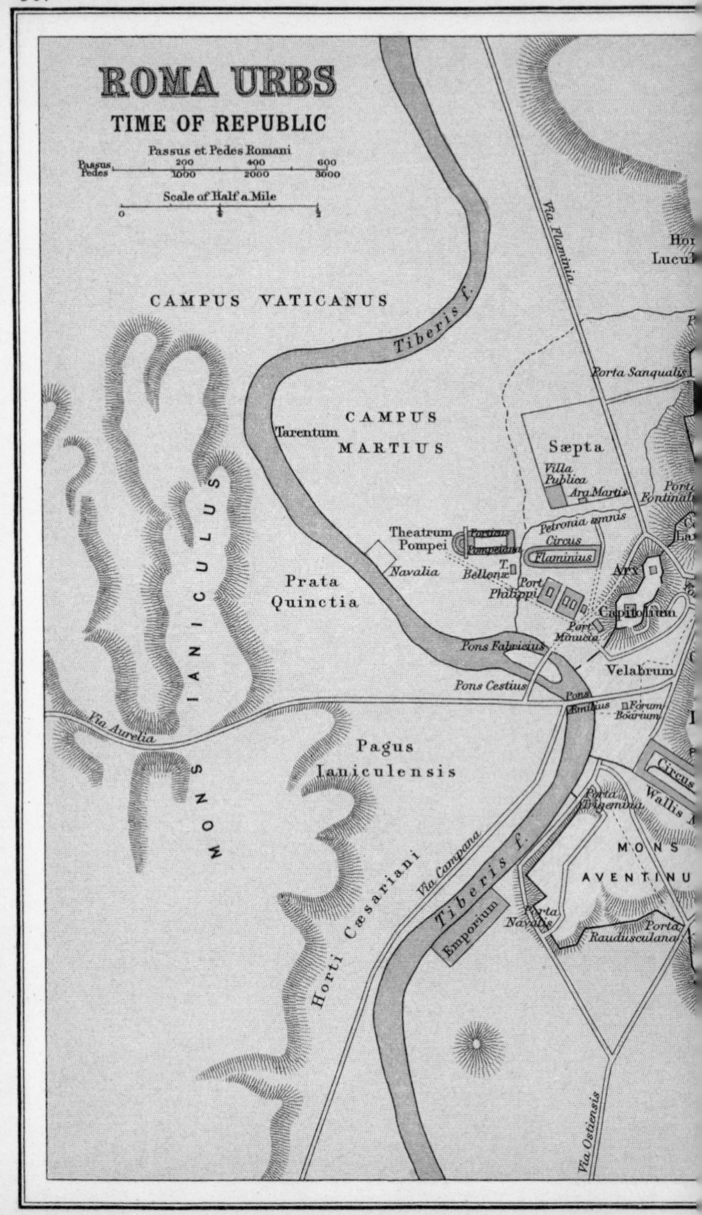
ROMA URBS
TIME OF REPUBLIC
Passus et Pedes Romani
Passus
Pedes
200
400
600
1000
2000
3000
Scale of Half a Mile
CAMPUS VATICANUS
Tiberis f.
Via Flaminia
CAMPUS
MARTIUS
Tarentum
Sæpta
Villa
Publica
Ara Martis
Porta Sanqualis
Petronia amnis
Circus
Flaminius
Theatrum
Pompei
Navalia
T. Bellonæ
Port. Philippi
Arx
Capitolium
Port. Minucia
Pons Fabricius
Pons Cestius
Velabrum
Pons Æmilius
Forum Boarium
IANICULUS
MONS
Via Aurelia
Prata
Quinctia
Pagus
Ianiculensis
Circus
Porta Trigemina
MONS
AVENTINU
Porta Navalis
Porta Raudusculana
Emporium
Tiberis f.
Via Campana
Horti Cæsariani
Via Ostiensis

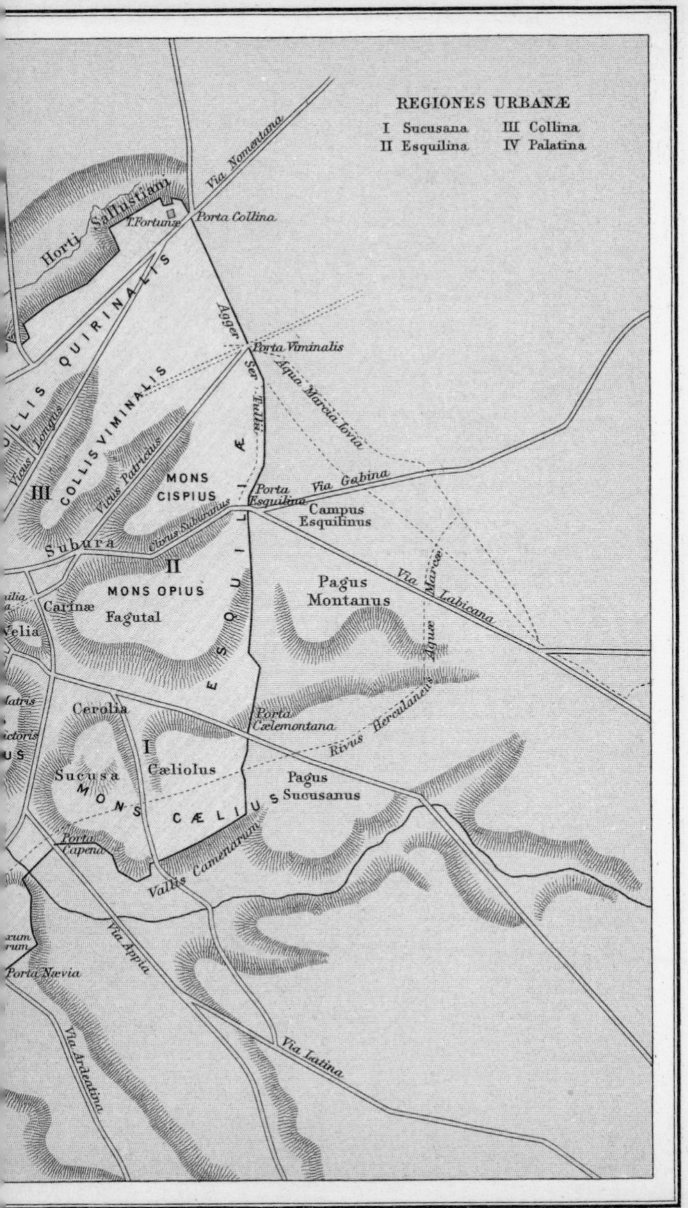
REGIONES URBANÆ
I Sucusana
II Esquilina
III Collina
IV Palatina
Via Nomentana
Horti Sallustiani
T. Fortunæ
Porta Collina
COLLIS QUIRINALIS
Agger
Porta Viminalis
Aqua Marcia Iovia
COLLIS VIMINALIS
Vicus Longus
Vicus Patricius
MONS CISPIUS
Ser. Tullii
III
Porta Esquilina
Via Gabina
Campus Esquilinus
Clivus Suburanus
Subura
II
MONS OPIUS
ESQUILIÆ
Pagus Montanus
Via Labicana
Aquæ Marcæ
Carinæ
Fagutal
Velia
Cerolia
Porta Cælemontana
Rivus Herculaneus
I
Cæliolus
Sucusa
MONS CÆLIUS
Pagus Sucusanus
Porta Capena
Vallis Camenarum
Via Appia
Porta Nævia
Via Latina
Via Ardeatina

John Bartholomew & Son, Ltd. Edinburgh

GRÆCIA
English Miles
0 10 20 30 40 50
Greek Stadia
0 100 200 300 400 500
20
21
22
23
40
39
38
37
ILLYRIA
MACEDONIA
EPIRUS
THESSALIA
DOLOPIA
ÆTOLIA
ACARNANIA
AMBRACIA
LOCRIS
DORIS
PHOCIS
ACHAIA
ELIS
ARCADIA
ARGOLIS
MESSENIA
LACONIA
PELOPONNESUS
MARE IONIUM
Apollonia
Antipatreia
Apsus
Byllis vel
Aulon
Aous
Oricum
Amantia
Antigoneia
Chaonia
Palæste
Chimæra
Othronus
Ericusa
Onchesmus
Malthace
Cassiope
Phœnice
Elæus
Hadrianopolis
Omphalium
Passaron
Buthrotum
Corcyra
Cestria, Ilium
Thyamis
Dodona
Thesprotia
Sybota
Cocytus
Acheron
Cheimerium Pr.
Torone
Ephyra
Pondosia
Paxus
Buchetium
Cassope
Nicopolis
Actium
Anactorium
Nericum
Leucas
Leucas, vel Leucadia
Phara
Taphiæ I.
Astacus
Ithaca
Samos, vel Cephallenia
Same
Pale
Cranii
Proni
Echinades I.
Parauæa
Aous
Castra Pyrrhi
Tymphæa
Orestis
Heraclea Lyncestis
Celetrum
Ægæ, vel Edessa
Eordæi
Emathia
Pella
Lydias
Bottiæis
Axius
Chalastra
Mygdonia
Aliacmon
Alorus
Beræa
Methone
Pieria
Pydna
Elima
Elimeia
Phylace
Olympus M.
Dium
Dolicha
Pythium
Heracleum
Thermaicus S.
Eritium
Perrhæbi
Gonnus
Cyretiæ
Oxyneia
Peneius
Mallæa
Europus
Tempe
Ossa M.
Ænea
Æginium
Histiæotis
Atrax
Phaloria
Tricca
Larissa
Magnesia
Gomphi
Pelasgiotis
Crannon
Pheræ
Iolcus
Ithome
Cierium
Enipeus
Apidanus
Scotussa
Pagasæ
Thessaliotis
Thebæ
Pharsalus
Phylace
Halos
Pagasæus S.
Thaumaci
Itonus
Achaia
Xyniæ
Pteleum
Othrys M.
Lamia
Echinus
Maliacus S.
Spercheius
Hypata
Œta M.
Heracleia
Thermopylæ
Daphnus
Athamania
Theudoria
Arachthus
Achelous
Charadrus
Argithea
Tetraphylia
Ambracia
Argos Amphilochicum
Agræi
Limnæa
Solium
Alyzia
Stratus
Agrinium
Eurytanes
Ophiones
Phyteum
Adopti
Thermon
Conope
Melite
Pleuron
Calydon
Œniadæ
Evenus
Amphissa
Crisa
Delphi
Daulis
Elateia
Cephissus
Parnassus M.
Naupactus
Phæstus
Anticyra
Chæroneia
Orchomenus
Coroneia
Helicon M.
Œantheia
Drepanum Pr.
Rhium Pr.
Patræ
Rhypæ
Ægium
Helice
Ægæ
Corinthiacus Sinus
Araxus Pr.
Dyme
Olenus
Pharæ
Leontium
Tritæa
Azania
Pellene
Sicyon
Cyllene
Chelonates Pr.
Peneius
Elis
Opus
Erymanthus M.
Pheneus
Cyllene M.
Clitor
Psophis
Stymphalis
Lechæum
Corinthus
Phlius
Cleonæ
Zacynthus
Pisatis
Letrini
Pisa
Ladon
Orchomenus
Orneæ
Mycenæ
Pitch springs
Ichthys Pr.
Olympia
Heræa
Argos
Tiryns
Macistus
Triphylia
Gortys
Mantineia
Nauplia
Cyparissius Sinus
Phigaleia
Lepreum
Alpheius
Tegea
Asine
Megalopolis
Thyrea
Argolicus S.
Strophades
Adania
Cyparissiæ
Eurotas
Parnon M.
Cynuria
Messene
Belemina
Messenia
Prasiæ
Prote
Pheræ
Taygetus M.
Sparta, vel Lacedæmon
Amyclæ
Pylas, vel Coryphasium
Sphacteria I.
Corone
Cardamyle
Methone
Leuctra
Gythium
Epidaurus L.
Œnussæ I.
Asine
Œtylus
Asopus
Acritas Pr.
Messeniacus S.
Teuthrone
Cænepolis
Laconicus S.
Tænarum Pr.
Scandeia

Amphipolis
Thasos
Samothrace
Imbros
Lemnos
Tenedos
Lesbos
Scyros
Chios
Psyra
Andros
Tenos
Ceos
Syros
Cythnos
Seriphos
Siphnos
Cimolos
Melos
Paros
Naxos
Mycones
Icaria
Samos
Patmos
Amorgos
Ios
Thera
Anaphe
Astypalæa
Calymna
Cos
Athenæ
Chalcis
Eretria
Smyrna
Clazomenæ
Teos
Phocæa
Adramyttium
Ilium, Troja
Hellespontus
Propontis
Icarium Mare
Doric
Ionic
Æolian & Achæan
Longitude East 24 of Greenwich
John Bartholomew & Son, Ltd. Edinburgh

GRÆCIA
SEPTENTRIONALIS
English Miles
0 5 10 20 30 40
Roman Miles
0 5 10 20 30 40
Stadia
0 50 100 200 300
20
21
39
40
Lyncestis
Cellæ
Begorritis L.
Pelium
Orestis
Celetrum
Castoria L.
Boius M.
Parauæa
Epirus
Antigonea
Eribœa
Chaonia
Elæus
Gitana
Phœnice
Onchesmus
Hadrianopolis
Cassiope
Buthrotum
Troia
Corcyra
Corcyra
Ilium
Molossis
Thyamis F.
Pyrrhi Castra
Auas
Tymphæa
Tyrissa
Elimea
Elimea
Æane
Chalcis
Peneus F.
Passaron
Pambotis L.
Tecmon
Dodona
Ægininum
Hestiæotis
Tricca
Gomphi
Ithome
Argithea
Athamania
Theudoria
Arachthus F.
Oropus F.
Thesprotia
Acheron
Pandosia
Ephyra
Cassope
Buchetium
Elæa
Toryne
Amphipyrgus Pr.
Sinus Thesprotius
Paxos
Propaxos
AMBRACIA
Dolopes
Campylus F.
Nicopolis
S. Ambracicus
Actium
Argos Amphilochicum
Agræi
Anactorium
Thyrrheum
Aperantia
Eurytanes
Achelous F.
Leucas
Sollium
ACARNANIA
Leucas
Taphos
Alyzia
Stratus
Agrinium
ÆT
Phara
Carnos
Rynchus L.
Phistyum
MARE
Leucate Pr.
Taphiæ Iæ
Astacus
Conope
Trichonis L.
Thermum
Echinades Iæ
Melite L.
IONIUM
Ithaca
Ithaca
Alalcomenæ
Œniadæ
Pleuron
Evenus F.
Naupactus
Calydon
Cynia L.
Rhium Pr.
Oxiæ Iæ
Sinus Calydonius
Araxus Pr.
Patræ
Pale
Same Samos
Cephallenia
Crane

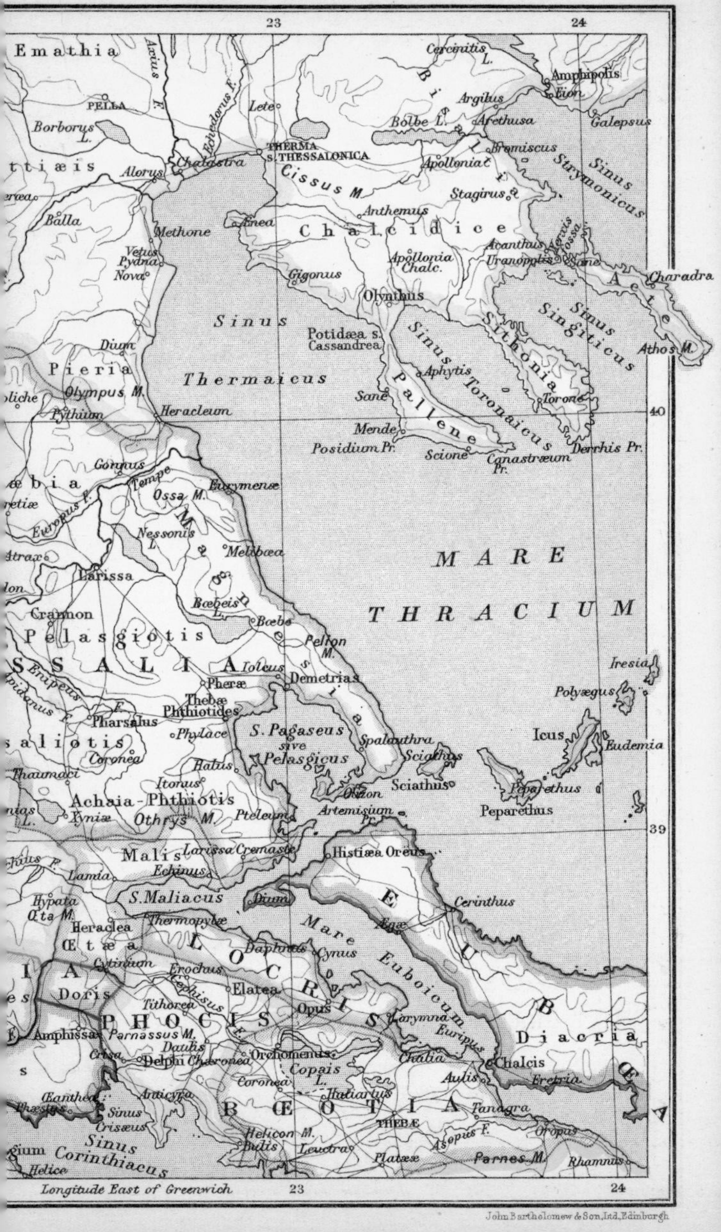
23
24
Emathia
Axius F.
Echedorus F.
Cercinitis L.
Bisaltia
Amphipolis
Eion
PELLA
Lete
Argilus
Borborus L.
Bolbe L.
Arethusa
Galepsus
THERMA
S. THESSALONICA
Bromiscus
Chalastra
Apollonia
Sinus Strymonicus
Alorus
Cissus M.
Stagirus
Balla
Anthemus
Aenea
Methone
Chalcidice
Acanthus
Xerxis Fossa
Vetus Pydna
Nova
Apollonia Chalc.
Uranopolis
Sane
Charadra
Gigonus
Acte
Olynthus
Sinus Singiticus
Sinus
Potidæa s. Cassandrea
Sithonia
Dium
Sinus Toronaicus
Athos M.
Pieria
Thermaicus
Aphytis
Olympus M.
Sane
Pallene
Torone
Pythium
Heracleum
40
Mende
Derrhis Pr.
Posidium Pr.
Scione
Canastræum Pr.
Gonnus
Tempe
Eurymenæ
Ossa M.
Europus F.
Nessonis L.
Magnesia
Melibœa
Larissa
MARE
Bœbeis L.
THRACIUM
Crannon
Bœbe
Pelasgiotis
Pelion M.
SSALIA
Iolcus
Iresia
Enipeus
Pheræ
Demetrias
Polyægus
Thebæ Phthiotides
Pharsalus
S. Pagaseus sive Pelasgicus
Icus
Phylace
Spalauthra
Eudemia
Coronea
Sciathus
Halus
Sciathus
Peparethus
Itonus
Olizon
Achaia-Phthiotis
Peparethus
Xyniæ
Othrys M.
Pteleum
Artemisium Pr.
39
Malis
Larissa Cremaste
Histiæa Oreus
Echinus
Lamia
Hypata
S. Maliacus
Dium
Cerinthus
Œta M.
Heraclea
Thermopylæ
Mare Euboicum
Œtæa
Ægæ
Euboea
Cytinium
Daphnus
Cynus
Doris
Erochus
Locris
Cephisus
Elatea
Tithorea
Opus
PHOCIS
Larymna
Amphissa
Parnassus M.
Euripus
Diacria
Daulis
Crisa
Delphi
Chæronea
Orchomenus
Chalia
Chalcis
Copais L.
Coronea
Aulis
Eretria
Œanthea
Anticyra
Haliartus
Sinus Crisæus
BŒOTIA
Tanagra
THEBÆ
Helicon M.
Oropus
Sinus Corinthiacus
Bulis
Leuctra
Asopus F.
Helice
Platææ
Parnes M.
Rhamnus
Longitude East of Greenwich
23
24
John Bartholomew & Son, Ltd, Edinburgh

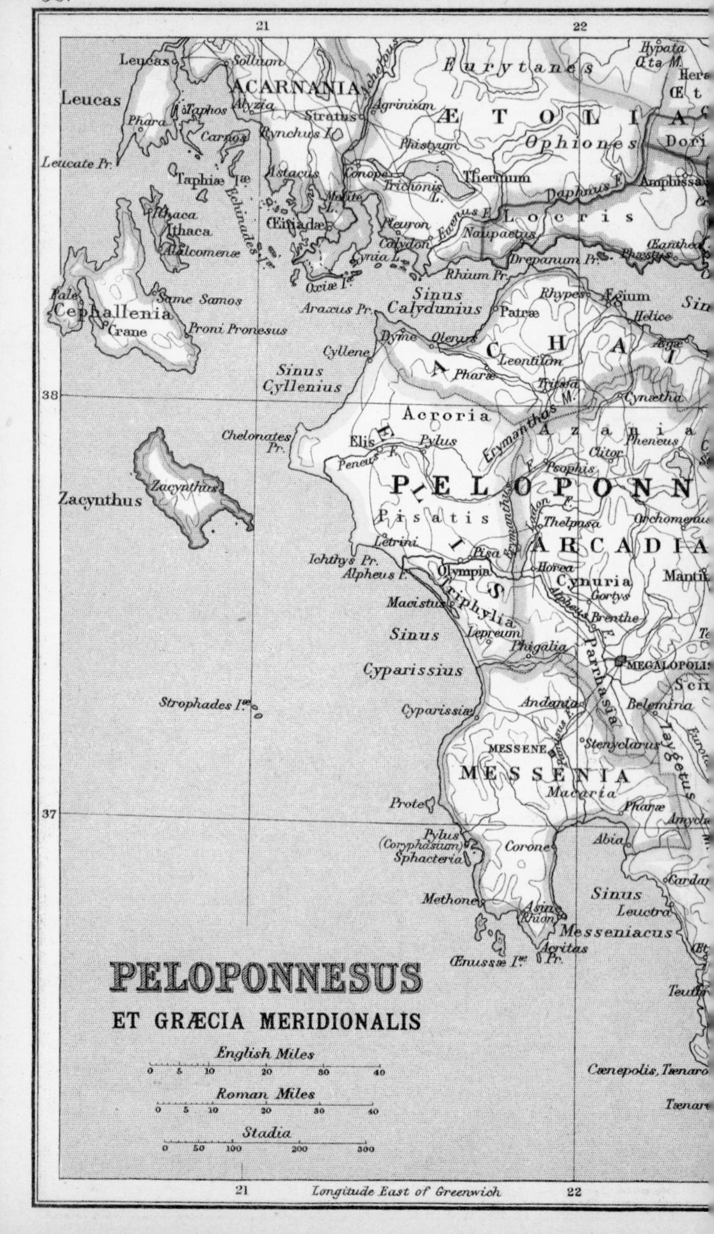
PELOPONNESUS
ET GRÆCIA MERIDIONALIS
English Miles
0 5 10 20 30 40
Roman Miles
0 5 10 20 30 40
Stadia
0 50 100 200 300
21
22
38
37
Longitude East of Greenwich
Leucas
Leucate Pr.
Sollium
ACARNANIA
Alyzia
Taphos
Phara
Carnos
Stratus
Agrinium
Rynchus L.
Eurytanes
ÆTOLIA
Ophiones
Phistyum
Thermum
Trichonis L.
Conope
Astacus
Taphiæ Iæ
Echinades Iæ
Œniadæ
Ithaca
Alalcomenæ
Pleuron
Calydon
Evenus F.
Naupactus
Locris
Daphnus F.
Amphissa
Drepanum Pr.
Rhium Pr.
Oxiæ Iæ
Pale
Cephallenia
Same Samos
Crane
Proni Pronesus
Araxus Pr.
Sinus Calydunius
Patræ
Rhypes
Ægium
Helice
Dyme
Olenus
Leontium
ACHAIA
Pharæ
Tritæa
Cynætha
Cyllene
Sinus Cyllenius
Acroria
Azania
Pheneus
Clitor
Psophis
Chelonates Pr.
Elis
Pylus
Peneus F.
Erymanthus
ELIS
PELOPONN
Zacynthus
Pisatis
Ladon F.
Thelpusa
Orchomenus
Letrini
Pisa
ARCADIA
Ichthys Pr.
Alpheus F.
Olympia
Horea
Cynuria
Gortys
Brenthe
Mantinea
Macistus
Triphylia
Sinus Cyparissius
Lepreum
Phigalia
Parrhasia
MEGALOPOLIS
Strophades Iæ
Cyparissiæ
Andania
Belemina
Stenyclarus
MESSENE
Pamisus F.
MESSENIA
Macaria
Taygetus
Pharæ
Prote
Pylus (Coryphasium)
Sphacteria
Corone
Abia
Methone
Asine Rhion
Sinus Messeniacus
Leuctra
Acritas Pr.
Œnussæ Iæ
Cænepolis, Tænaro

John Bartholomew & Son Ltd. Edinburgh

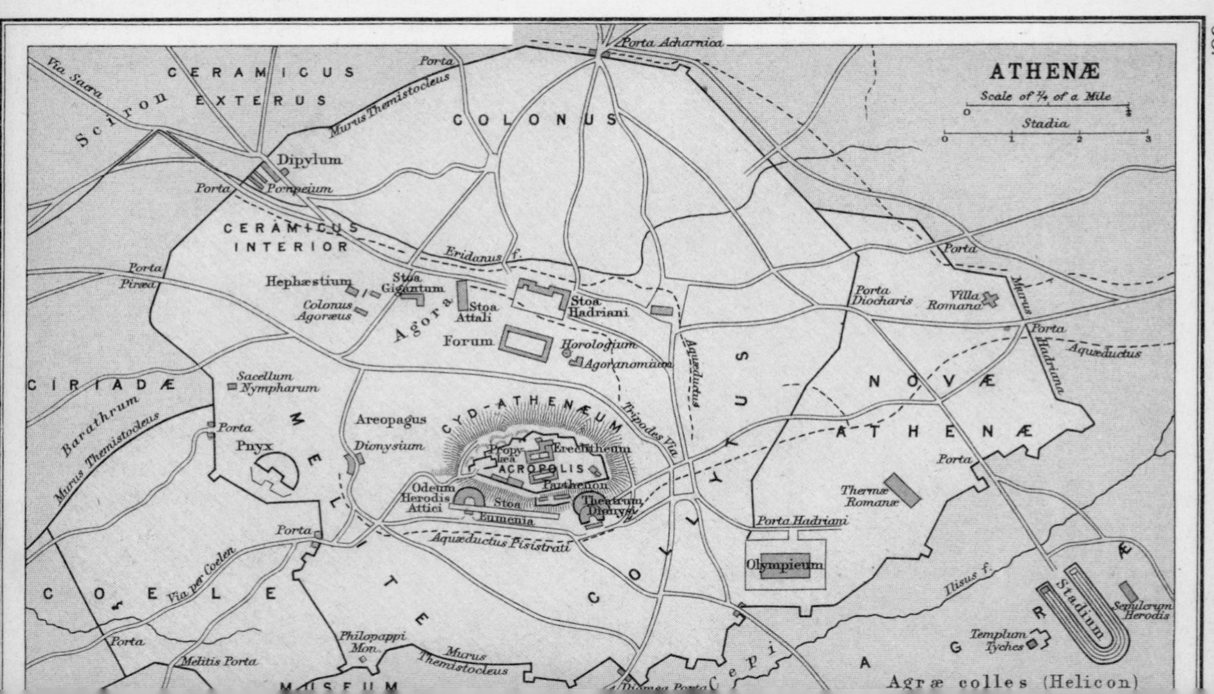
ATHENÆ
Scale of 3/4 of a Mile
Stadia
0
1
2
3
CERAMICUS EXTERUS
Via Sacra
Sciron
COLONUS
Porta Acharnica
Porta
Murus Themistocleus
Dipylum
Pompeium
CERAMICUS INTERIOR
Eridanus f.
Porta Piræa
Hephæstium
Stoa Gigantum
Colonus Agoræus
Agora
Stoa Attali
Stoa Hadriani
Forum
Horologium
Agoranomium
Aquæductus
Porta Diocharis
Villa Romana
Murus
Porta Hadriana
NOVÆ ATHENÆ
CIRIADÆ
Sacellum Nympharum
Barathrum
Pnyx
MELITE
Areopagus
Dionysium
CYD-ATHENÆUM
Tripodes Via
Propylæa
Erechtheum
ACROPOLIS
Parthenon
Odeum Herodis Attici
Stoa
Eumenia
Theatrum Dionysi
Aquæductus Pisistrati
COLLYTUS
Thermæ Romanæ
Porta Hadriani
Olympieum
Ilisus f.
Stadium
Sepulcrum Herodis
Templum Tyches
AGRÆ
COELE
Via per Coelen
Melitis Porta
Philopappi Mon.
Murus Themistocleus
MUSEUM
Cepi
Agræ colles (Helicon)

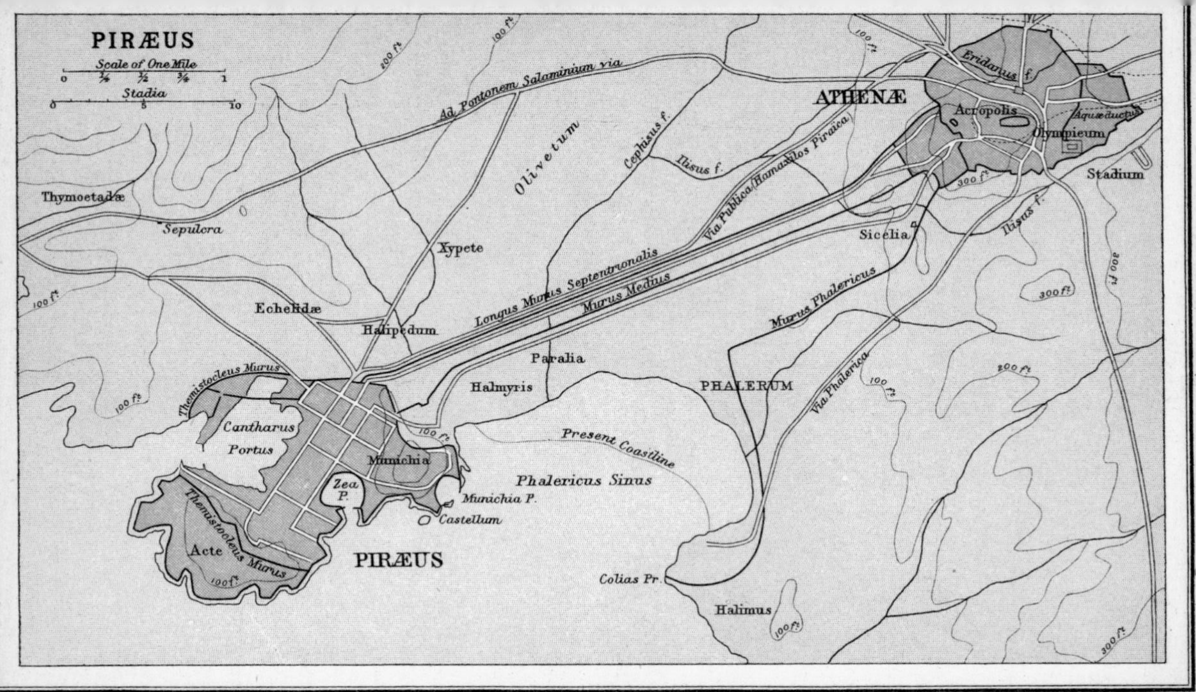
PIRÆUS
Scale of One Mile
0 ¼ ½ ¾ 1
Stadia
0 5 10
Ad Pontonem Salaminium via
Thymoetadæ
Sepulcra
Olivetum
Cephisus f.
Ilisus f.
Via Publica/Hamaxitos Piraica
ATHENÆ
Eridanus f.
Acropolis
Aquæductus
Olympieum
Stadium
300 ft.
Ilisus f.
Sicelia
Xypete
Echelidæ
Halipedum
Longus Murus Septentrionalis
Murus Medius
Murus Phalericus
200 ft.
100 ft.
Paralia
Halmyris
PHALERUM
Via Phalerica
Themistocleus Murus
Cantharus
Portus
Munichia
Zea P.
Present Coastline
Phalericus Sinus
Munichia P.
Castellum
Acte
Themistocleus Murus
PIRÆUS
Colias Pr.
Halimus
John Bartholomew & Son, Ltd. Edinburgh

Caledonia
INSULÆ
BRITANNICÆ
Ierne
Albion
OCEANUS ATLANTICUS
OCEANUS GERMANICUS
Rhenus
G E R
Danuv
CELTICA
Ligeris F.
Lugudunum
Genava
Rhodanus
Ræti a
Venetia
Padus F.
Liguria
Etruria
Umbria
ADRI
Avennio
Agatha
Narbo
Massalia
Monœci
Antipolis
Nicæa
Athenopolis
Olbia
Emporiæ
Rhode
Cyrnos
Alalia
(Corsica)
Punicum
Roma
Latium
Circei
IBERIA
Durius F.
Iber F.
Tagus F.
Anas F.
Bætis F.
Tarraco
Baleares Iæ
(Gymnesiæ)
Saguntum
Hemeroscopium
Alonæ
Lucentum
Ebusus
(Pityusæ)
Onoba
Gades
Malaca
Abdera
Mænaca
Fr. Gaditanum
Carteia
Columnæ Herculis
Tingis
Lixus
Rusaddir
Cartenna
Icosium
Iol
Iomnium
Chullu
Hippo
Diarrhytus
Utica
Carthago
Sardo
Tharrus
(Sardinia)
Sulci
Carales
MARE TYRRHENU
Posidon
M A R E
Panhormus
Iæ Æoli
Motya
Sicili
Agrigentum
(Acragas)
Camarina
Hadrumetum
Thapsus
Tacapes
Sabrata
G Æ T U L I
English Miles
Stadia
10
0
50
30

GRECIAN & PHŒNICIAN COLONIES
Greek Colonies
Phœnician Colonies
20
30
40
50
40
30
Borysthenes F.
Scythæ
Olbia
Mæotis L.
Phanagoria
Ophiusa
Panticapæum
Theudosia
Chersonesus
Colchis
Pityus
Dioscurias
Phasis
Getæ
Ister F.
Istrus
Tomis
Callatis
Odessus
Mesembria
PONTUS EUXINUS
Sinope
Cytorus
Carusa
Amisus
Themiscyra
Cotyora
Cerasus
Hermonassa
Trapezus
Heraclea
Bosporus Thracicus
THRACE
Byzantium
Perinthus
Calchedon
Astacus
Propontis
Cius
Cyzicus
Lissus
Crenides
Abdera
Neapolis
Amphipolis
Thasos
Ænus
Apollonia
Methone
Olynthus
Potidæa
Abydus
Ilium
Assus
Lemnos
Cappadocia
Epidamnus
Tarentum
Hydruntum
Siris
Sybaris
Epirus
Corcyra
Croton
Scylletium
Caulonia
Cephallenia
Ambracia
Chalcis
Chios
Lesbos
Atarneus
Cyme
Phrygia
Smyrna
Ephesus
Samos
Miletus
Tarsus
Soli
Myriandus
Rhosus
Cilicia
GRÆCIA
Athenæ
Peloponnesus
Sparta
Naxos
Halicarnassus
Phaselis
Side
Celenderis
MARE IONIUM ET SICULUM
Melos
Rhodus
Cythera
Cydonia
Cnosus
Creta
Carpathus
Lapethus
Salamis
Soli
Citium
Cyprus
Paphos
Curium
Amathus
Aradus
Byblus
Berytus
Sidon
Tyrus
Ace
Damascus
PHŒNICE
Iope
Hierosolyma
INTERNUM
Apollonia
Cyrene
Taucheira
Paliurus
Barca
Euhesperides
Milesiorum castellum
Naucratis
Memphis
ÆGYPTUS
LIBYA
Longitude East 20 of Greenwich
John Bartholomew & Son, Ltd, Edinburgh

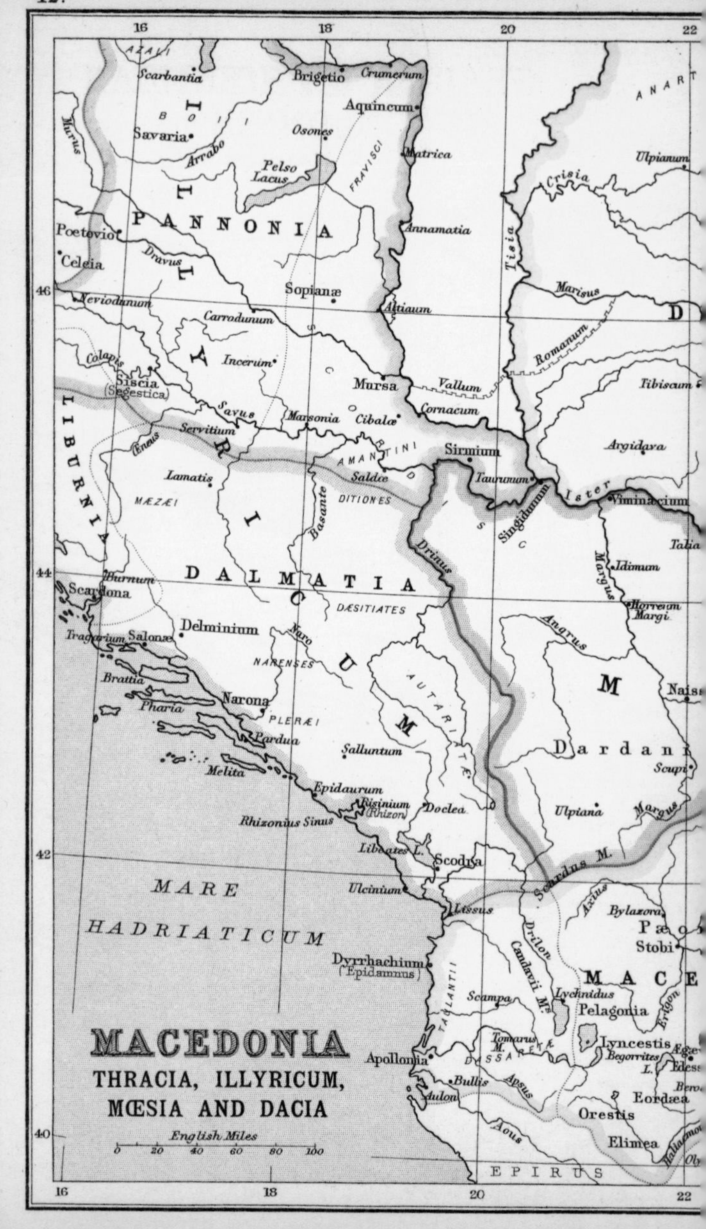
MACEDONIA
THRACIA, ILLYRICUM,
MŒSIA AND DACIA
English Miles
0 20 40 60 80 100
16
18
20
22
46
44
42
40
AZALI
Scarbantia
Brigetio
Crumerum
Aquincum
BOII
Savaria
Osones
Murus
Arrabo
Pelso Lacus
FRAVISCI
Matrica
Ulpianum
Crisia
PANNONIA
Poetovio
Celeia
Dravus
Annamatia
Tisia
Sopianæ
Marisus
Neviodunum
Altiaum
Carrodunum
Romanum
Colapis
Incerum
Siscia
(Segestica)
Mursa
Vallum
Tibiscum
LIBURNIA
Savus
Marsonia
Cibalæ
Cornacum
Servitium
Œneus
AMANTINI
Sirmium
Argidava
Lamatis
Saldæ
Taurunum
MÆZÆI
Basante
DITIONES
Singidunum
Ister
Viminacium
Drinus
Talia
Margus
Idimum
Burnum
Scardona
DALMATIA
DÆSITIATES
Horreum Margi
Tragurium
Salonæ
Delminium
Naro
Angrus
NARENSES
Brattia
Pharia
Narona
AUTARIATÆ
Naiss
PLERÆI
Pardua
Dardani
Salluntum
Scupi
Melita
Epidaurum
Risinium
(Rhizon)
Doclea
Ulpiana
Margus
Rhizonius Sinus
Libeates L.
Scodra
Scardus M.
MARE
HADRIATICUM
Ulcinium
Lissus
Axius
Bylazora
Drilon
Stobi
Dyrrhachium
(Epidamnus)
Candavii Ms.
MACE
TAULANTII
Scampa
Lychnidus
Pelagonia
Erigon
Tomarus M.
DASSARETÆ
Lyncestis
Apollonia
Begorrites L.
Bullis
Apsus
Aulon
Eordæa
Orestis
Aous
Elimea
EPIRUS
ILLYRICUM
MŒSIA
SCORDISCI

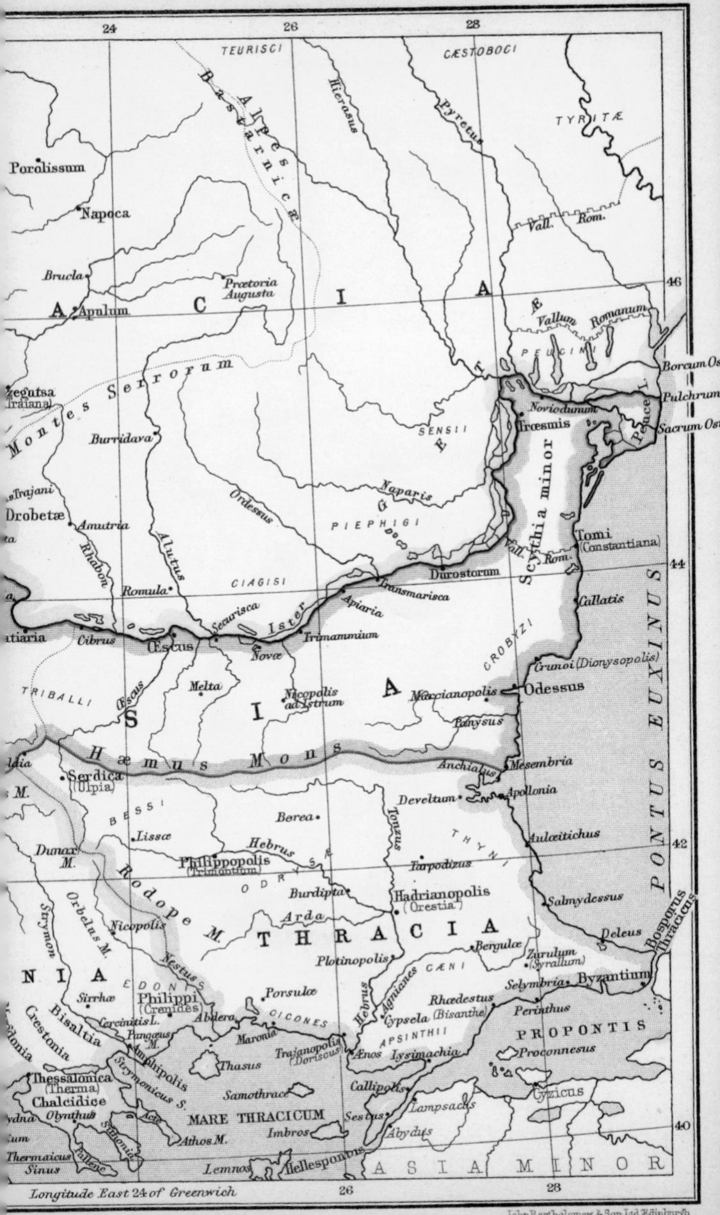
TEURISCI
CÆSTOBOCI
TYRITÆ
Porolissum
Napoca
Brucla
Prætoria Augusta
Apulum
Montes Serrorum
Burridava
Drobetæ
Amutria
Rhabon
Alutus
Romula
Ordessus
Naparis
PIEPHIGI
CIAGISI
SENSII
Pyretus
Hierasus
Vall. Rom.
Vallum Romanum
PEUCINI
Borcum Ost.
Pulchrum
Sacrum Ost.
Peuce I.
Noviodunum
Trœsmis
Scythia minor
Tomi
(Constantiana)
Durostorum
Transmarisca
Apiaria
Ister
Sucurisca
Cibrus
Œscus
Novæ
Trimammium
Callatis
CROBYZI
Grunoi (Dionysopolis)
Odessus
Marcianopolis
Nicopolis ad Istrum
Melta
TRIBALLI
Panysus
Hæmus Mons
Anchialus
Mesembria
Apollonia
Develtum
Serdica
(Ulpia)
BESSI
Berea
Tonzus
THYNI
Aulæitichus
Lissæ
Hebrus
Philippopolis
(Trimontium)
ODRYSÆ
Tarpodizus
Burdipta
Hadrianopolis
(Orestia)
Salmydessus
Rodope M.
Arda
THRACIA
Nicopolis
Orbelus M.
Strymon
Deleus
Bosporus Thracicus
Bergulæ
Plotinopolis
CÆNI
Zurulum
(Syrallum)
Agrianes
Nestus
EDONES
Porsulæ
Philippi
(Crenides)
Sirrhæ
Selymbria
Byzantium
Rhædestus
(Bisanthe)
Perinthus
Cypsela
PROPONTIS
CICONES
Abdera
Maronia
Cercinitis L.
Pangæus M.
Bisaltia
Crestonia
Amphipolis
Thasus
Trajanopolis
(Doriscus)
Ænos
APSINTHII
Lysimachia
Proconnesus
Strymonicus S.
Thessalonica
(Therma)
Chalcidice
Olynthus
Samothrace
Callipolis
Cyzicus
Lampsacus
MARE THRACICUM
Sestus
Abydus
Imbros
Athos M.
Acte
Sithonia
Pallene
Thermaicus Sinus
Lemnos
Hellespontus
ASIA MINOR
Longitude East 24 of Greenwich
24
26
28
46
44
42
40
John Bartholomew & Son, Ltd. Edinburgh

BRITANNIA
English Miles
0 10 20 40 60 80 100 120
Roman Miles
0 10 20 40 60 80 100 120
OCEANUS ATLANTICUS
OCEANUS GERMANICUS
Taruedum s. Orcas Pr.
Veruedrum Pr.
Verubium Pr.
CORNAVII
CAERENI
CARNONACAE OR CAERENI
SMERTAE
LUGI
DECANTAE
CREONES
CERONES
Volas S.?
Hebudae
Scetis
Malaeus
Ricina
TAEZALI
CALEDONII
Tuësis
VACOMAGI
Deva
VENICONES
CALEDONIA
Saltus Caledonius
Horrea
Taus
M. Graupius?
HORESTI
?Lindum
Bodotria
Vallum Antonini
EPIDII
Clota
DAMNONII
Coria?
Watling Street
OTADINI
Newstead
Novius
SELGOVAE
Bremenium
Epidium Pr.
Blatum Bulgium
Vallum Hadriani
NOVANTAE
Pons Aelii
(Newcastle)
Novantarum Paeninsula
Ituna
Luguvallium
(Carlisle)
Vinovia
Venniconium Pr.
Pr. Septentrionale
VENNICONII
Vidua
Argitas
ROBOGDII
Ravius
8
6
2
0
2
58
56

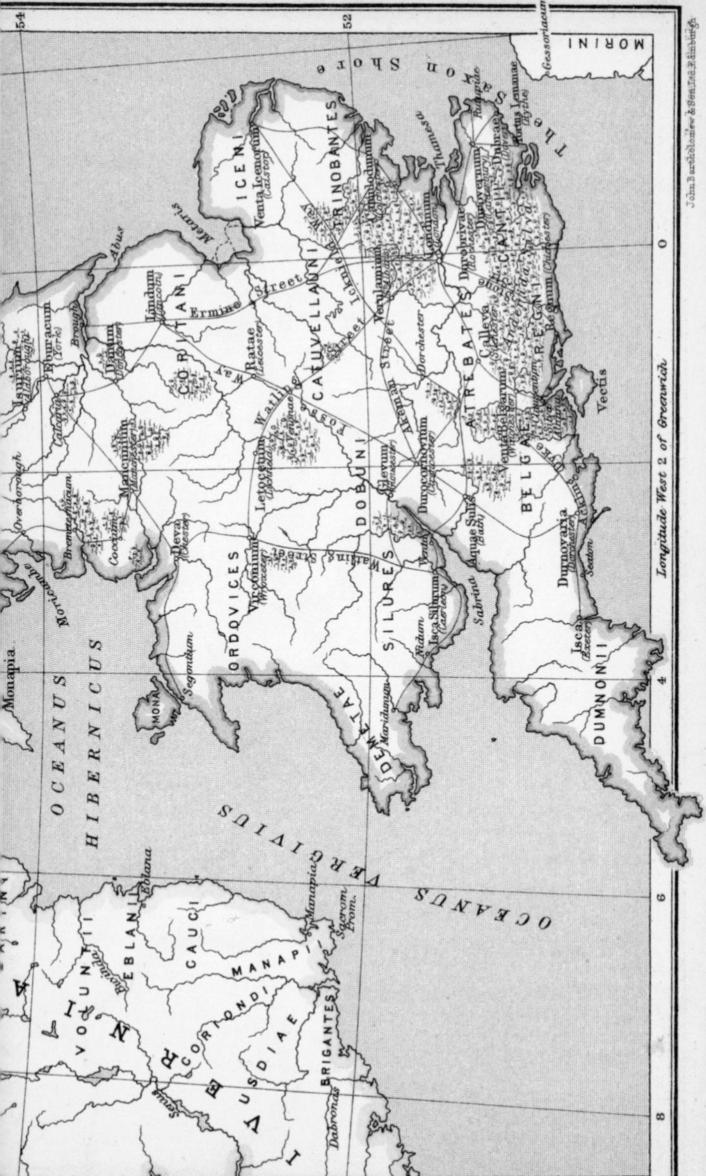

Monapia
Overborough
Isurium (Aldborough)
Eburacum (York)
Calcaria
Brough
Bremetennacum
Moricambe
OCEANUS HIBERNICUS
IVERNIA
VOLUNTII
Buvinda
EBLANII
Eblana
Senus
CORIONDI
CAUCI
USDIAE
MANAPII
Manapia
BRIGANTES
Dabronas
Sacrom Prom.
OCEANUS VERGIVIUS
MONA
Segontium
Coccium
Mancunium (Manchester)
Danum (Doncaster)
Abus
Lindum (Lincoln)
CORITANI
Deva (Chester)
Metaris
ORDOVICES
Viroconium (Wroxeter)
Letocetum (Lichfield)
Venonae
Watling Street
Ratae (Leicester)
Ermine Street
Way
ICENI
Venta Icenorum (Caistor)
Foss Way
CATUVELLAUNI
Icknield Way
TRINOBANTES
DEMETAE
Maridunum
SILURES
DOBUNI
Glevum (Gloucester)
Verulamium (St Albans)
Camulodunum (Colchester)
Akeman Street
Nidum
Isca Silurum (Caerleon)
Venta
Durocornovium (Cirencester)
Dorchester
Londinium (London)
Thamesa
Sabrina
Aquae Sulis (Bath)
ATREBATES
Durobrivae (Rochester)
Calleva (Silchester)
Stone Street
Durovernum (Canterbury)
Rutupiae
Venta Belgarum (Winchester)
Anderida Silva
CANTII
Dubrae (Dover)
Portus Lemanae (Hythe)
BELGAE
Clausentum
Silva Ampla
REGNI
Regnum (Chichester)
Gessoriacum
The Saxon Shore
MORINI
Durnovaria (Dorchester)
Ackling Dyke
Isca (Exeter)
Seaton
Vectis
DUMNONII
54
52
8
6
4
0
Longitude West 2 of Greenwich
John Bartholomew & Son, Ltd. Edinburgh

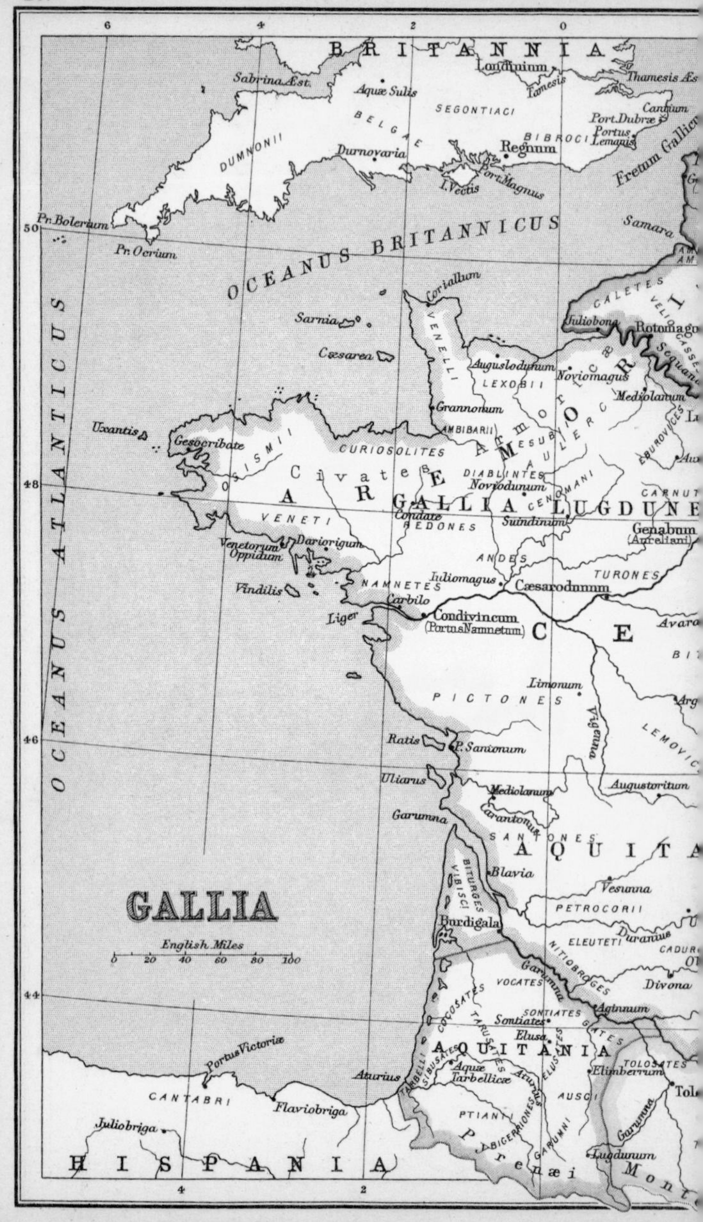
GALLIA
English Miles
0 20 40 60 80 100
BRITANNIA
Londinium
Sabrina Æst.
Aquæ Sulis
Tamesis
Thamesis Æs
SEGONTIACI
BELGAE
Cantium
Port.Dubræ
Portus Lemanis
BIBROCI
Regnum
DUMNONII
Durnovaria
Fretum Gallic
Port.Magnus
I.Vectis
Pr.Bolerium
Pr.Ocrium
OCEANUS BRITANNICUS
Samara
OCEANUS ATLANTICUS
Coriallum
Sarnia
Cæsarea
VENELLI
CALETES
VELIOCASSES
Juliobona
Rotomagu
Sequana
Augustodurum
Noviomagus
LEXOBII
Mediolanum
Grannonum
AMBIBARII
EBUROVICES
Uxantis
Gesocribate
OSISMII
CURIOSOLITES
MESUBII
AULERCI
Armorica
Civitates
ARMORICÆ
DIABLINTES
Noviodunum
CENOMANI
CARNUT
GALLIA LUGDUNE
VENETI
Condate
REDONES
Suindinum
Genabum
(Aureliani)
Venetorum Oppidum
Dariorigum
ANDES
Iuliomagus
Cæsarodunum
TURONES
Vindilis
NAMNETES
Carbilo
Liger
Condivincum
(Portus Namnetum)
CE
Avara
Limonum
PICTONES
Vigenna
LEMOVIC
Ratis
P.Santonum
Uliarus
Mediolanum
Augustoritum
Garumna
Carantonus
SANTONES
AQUITA
BITURGES VIBISCI
Blavia
Vesunna
PETROCORII
Burdigala
Duranius
ELEUTETI
NITIOBROGES
CADUR
VOCATES
Garumna
Divona
COCOSATES
TARUSATES
SONTIATES
Sontiates
Aginnum
Elusa
ELUSATES
GATES
AQUITANIA
Portus Victoriæ
SIBUSATES
Aquæ Tarbellicæ
Aturus
Elimberrum
TOLOSATES
Aturius
TARBELLI
AUSCI
Tol
CANTABRI
Flaviobriga
PTIANII
BIGERRIONES
GARUMNI
Garumna
Juliobriga
Pyrenæi
Lugdunum
Mont
HISPANIA
6
4
2
0
50
48
46
44

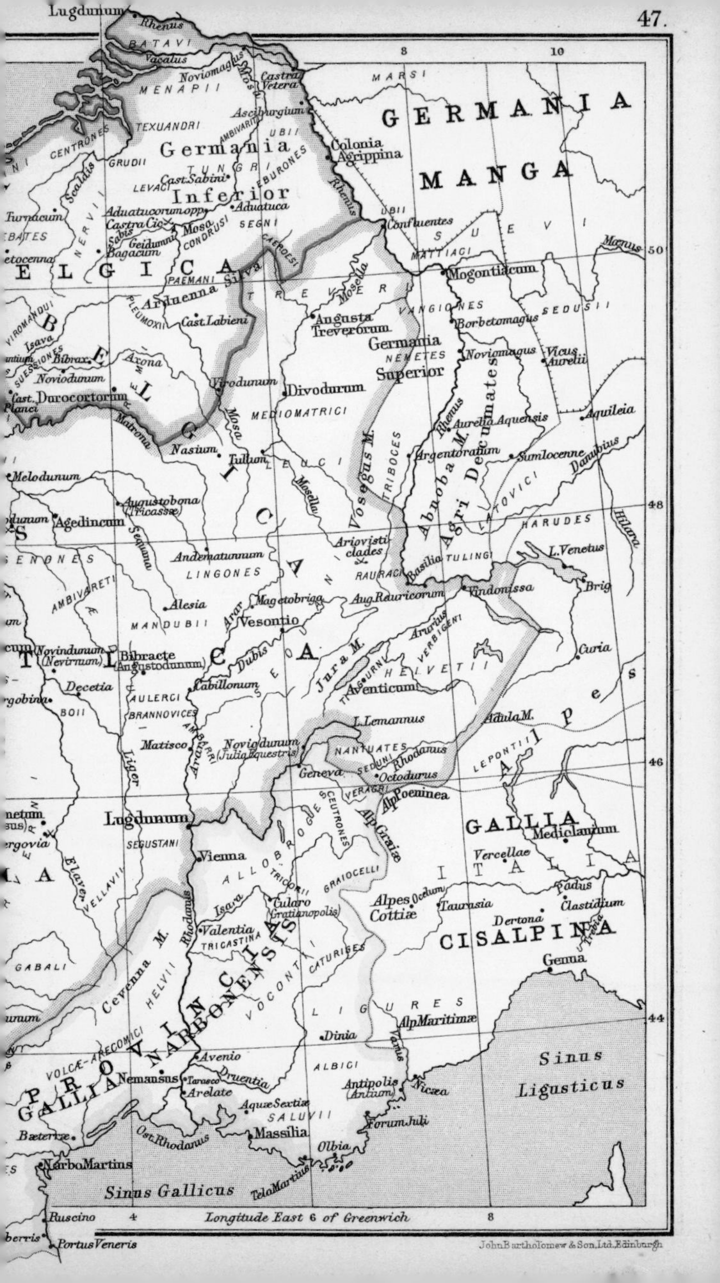
Lugdunum
Rhenus
BATAVI
Vacalus
Noviomagus
MENAPII
Mosa
Castra Vetera
MARSI
GERMANIA
Asciburgium
TEXUANDRI
AMBIVARITI
UBII
CENTRONES
Germania
Colonia Agrippina
MANGA
TUNGRI
EBURONES
GRUDII
Scaldis
Cast.Sabini
LEVACI
Inferior
NERVII
Rhenus
Turnacum
Aduatucorum opp.
Aduatuca
Castra Cic.
Sabis
Mosa
CONDRUSI
SEGNI
UBII
Confluentes
SUEVI
Geidumni
Bagacum
CAEROESI
MATTIACI
Mœnus
50
BELGICA
PAEMANI
Silva
Mogontiacum
Arduenna
TREVERI
Mosella
VANGIONES
SEDUSII
VIROMANDUI
PLEUMOXII
Cast.Labieni
Augusta Treverorum
Borbetomagus
Isava
Germania
NEMETES
Noviomagus
Vicus Aurelii
SUESSIONES
Bibrax
Axona
REMI
Superior
Noviodunum
Virodunum
Divodurum
Decumates
Durocortorum
MEDIOMATRICI
Aurelia Aquensis
Aquileia
Matrona
Mosa
Rhenus
Nasium
Tullum
LEUCI
Vosegus M.
TRIBOCES
Argentoratum
Sumlocenne
Danubius
Melodunum
Mosella
Abnoba M.
LATOVICI
Agri
Augustobona (Tricassæ)
48
Agedincum
Sequana
HARUDES
Hilara
SENONES
Ariovisti clades
L.Venetus
Andematunnum
LINGONES
RAURACI
Basilia
TULINGI
Vindonissa
Brig
AMBIVARETI
Alesia
Arar
Magetobriga
Aug.Rauricorum
MANDUBII
Vesontio
Aruras
VERBIGENI
Novindunum (Nevirnum)
Bibracte Augustodunum
Dubis
SEQUANI
Jura M.
Curia
HELVETII
Decetia
Cabillonum
TIGURINI
Aventicum
BOII
AULERCI BRANNOVICES
L.Lemannus
Adula M.
Alpes
Matisco
AMBARRI
Noviodunum (Julia Equestris)
NANTUATES
Rhodanus
LEPONTII
Liger
Arar
SEDUNI
Octodurus
46
Geneva
VERAGRI
Alp.Pœninea
CEUTRONES
ALLOBROGES
Alp.Graiæ
GALLIA
Lugdunum
Mediolanum
SEGUSTANI
Vercellae
Vienna
ITALIA
Elaver
VELLAVII
TRICORII
GRAIOCELLI
Padus
Alpes Cottiæ
Ocelum
Taurasia
Clastidium
Isara
Cularo (Gratianopolis)
Dertona
Rhodanus
Valentia
CISALPINA
Trebia
TRICASTINA
CATURIGES
Genua
GABALI
Cevenna M.
HELVII
VOCONTII
LIGURES
Alp.Maritimæ
44
Dinia
Varus
Sinus
Ligusticus
VOLCÆ-ARECOMICI
Avenio
ALBICI
PROVINCIA
NARBONENSIS
GALLIA
Nemausus
Tarasco
Druentia
Antipolis (Antium)
Nicæa
Arelate
Aquæ Sextiæ
SALUVII
Forum Juli
Bæterræ
Ost.Rhodanus
Massilia
Olbia
Narbo Martius
Sinus Gallicus
Tela Martius
Ruscino
4
Longitude East 6 of Greenwich
8
Portus Veneris
John Bartholomew & Son, Ltd. Edinburgh

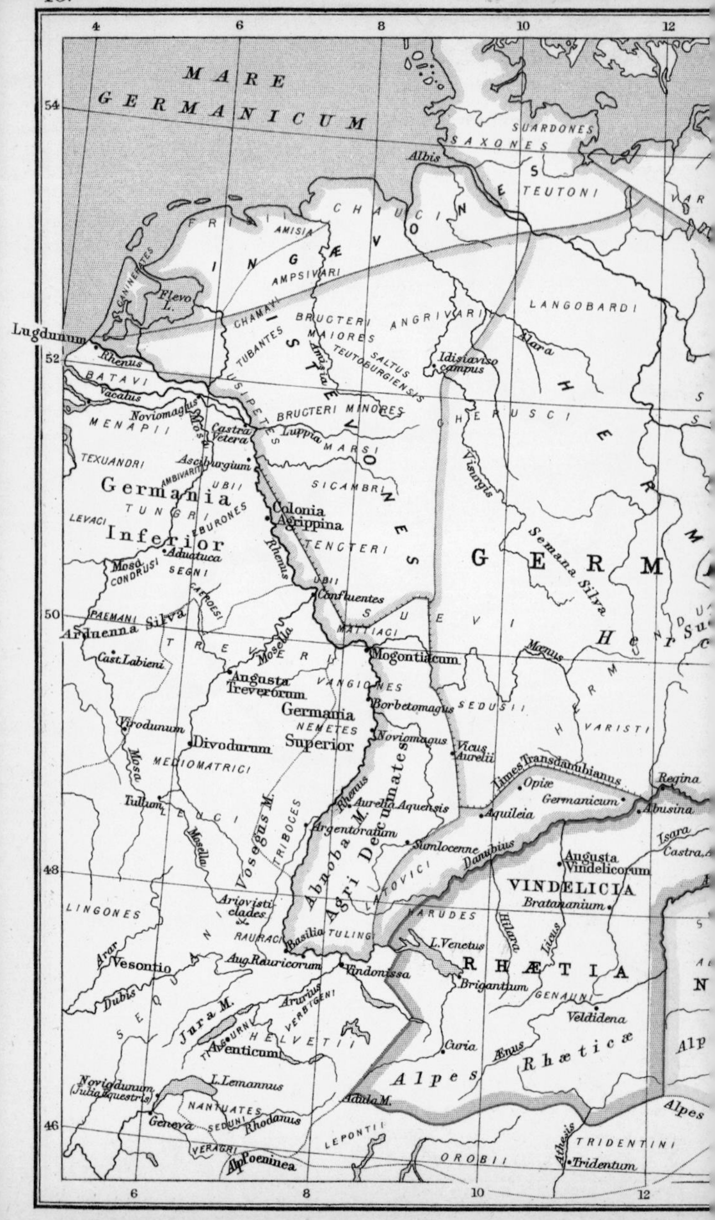
MARE GERMANICUM
SAXONES
SUARDONES
TEUTONI
Albis
CHAUCI
FRISII
AMISIA
INGÆVONES
AMPSIVARI
CANINEFATES
Flevo L.
CHAMAVI
TUBANTES
BRUCTERI MAIORES
ANGRIVARII
LANGOBARDI
Lugdunum
Rhenus
BATAVI
Vacalus
Amisia
SALTUS TEUTOBURGIENSIS
Idisiaviso campus
Alara
HERMINONES
ISTÆVONES
USIPETES
Noviomagus
MENAPII
Mosa
Castra Vetera
Luppia
BRUCTERI MINORES
CHERUSCI
MARSI
TEXUANDRI
Asciburgium
AMBIVARITI
UBII
SICAMBRI
Visurgis
Germania Inferior
TUNGRI
EBURONES
LEVACI
Colonia Agrippina
TENCTERI
Semana Silva
Aduatuca
Mosa
CONDRUSI
SEGNI
CAEROESI
GERMANIA
UBII
Confluentes
SUEVI
PAEMANI
Arduenna Silva
MATTIACI
TREVERI
Moenus
Mogontiacum
Cast. Labieni
Mosella
Augusta Treverorum
VANGIONES
Borbetomagus
SEDUSII
Germania Superior
NEMETES
Virodunum
Divodurum
Noviomagus
VARISTI
Vicus Aurelii
Mosa
MEDIOMATRICI
Decumates
Limes Transdanubianus
Opiæ
Regina
Tullum
LEUCI
Vosegus M.
TRIBOCES
Rhenus
Aurelia Aquensis
Germanicum
Abusina
Aquileia
Mosella
Argentoratum
Isara
Abnoba M.
Agri Decumates
Sumlocenne
Danubius
Castra
Augusta Vindelicorum
LATOVICI
VINDELICIA
Ariovisti clades
Bratananium
LINGONES
HARUDES
Hilara
RAURACI
Basilia
TULINGI
L. Venetus
Licus
Arar
Vesontio
SEQUANI
Aug. Rauricorum
Vindonissa
RHÆTIA
Brigantium
N
Dubis
Jura M.
Arurius
VERBIGENI
GENAUNI
Veldidena
Aventicum
HELVETII
Alp
Curia
Ænus
Rhætice
Noviodunum (Julia Equestris)
L. Lemannus
Alpes
Adula M.
Alpes
NANTUATES
Geneva
SEDUNI
Rhodanus
LEPONTII
TRIDENTINI
VERAGRI
Alp. Poeninea
OROBII
Athesis
Tridentum
4
6
8
10
12
54
52
50
48
46

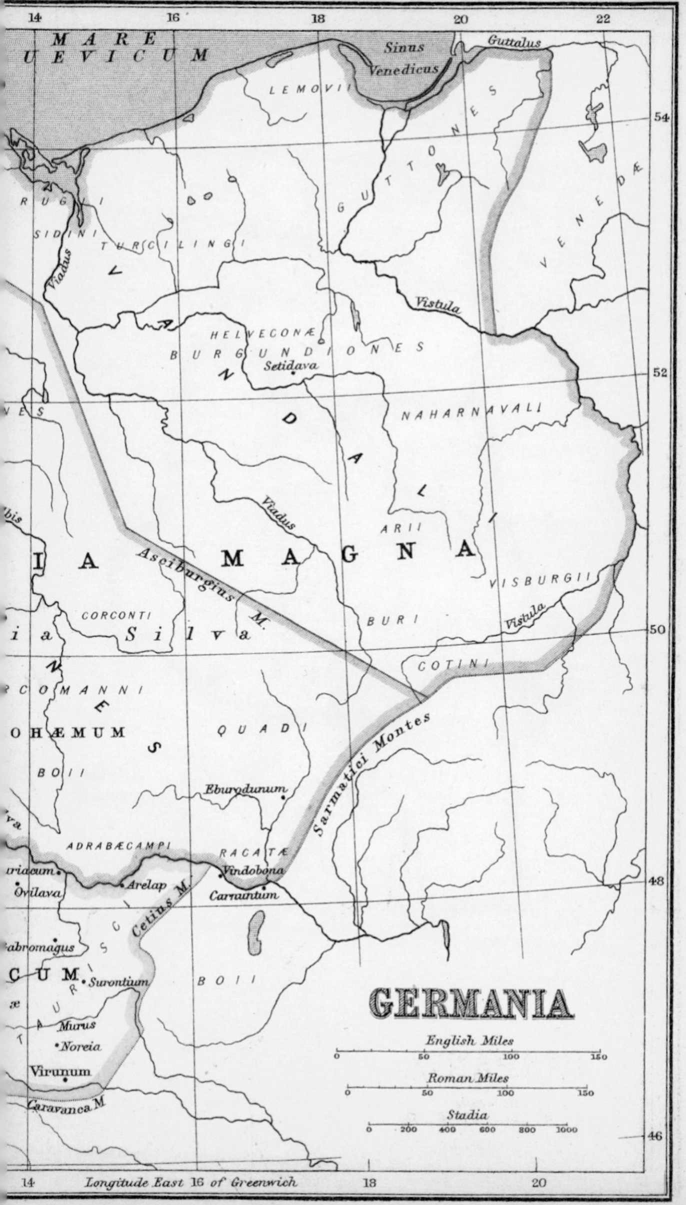
GERMANIA
MARE SUEVICUM
Sinus Venedicus
Guttalus
LEMOVII
GUTTONES
VENEDÆ
RUGII
SIDINI
TURCILINGI
Viadus
VANDALI
Vistula
HELVECONÆ
BURGUNDIONES
Setidava
NAHARNAVALI
Viadus
ARII
MAGNA
Asciburgius M.
VISBURGII
CORCONTI
Silva
BURI
Vistula
COTINI
MARCOMANNI
QUADI
Sarmatici Montes
BOHÆMUM
BOII
Eburodunum
ADRABÆCAMPI
RACATÆ
Vindobona
Arelap
Ovilava
Carnuntum
Cetius M.
Surontium
BOII
Murus
Noreia
Virunum
Caravanca M.
English Miles
Roman Miles
Stadia
Longitude East 16 of Greenwich
John Bartholomew & Son, Ltd. Edinburgh

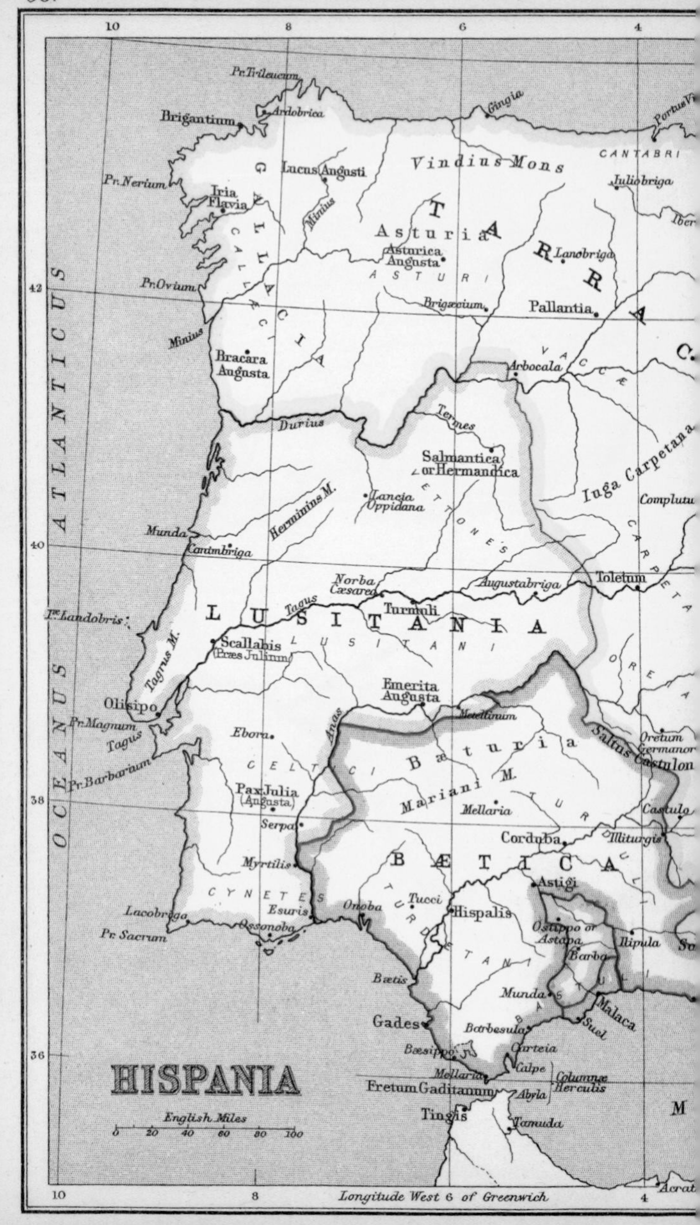
HISPANIA
OCEANUS ATLANTICUS
GALLÆCIA
Asturia
TARRAC.
LUSITANIA
Bæturia
BÆTICA
Vindius Mons
Iuga Carpetana
Herminius M.
Mariani M.
Saltus Castulon
Pr. Trileucum
Ardobrica
Brigantium
Pr. Nerium
Iria Flavia
Lucus Augusti
Minius
Pr. Ovium
Bracara Augusta
Gingia
CANTABRI
Juliobriga
Asturica Augusta
ASTURI
Lanobriga
Brigæcium
Pallantia
VACCÆ
Arbocala
Durius
Termes
Salmantica or Hermandica
Lancia Oppidana
VETTONES
Complutum
CARPETANI
Munda
Conimbriga
Norba Cæsarea
Augustabriga
Toletum
Tagus
Turmuli
Pr. Landobris
Tagrus M.
Scallabis (Præs Julium)
LUSITANI
Emerita Augusta
Metellinum
Olisipo
Pr. Magnum
Pr. Barbarium
Ebora
Anas
CELTICI
Pax Julia (Augusta)
Serpa
Myrtilis
CYNETES
Esuris
Lacobriga
Pr. Sacrum
Ossonoba
Onoba
Tucci
TURDETANI
Hispalis
Mellaria
TURDULI
Corduba
Illiturgis
Castulo
Oretum Germanorum
ORETANI
Astigi
Ostippo or Astapa
Barba
Ilipula
Bætis
Munda
Malaca
Suel
Gades
Barbesula
Bæsippo
Carteia
Calpe
Mellaria
Columnæ Herculis
Fretum Gaditanum
Abyla
Tingis
Tamuda
Acrat
English Miles
0 20 40 60 80 100
Longitude West 6 of Greenwich
10
8
6
4
42
40
38
36

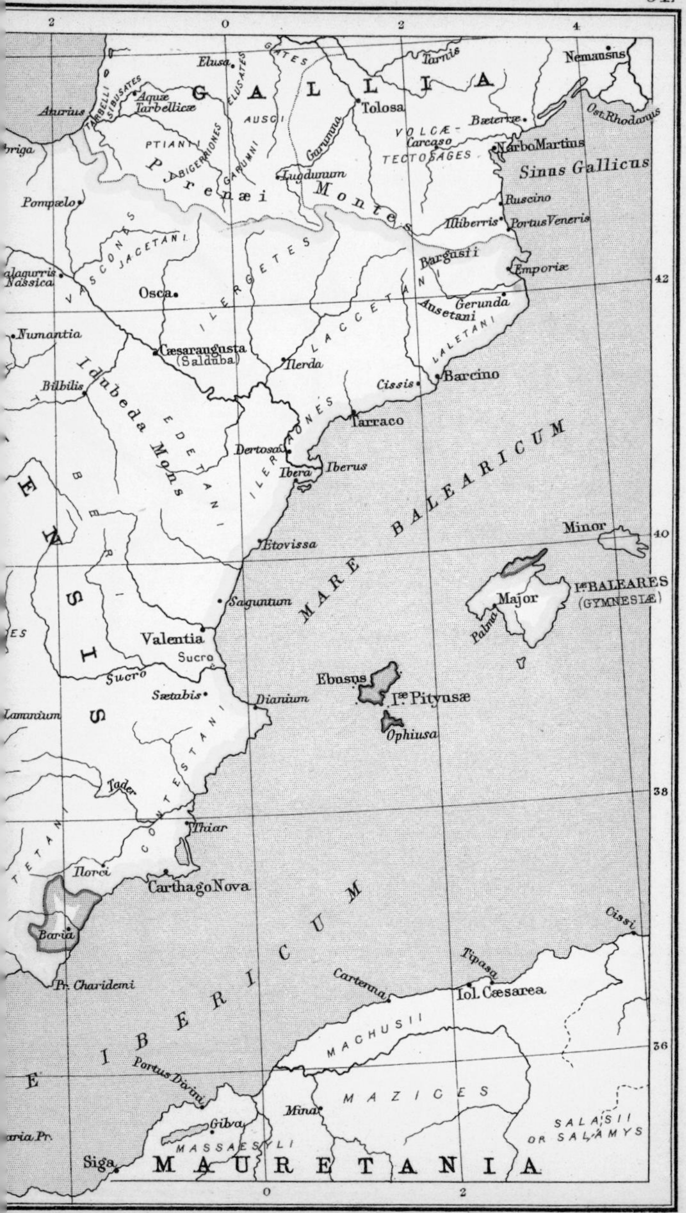

John Bartholomew & Son, Ltd. Edinburgh

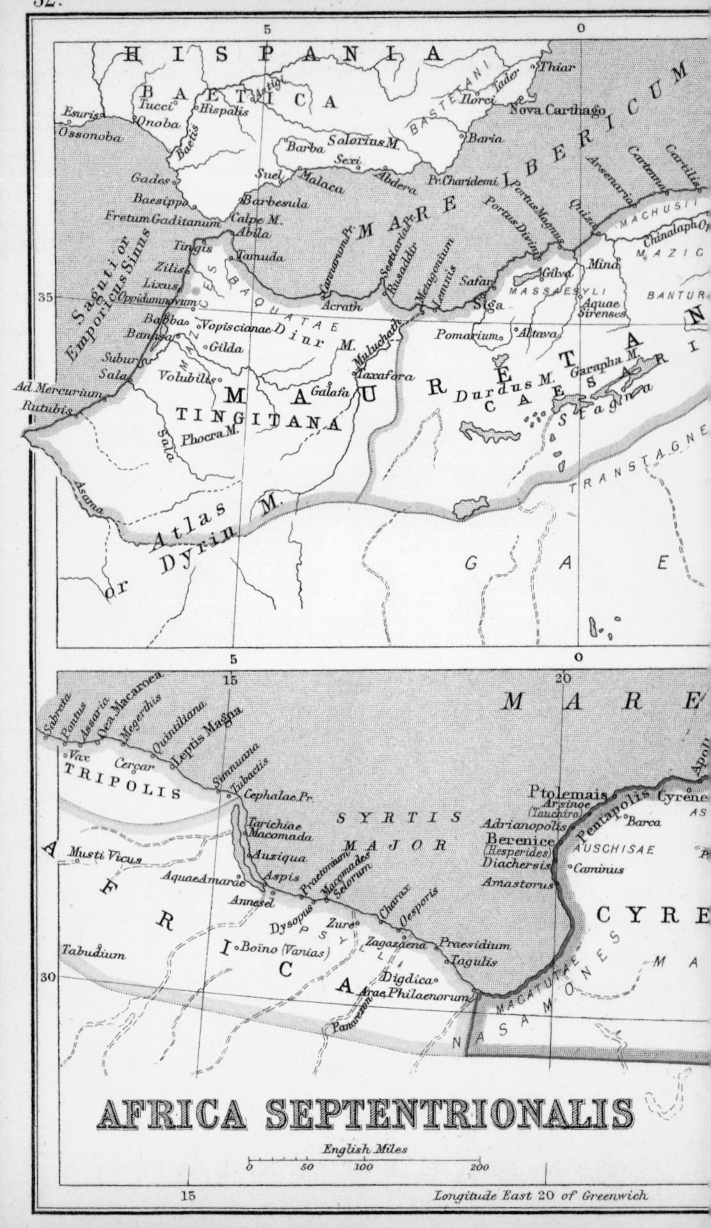
HISPANIA
BAETICA
Tucci
Onoba
Hispalis
Astigi
Esuris
Ossonoba
Baetis
Barba
Solorius M.
Sexi
Suel
Malaca
Abdera
Gades
Baesippo
Barbesula
Fretum Gaditanum
Calpe M.
Abila
Tingis
Tamuda
Zilis
Lixus
Oppidum novum
Babba
Banasa
Subur
Sala
Ad Mercurium
Rutubis
Sagunti or Emporicus Sinus
BASTETANI
Tader
Thiar
Ilorci
Nova Carthago
Baria
Pr. Charidemi
MARE IBERICUM
Arsenaria
Cartennas
Cartilis
Portus Magnus
Portus Divini
Quiza
MACHUSII
Chinalaph
MAZICES
Mina
BANTUR
Russaddir
Sestiaria Pr.
Metagonium
Lemnis
Acrath
Safar
Siga
Gilva
MASSAESYLI
Aquae Sirenses
Pomarium
Altava
BAQUATAE
Vopiscianae
Diur M.
Gilda
Muluchath
Taxafora
MAURETANIA
TINGITANA
CAESARIENSIS
Volubilis
Galafa
Durdus M.
Garapha M.
Stagna
Phocra M.
Sala
Asama
Atlas M.
or Dyrin
TRANSTAGNENSES
GAETULIA
5
0
35
MARE
Sabrata
Pontus
Assaria
Oea Macaroea
Megerthis
Quintiliana
Leptis Magna
Vax
Cercar
TRIPOLIS
Simnuana
Tubactis
Cephalae Pr.
SYRTIS MAJOR
Tarichiae
Macomada
Auxiqua
Aspis
Praetorium
Macomades Selorum
Charax
Oesporis
Annesel
Musti Vicus
Aquae Amarae
AFRICA
Dysopus
Zure
PSYLLI
Zagazaena
Praesidium
Tagulis
Boïno (Varias)
Tabudium
Digdica
Arae Philaenorum
Panorezon
Ptolemais
Arsinoe (Tauchira)
Pentapolis
Cyrene
Apollonia
Barca
Adrianopolis
Berenice (Hesperides)
Diachersis
Amastorus
AUSCHISAE
Caminus
CYRENAICA
MACATUTAE
NASAMONES
MARMARICA
15
20
30
AFRICA SEPTENTRIONALIS
English Miles
0
50
100
200
Longitude East 20 of Greenwich

SICILIA
INTERNUM
Saldae
Choba
Cirta
Hippo Regius
Utica
CARTHAGO
Clypea
Cossyra I.
ZEUGITANA
Curubis
Neapolis
Horrea Caelia
Hadrumetum
Leptis Minor
Thapsus
Acholla
Brachodes Pr.
BYZACIUM
Thysdrus
Sufetula
Theveste
Lambasa
Tubunae
Aurasius M.
Sitifis
Auzia
Thaenae
Cercina I.
Macomades
SYRTIS MINOR
Tacape
Girba
I. Meninx
Githis
Capsa
NUMIDIA
Ad Maiores
Libyca Palus
Tritonis Palus
Nepte
Bescera
Ad Badias
Cerva
Thelepte
Ubaza
Scillium
MACHLYES
AUSENSES
LOTOPHAGI
Sabrata
Pontus
Locri
Pisida
Sicca Veneria
Zama Regia
Thala
Sufes
Madaura
Thagaste
Naraggara
Bulla
Thuburbo
Thignica
Thacia
Carpis
Pr. Mercurii
Saltinae Tubunenses
Aquae Herculis
Cellae
Tamannuna
Arae
Nasavath
Satafi
Mileum
Sigus
Macomades
Lamasba
INTERNUM
Darnis
Chersonnesus
Petras Minor
Antipyrgos
Gereatis
Panormus
Catabathmus Major
Tigrae
Apis
Drepanum Pr.
Paraetonium
Catabathmus Minor
Hermaeum Pr.
Phoenicus
ALEXANDRIA
Mareotis L.
Canopus
Pharos I.
Nili Ostia
Buto
Sais
Busiris
Mendes
Pelusium
Bubastis
Athribis
Heliopolis
Prosopis
Letopolis
Memphis
DELTA
Aphroditopolis
AEGYPTUS
Arsinoe
Tacona
Hipponon
Nilus
Ammonium
Deserta Libyca
ADYRMACHIDAE
ICA
5
10
35
25
30

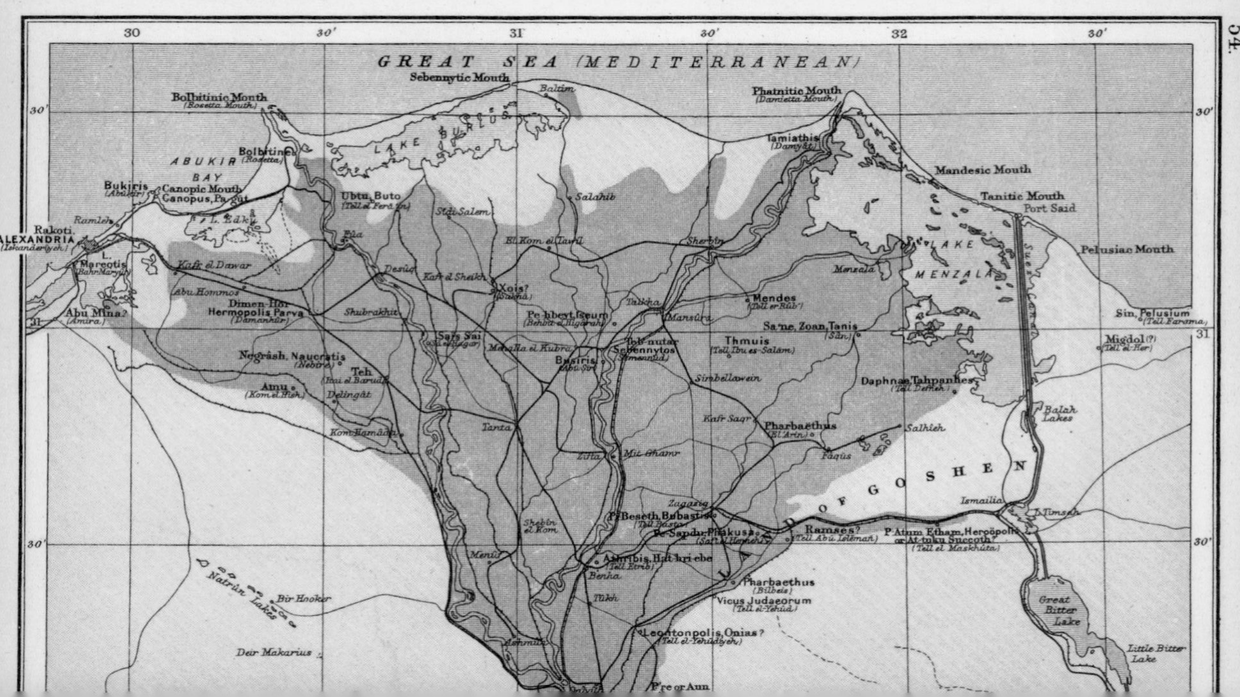

GREAT SEA (MEDITERRANEAN)
Sebennytic Mouth
Baltim
Bolbitinic Mouth
(Rosetta Mouth)
Phatnitic Mouth
(Damietta Mouth)
LAKE BURLUS
Tamiathis
Bolbitine
(Rosetta)
ABUKIR BAY
Mandesic Mouth
Tanitic Mouth
Port Said
Bukiris
Canopic Mouth
Canopus, Pa-gut
Ubtu, Buto
Salahib
Sidi Salem
Ramleh
L. Edku
Rakoti.
ALEXANDRIA
L. Mareotis
Kafr el Dawar
Desuq
Kafr el Sheikh
El Kom el Tawil
Sherbin
LAKE MENZALA
Menzala
Pelusiac Mouth
Abu Hommos
Dimen-Hor
Hermopolis Parva
(Damanhur)
Abu Mina?
Shubrakhit
Xois?
Mendes
Talkha
Mansura
Sin, Pelusium
(Tell Farama)
Sa'ne, Zoan, Tanis
(San)
Thmuis
Migdol (?)
(Tell el-Her)
Sais Sai
Mehalla el Kubra
Sebennytos
Busiris
Negrâsh, Naucratis
(Nebira)
Teh
Amu
(Kom el Hish)
Delingât
Simbellawein
Daphnae, Tahpanhes
(Tell Defneh)
Balah Lakes
Kafr Saqr
Pharbaethus
Salhieh
Tanta
Kom Hamâda
Zifta
Mit Ghamr
Faqus
LAND OF GOSHEN
Ismailia
L. Timsah
Zagazig
P. Beseth, Bubastis
(Tell Basta)
Shebin el Kom
Ramses?
(Tell Abu Islêman)
P. Atum Etham, Heroöpolis
or At-tuku Succoth?
(Tell el Maskhuta)
Menuf
Athribis, Hat-hri-ebe
(Tell Atrib)
Benha
Pharbaethus
(Bilbeis)
Vicus Judaeorum
(Tell el-Yehud)
Natrûn Lakes
Bir Hooker
Tukh
Great Bitter Lake
Leontonpolis, Onias?
(Tell el-Yehudiyeh)
Deir Makarius
Ashmun
Little Bitter Lake
P're or Aun
30
30'
31
32

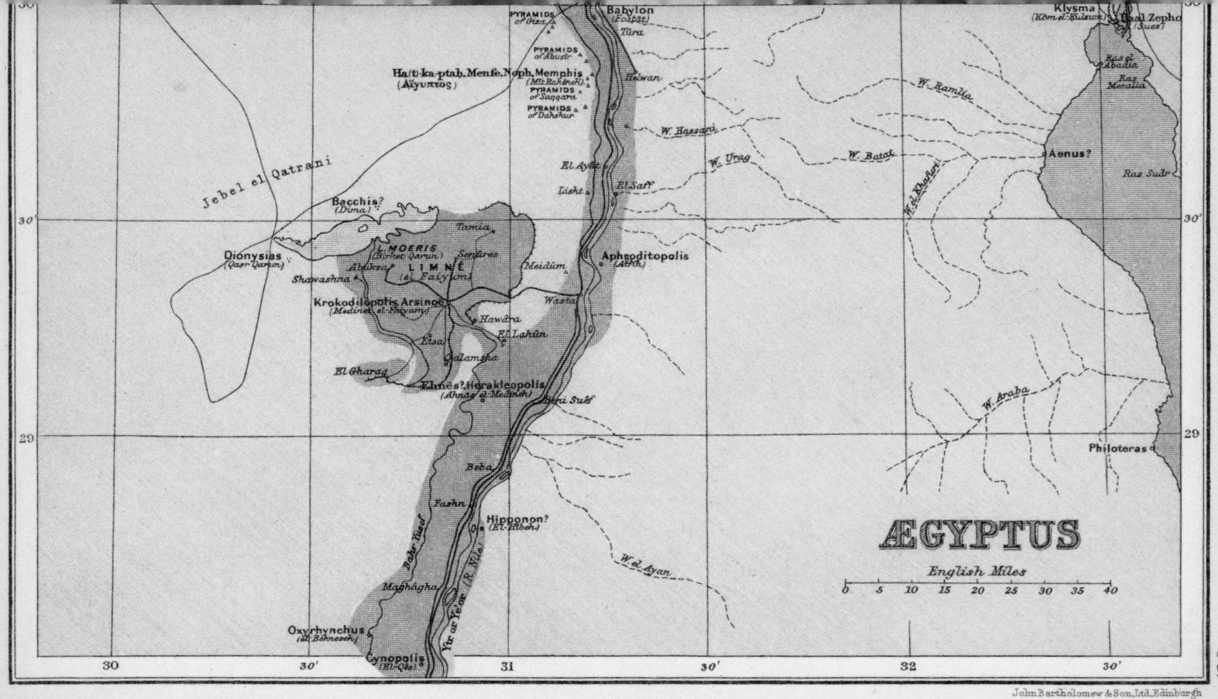
ÆGYPTUS
English Miles
0 5 10 15 20 25 30 35 40
Babylon
(Fostât)
Tura
Helwan
PYRAMIDS of Giza
PYRAMIDS of Abusir
Ha(t)-ka-ptah, Menfe, Noph, Memphis
(Aἴγυπτος)
(Mit Rahêneh)
PYRAMIDS of Saqqara
PYRAMIDS of Dahshur
Klysma
(Kôm el-Kulzum)
Baal Zepho
(Suez)
Ras el Abadia
Ras Mesalla
Ras Sudr
Aenus?
W. Ramlia
W. Hassani
W. Urag
W. Batat
W. el Khafuri
W. Araba
W. el Ayan
Philoteras
El Ayat
Lisht
El Saff
Jebel el Qatrani
Bacchis?
(Dima)
Dionysias
(Qasr Qarun)
L. MOERIS
(Birket Qarun)
LIMNÉ
(el Faiyum)
Tamia
Senfires
Abuksa
Shawashna
Meidûm
Aphroditopolis
(Atfih)
Wasta
Krokodilopolis Arsinoe
(Medinet el-Faiyum)
Hawâra
El Lahûn
Etsa
Qalamsha
El Gharaq
Ehnês? Herakleopolis
(Ahnas el Medineh)
Beni Suef
Beba
Fashn
Hipponon?
(El-Hibeh)
Bahr Yusef
(R. Nile)
Yir or Ye'or
Maghâgha
Oxyrhynchus
(el Behneseh)
Cynopolis
(El-Qês)
30
30'
31
32
29
John Bartholomew & Son, Ltd, Edinburgh

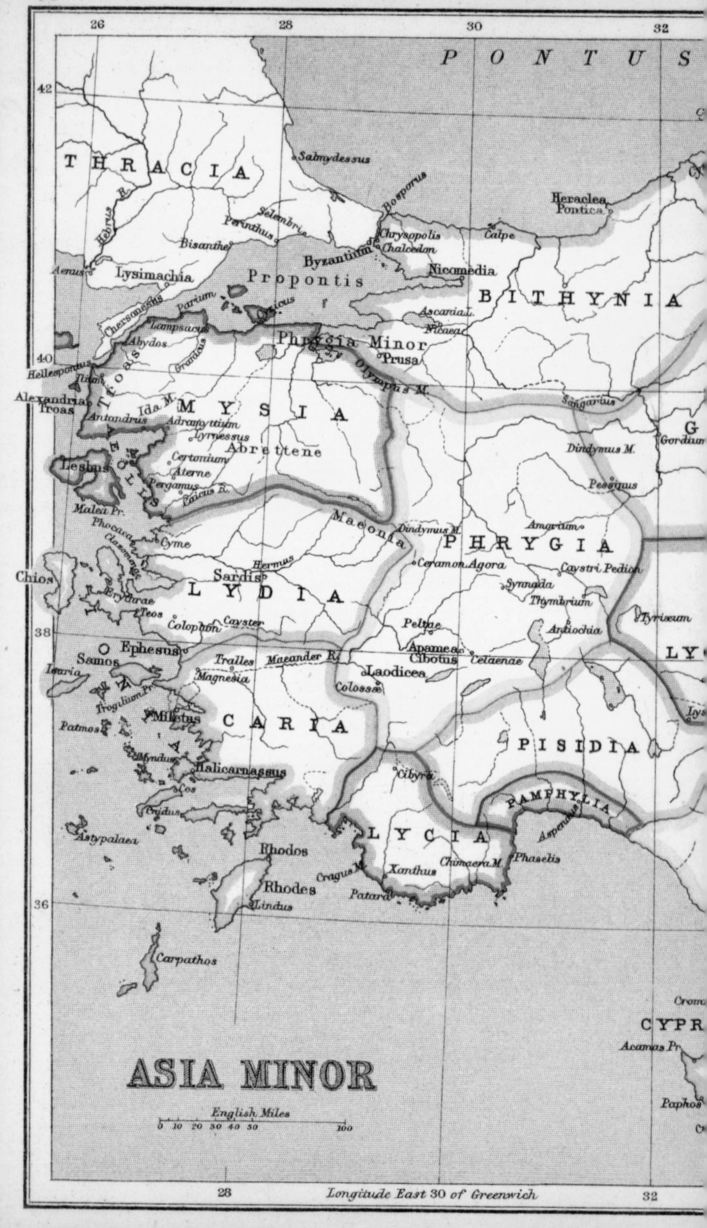

PONTUS
THRACIA
Salmydessus
Hebrus R.
Selembria
Perinthus
Bisanthe
Bosporus
Chrysopolis
Chalcedon
Byzantium
Heraclea Pontica
Calpe
Aenus
Lysimachia
Propontis
Nicomedia
BITHYNIA
Chersonesus
Parium
Cyzicus
Ascania L.
Nicaea
Lampsacus
Abydos
Phrygia Minor
Prusa
Hellespontus
Ilium
Troas
Granicus
Olympus M.
Alexandria Troas
Ida M.
MYSIA
Antandrus
Adramyttium
Lyrnessus
Sangarius
Gordium
Dindymus M.
Abrettene
Certonium
Aterne
Lesbos
Pergamus
Caicus R.
Pessinus
Malea Pr.
Phocaea
Maeonia
Dindymus M.
Amorium
Cyme
PHRYGIA
Clazomenae
Hermus
Ceramon Agora
Caystri Pedion
Chios
Sardis
Synnada
LYDIA
Erythrae
Thymbrium
Teos
Colophon
Cayster
Tyriaeum
Peltae
Antiochia
Ephesus
Apamea
Cibotus
Celaenae
Samos
Tralles
Maeander R.
Laodicea
Icaria
Magnesia
Colossae
Trogilium Pr.
Miletus
CARIA
Patmos
PISIDIA
Myndus
Halicarnassus
Cibyra
Cos
PAMPHYLIA
Cnidus
Aspendus
Astypalaea
LYCIA
Phaselis
Rhodos
Chimaera M.
Cragus M.
Xanthus
Rhodes
Patara
Lindus
Carpathos
CYPR
Acamas Pr.
Paphos
ASIA MINOR
English Miles
0 10 20 30 40 50 100
Longitude East 30 of Greenwich
26
28
30
32
42
40
38
36

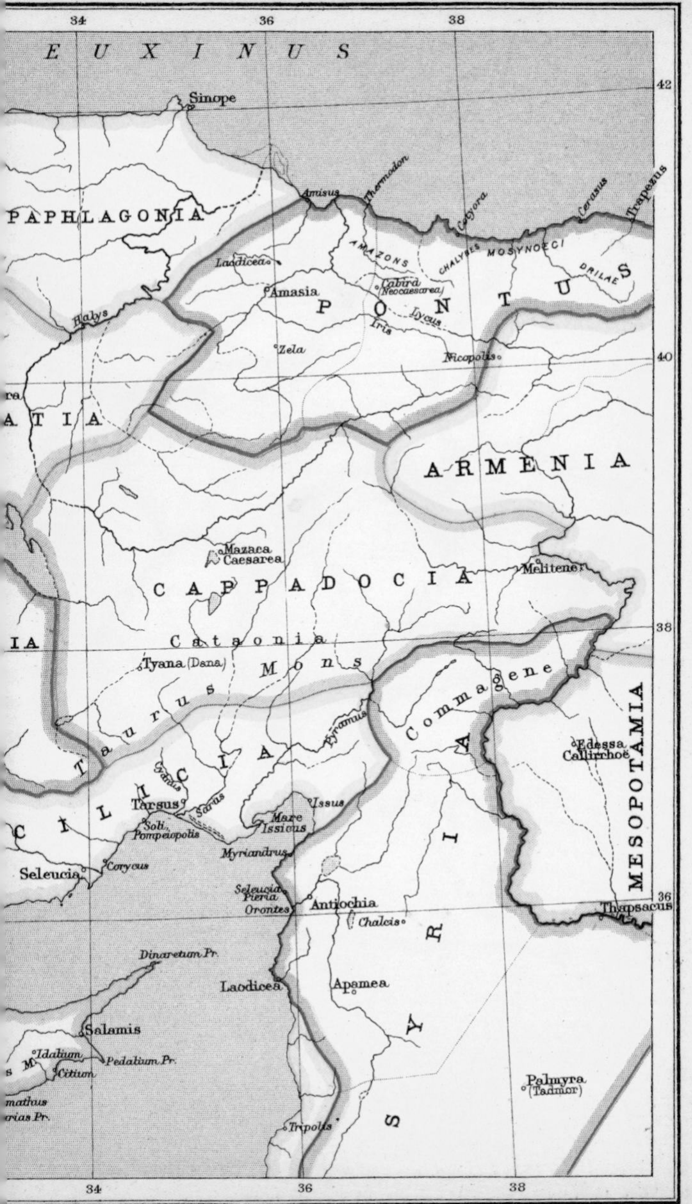
E U X I N U S
Sinope
PAPHLAGONIA
Amisus
Thermodon
Cotyora
Cerasus
Trapezus
AMAZONS
CHALYBES
MOSYNOECI
DRILAE
Laodicea
Cabira (Neocaesarea)
Amasia
P O N T U S
Halys
Lycus
Iris
Zela
Nicopolis
ATIA
ARMENIA
Mazaca Caesarea
Melitene
CAPPADOCIA
Cataonia
IA
Tyana (Dana)
Taurus Mons
Commagene
Pyramus
CILICIA
Cydnus
Sarus
Tarsus
Issus
Mare Issicus
Soli, Pompeiopolis
Myriandrus
Seleucia
Corycus
Edessa Callirrhoë
MESOPOTAMIA
SYRIA
Seleucia Pieria
Orontes
Antiochia
Chalcis
Thapsacus
Dinaretum Pr.
Laodicea
Apamea
Salamis
Idalium
Pedalium Pr.
Citium
Palmyra (Tadmor)
Tripolis
34
36
38
42
40
38
36

John Bartholomew & Son, Ltd. Edinburgh

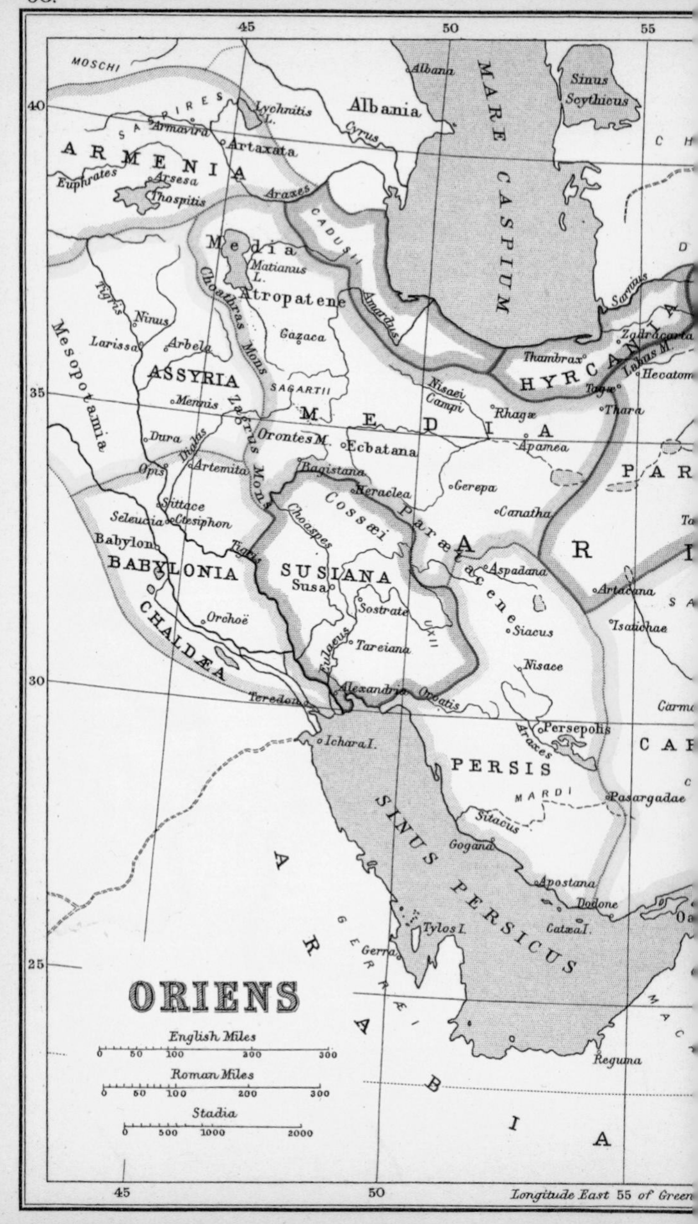
ORIENS
English Miles
Roman Miles
Stadia
MARE CASPIUM
SINUS PERSICUS
ARMENIA
ASSYRIA
Mesopotamia
BABYLONIA
CHALDÆA
SUSIANA
PERSIS
HYRCANIA
MEDIA
Media Atropatene
ARABIA
Albania
Sinus Scythicus
Longitude East 55 of Green

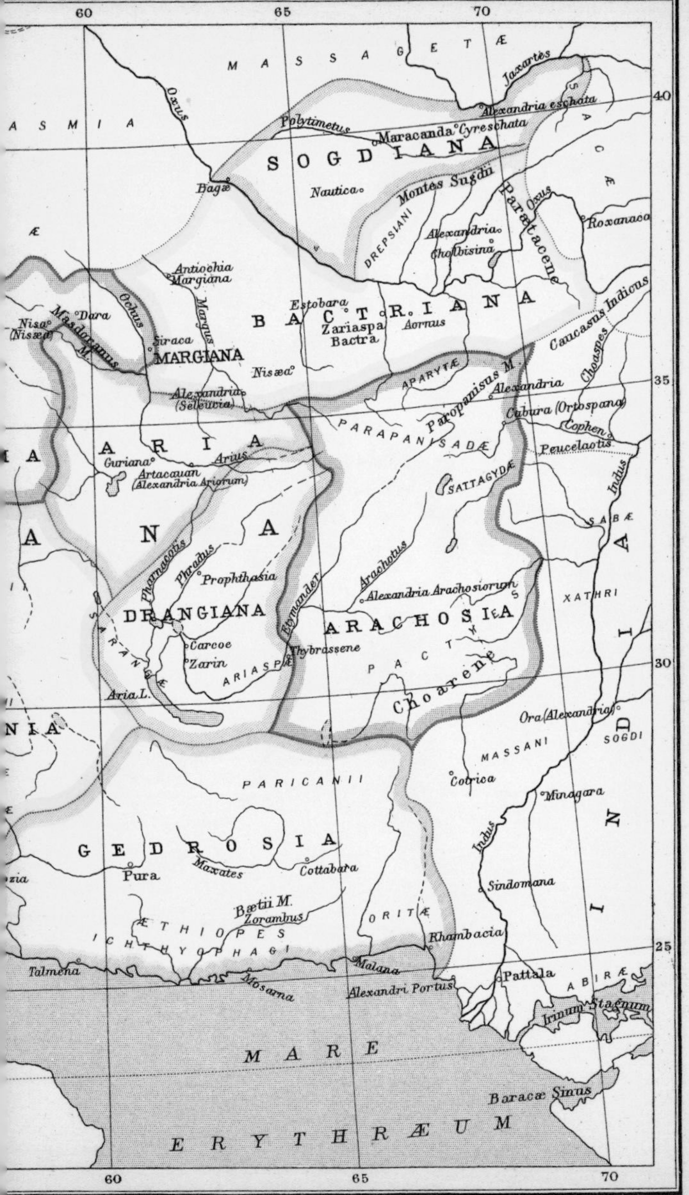
MASSAGETÆ
Jaxartes
Oxus
Polytimetus
Alexandria eschata
Maracanda
Cyreschata
SOGDIANA
SACÆ
Bagæ
Nautica
Montes Sugdii
Paratacene
Roxanaca
DREPSIANI
Alexandria
Cholbisina
Antiochia Margiana
Ochus
Margus
Estobara
BACTRIANA
Zariaspa Bactra
Aornus
Caucasus Indicus
Dara
Nisa (Nisæa)
Masdoranus M.
Siraca
MARGIANA
Nisæa
APARYTÆ
Paropanisus M.
Alexandria
Choaspes
Alexandria (Seleucia)
Cabura (Ortospana)
PARAPANISADÆ
Cophen
Peucelaotis
ARIA
Guriana
Arius
Artacauan (Alexandria Ariorum)
SATTAGYDÆ
Indus
SABÆ
ANA
Pharnacotis
Phradus
Prophthasia
Arachotus
Etymander
Alexandria Arachosiorum
XATHRI
DRANGIANA
ARACHOSIA
PACTYES
SARANGÆ
Carcoe
Zarin
Thybrassene
ARIASPÆ
Aria L.
Choarene
Ora (Alexandria)
SOGDI
NIA
MASSANI
PARICANII
Cotrica
Minagara
GEDROSIA
INDIA
Indus
Maxates
Pura
Cottabara
Sindomana
Bætii M.
Zorambus
ORITÆ
ÆTHIOPES
ICHTHYOPHAGI
Rhambacia
Talmena
Malana
Mosarna
Alexandri Portus
Pattala
ABIRÆ
Irinum Stagnum
MARE
ERYTHRÆUM
Baracæ Sinus
60
65
70
40
35
30
25
John Bartholomew & Son, Ltd., Edinburgh

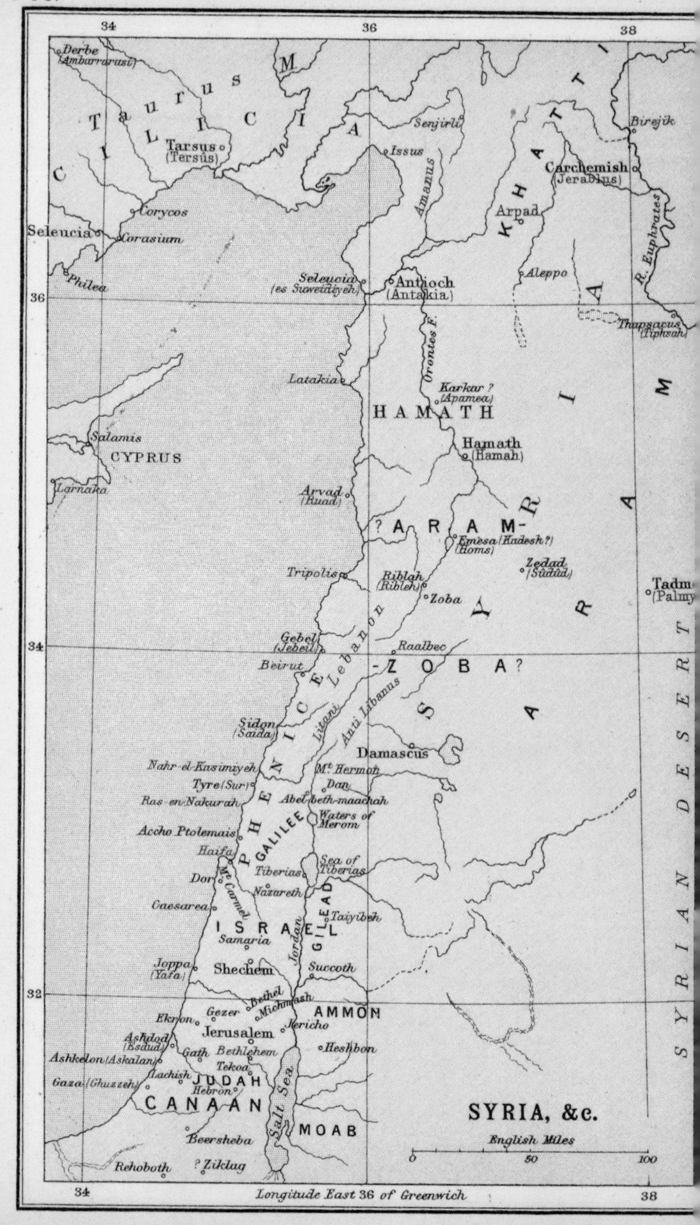
SYRIA, &c.
English Miles
0
50
100
Longitude East 36 of Greenwich
34
36
38
32
Derbe (Amburrarasi)
Taurus
CILICIA
Tarsus (Tersûs)
Corycos
Seleucia
Corasium
Philea
Senjirli
Issus
Amanus
Birejik
Carchemish (Jerablus)
KHATTI
Arpad
Aleppo
R. Euphrates
Seleucia (es Suweidiyeh)
Antioch (Antakia)
Thapsacus (Tiphsah)
Orontes F.
Latakia
Karkar ? (Apamea)
HAMATH
Salamis
CYPRUS
Hamath (Hamah)
Larnaka
Arvad (Ruad)
? ARAM-
Emesa (Kadesh?) (Homs)
Zedad (Sûdûd)
Tripolis
Riblah (Ribleh)
Zoba
Tadm (Palmy
Gebel (Jebeil)
Raalbec
Lebanon
-ZOBA?
Beirut
Anti Libanus
Litani
Sidon (Saida)
Damascus
Nahr-el-Kasimiyeh
Mt. Hermon
Tyre (Sur)
Dan
Ras-en-Nakurah
Abel-beth-maachah
Waters of Merom
Acco Ptolemais
PHENICE
GALILEE
Haifa
Sea of Tiberias
Tiberias
Dor
Mt. Carmel
Nazareth
Caesarea
GILEAD
Taiyibeh
ISRAEL
Samaria
Jordan
Joppa (Yafa)
Shechem
Succoth
Bethel
Michmash
Gezer
AMMON
Ekron
Jericho
Jerusalem
Ashdod (Esdud)
Heshbon
Gath
Bethlehem
Ashkelon (Askalan)
Tekoa
Lachish
JUDAH
Gaza (Ghuzzeh)
Hebron
CANAAN
Salt Sea
MOAB
Beersheba
Rehoboth
? Ziklag
SYRIA
SYRIAN DESERT

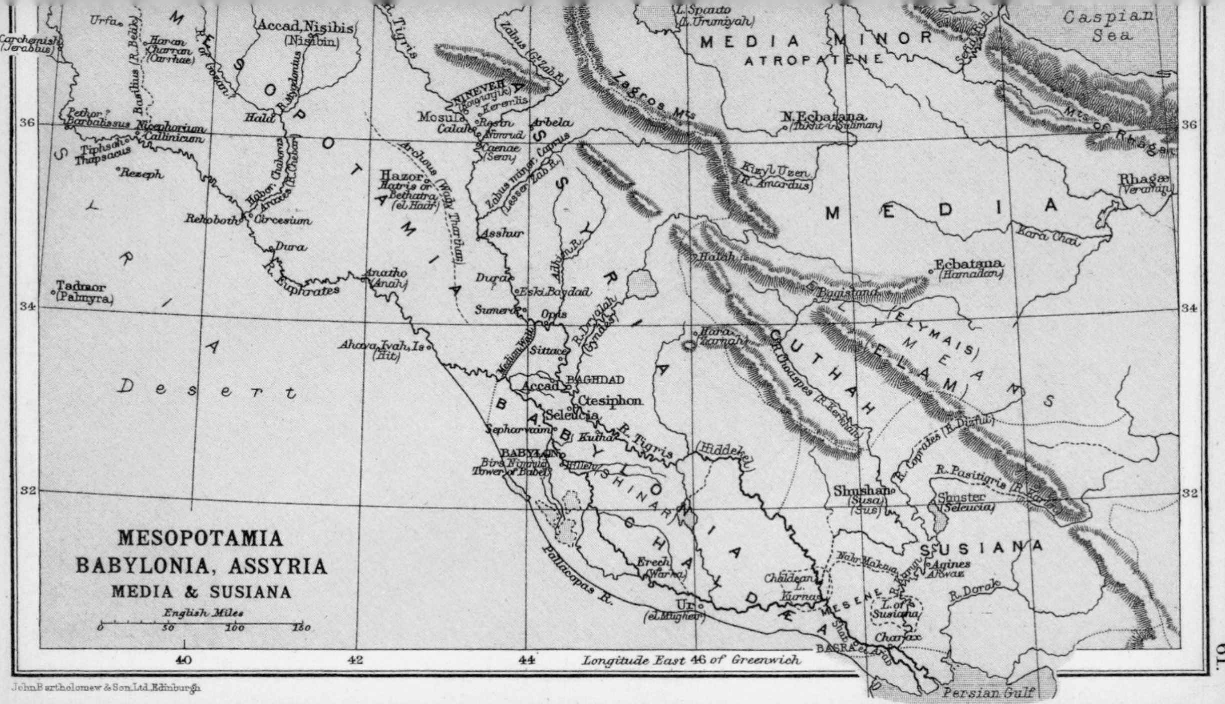

John Bartholomew & Son Ltd. Edinburgh

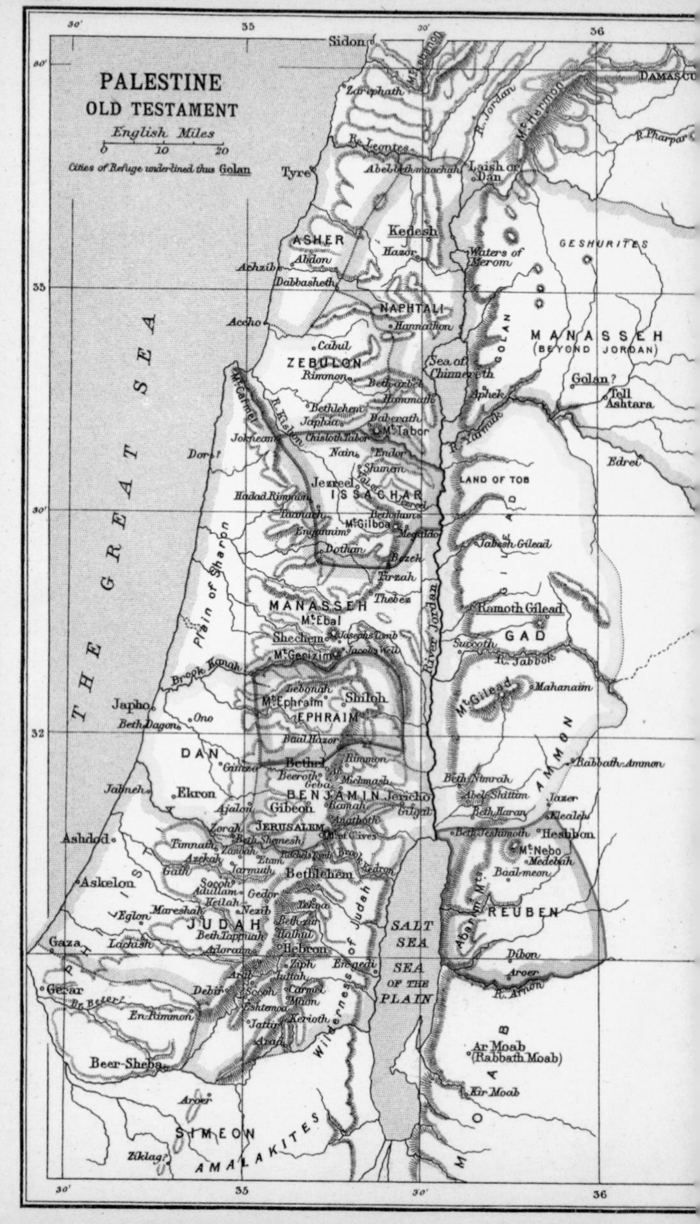
PALESTINE
OLD TESTAMENT
English Miles
0 10 20
Cities of Refuge underlined thus Golan
THE GREAT SEA
Sidon
Zarephath
Mt Lebanon
R. Jordan
Mt Hermon
DAMASCUS
R. Pharpar
R. Leontes
Tyre
Abel-beth-maachah
Laish or Dan
Kedesh
Hazor
ASHER
Abdon
Achzib
Dabbasheth
Waters of Merom
GESHURITES
Accho
NAPHTALI
Hannathon
MANASSEH
(BEYOND JORDAN)
GOLAN
Cabul
ZEBULON
Rimmon
Sea of Chinnereth
Golan?
Tell Ashtara
Aphek
Mt Carmel
R. Kishon
Bethlehem
Japhia
Daberath
Mt Tabor
Chisloth Tabor
Jokneam
R. Yarmuk
Dor
Nain
Endor
Shunem
Edrei
Jezreel
ISSACHAR
Vale of Jezreel
LAND OF TOB
Hadad Rimmon
Taanach
Mt Gilboa
Engannim
Megiddo
Plain of Sharon
GILEAD
Jabesh Gilead
Dothan
Bezek
Tirzah
Thebez
MANASSEH
Mt Ebal
Ramoth Gilead
Shechem
Joseph's Tomb
Jacob's Well
Mt Gerizim
GAD
Succoth
River Jordan
R. Jabbok
Brook Kanah
Lebonah
Shiloh
Mt Ephraim
EPHRAIM
Mt Gilead
Mahanaim
Japho
Beth Dagon
Ono
Baal Hazor
AMMON
DAN
Gimzo
Bethel
Rimmon
Rabbath-Ammon
Beeroth
Geba
Michmash
Beth Nimrah
Jabneh
Ekron
BENJAMIN
Jericho
Abel-Shittim
Jazer
Ajalon
Gibeon
Ramah
Gilgal
Anathoth
Beth Haran
Elealeh
Zorah
JERUSALEM
Mt of Olives
Beth Jeshimoth
Heshbon
Ashdod
Timnath
Beth Shemesh
Zanoah
Azekah
Etam
Rachel's Tomb
Brook Kedron
Mt Nebo
Medebah
Gath
Jarmuth
Bethlehem
Baal-meon
Askelon
Socoh
Adullam
Gedor
Keilah
Tekoa
Nezib
Wilderness of Judah
Eglon
Mareshah
Beth-zur
REUBEN
JUDAH
Halhul
Abarim Mts
Beth Tappuah
Hebron
SALT SEA
Gaza
Lachish
Adoraim
Ziph
Engedi
Dibon
SEA OF THE PLAIN
Arab
Juttah
Aroer
Gerar
Debir
Socoh
Carmel
R. Arnon
Br. Besor
Maon
Eshtemoa
En-Rimmon
Kerioth
Jattir
Anab
MOAB
Ar Moab
(Rabbath Moab)
Beer-Sheba
Kir Moab
Aroer
SIMEON
AMALAKITES
Ziklag?
30' 35 30' 36

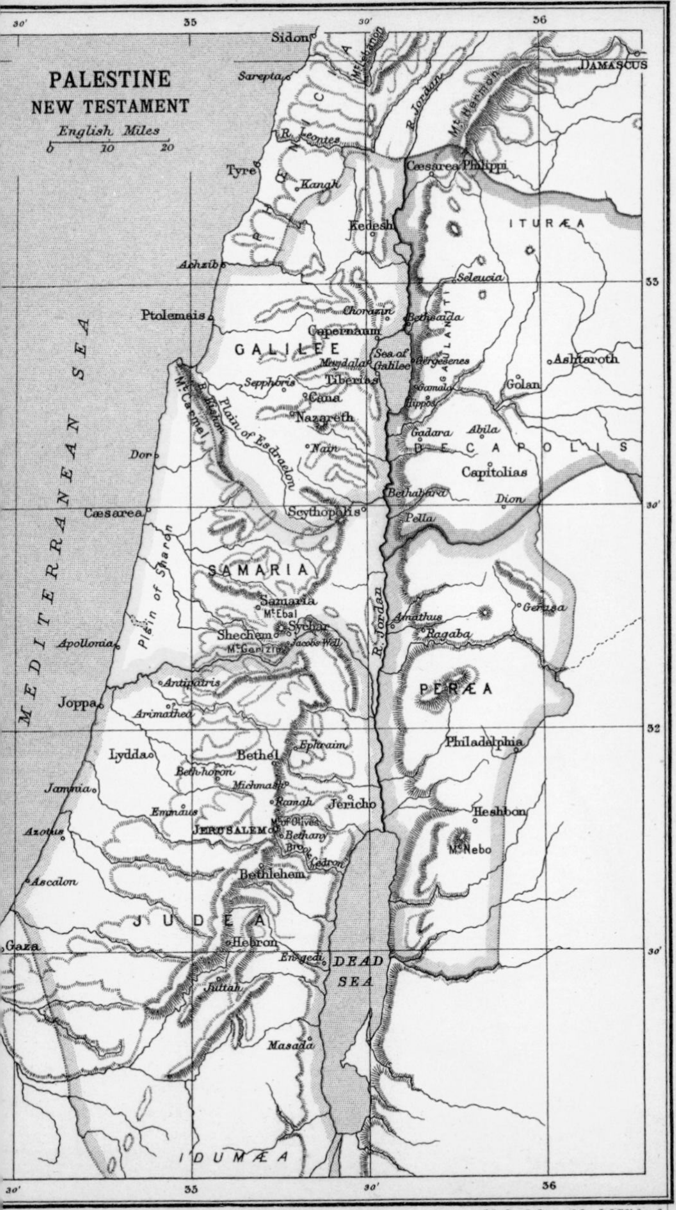

John Bartholomew & Son, Ltd. Edinburgh

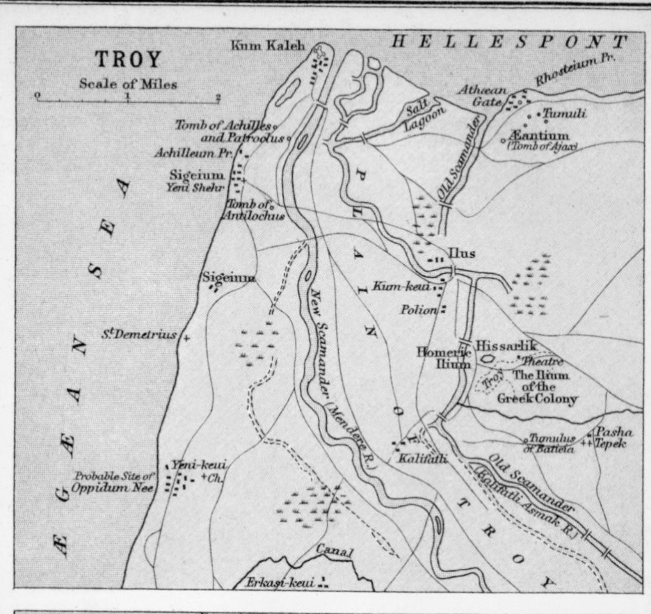
TROY
Scale of Miles
0
1
2
HELLESPONT
Kum Kaleh
Rhosteium Pr.
Athæan Gate
Tumuli
Æantium
(Tomb of Ajax)
Salt Lagoon
Old Scamander
Tomb of Achilles and Patroclus
Achilleum Pr.
Sigeium
Yeni Shehr
Tomb of Antilochus
ÆGÆAN SEA
PLAIN OF TROY
Ilus
Sigeium
Kum-keui
Polion
New Scamander (Mendere R.)
St Demetrius
Homeric Ilium
Hissarlik
Theatre
Troy
The Ilium of the Greek Colony
Tumulus of Batieia
Pasha Tepek
Kalifatli
Old Scamander (Kalifatli Asmak R.)
Yeni-keui
Ch.
Probable Site of Oppidum Nee
Canal
Erkasi-keui

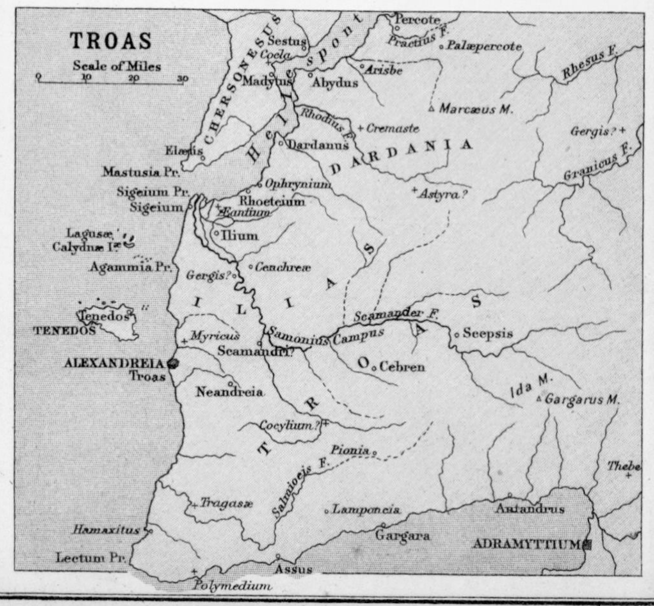
TROAS
Scale of Miles
0
10
20
30
Percote
Practius F.
Palæpercote
Sestus
Coela
Hellespont
Madytus
Abydus
Arisbe
Rhesus F.
CHERSONESUS
Marcæus M.
Rhodius F.
Cremaste
Gergis?
Elæus
Dardanus
DARDANIA
Granicus F.
Mastusia Pr.
Ophrynium
Sigeium Pr.
Sigeium
Rhoeteium
Æantium
Astyra?
Ilium
Lagusæ
Calydnæ Is.
Agammia Pr.
Cenchreæ
Gergis?
ILIAS
Tenedos
TENEDOS
Scamander F.
Myricus
Samonius Campus
Scepsis
Scamandria?
ALEXANDREIA Troas
Cebren
Neandreia
Ida M.
Gargarus M.
Cocylium?
TROAS
Pionia
Thebe
Satnioeis F.
Tragasæ
Lamponeia
Antandrus
Hamaxitus
Gargara
ADRAMYTTIUM
Lectum Pr.
Assus
Polymedium

MAPS AND PLANS

OF

NOTABLE BATTLES AND DISTRICTS

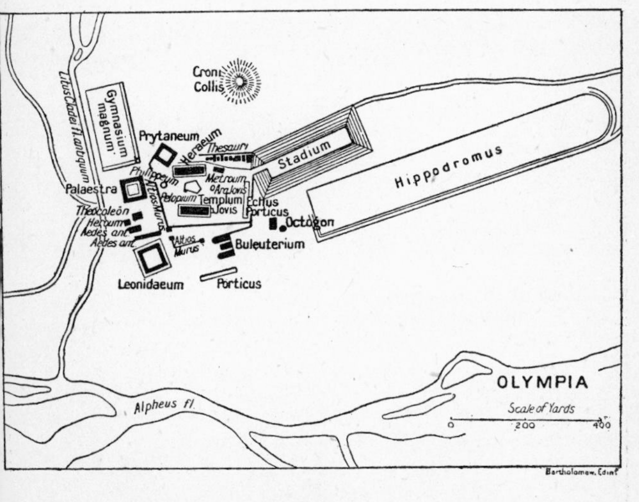

OLYMPIA

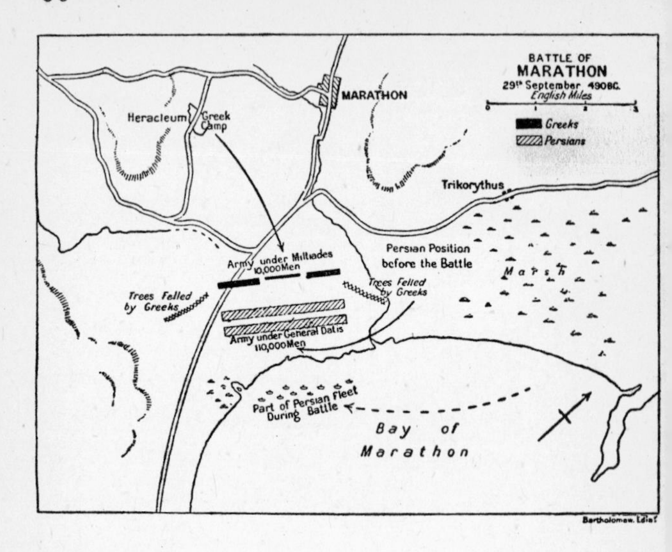
BATTLE OF
MARATHON
29th September 490BC.
English Miles
Greeks
Persians
MARATHON
Heracleum
Greek Camp
Trikorythus
Persian Position before the Battle
Marsh
Army under Miltiades 10,000 Men
Trees Felled by Greeks
Trees Felled by Greeks
Army under General Datis 110,000 Men
Part of Persian Fleet During Battle
Bay of Marathon
Bartholomew. Edin.

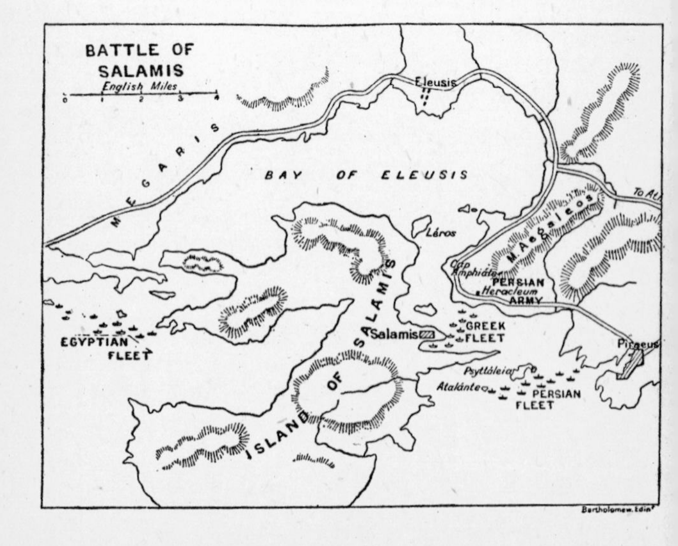
BATTLE OF
SALAMIS
English Miles
Eleusis
MEGARIS
BAY OF ELEUSIS
Léros
Aegaleos
Cap Amphiále
PERSIAN ARMY
Heracleum
ISLAND OF SALAMIS
Salamis
GREEK FLEET
EGYPTIAN FLEET
Psyttáleia
Atalánte
PERSIAN FLEET
Piraeus
Bartholomew. Edin.

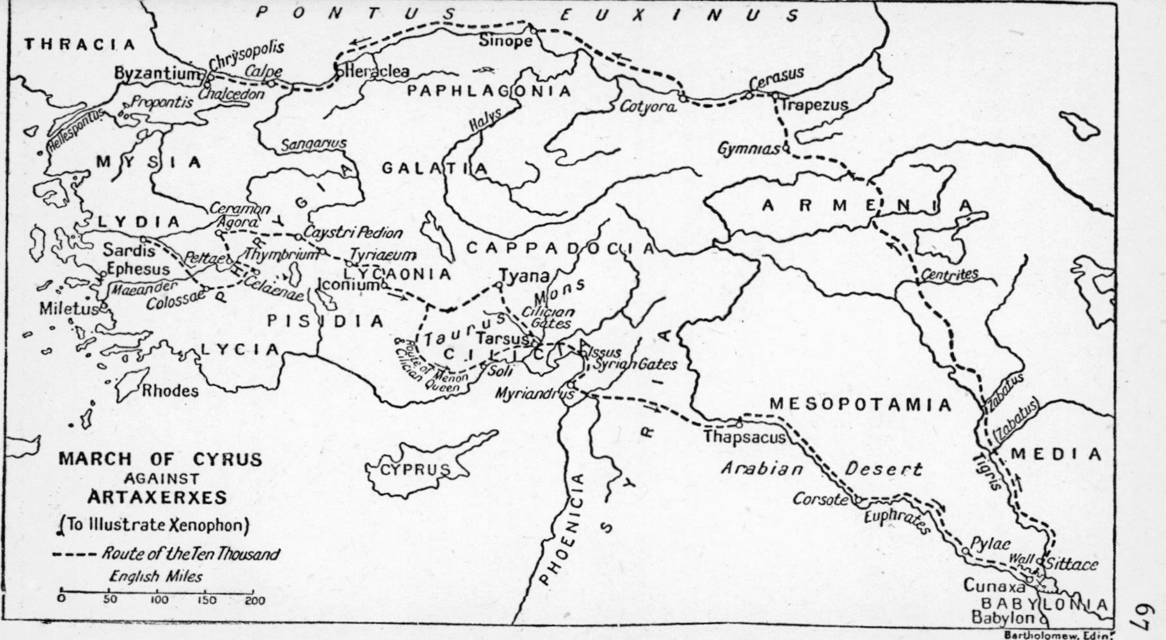
PONTUS EUXINUS
THRACIA
Byzantium
Chrysopolis
Calpe
Chalcedon
Propontis
Hellespontus
Heraclea
Sinope
PAPHLAGONIA
Cotyora
Cerasus
Trapezus
Halys
Sangarius
Gymnias
MYSIA
GALATIA
ARMENIA
PHRYGIA
LYDIA
Ceramon Agora
Caystri Pedion
Sardis
Peltae
Thymbrium
Tyriaeum
Ephesus
LYCAONIA
CAPPADOCIA
Tyana
Iconium
Maeander
Colossae
Celaenae
Miletus
Mons
Cilician Gates
PISIDIA
Taurus
Tarsus
Centrites
LYCIA
CILICIA
Issus
Syrian Gates
Route of Menon & Cilician Queen
Soli
Rhodes
Myriandrus
SYRIA
MESOPOTAMIA
Zabatus
(Zabatus)
Thapsacus
MEDIA
CYPRUS
Arabian Desert
Tigris
PHOENICIA
Corsote
Euphrates
Pylae
Wall
Sittace
Cunaxa
BABYLONIA
Babylon
MARCH OF CYRUS
AGAINST
ARTAXERXES
(To Illustrate Xenophon)
Route of the Ten Thousand
English Miles
0
50
100
150
200
Bartholomew, Edin.

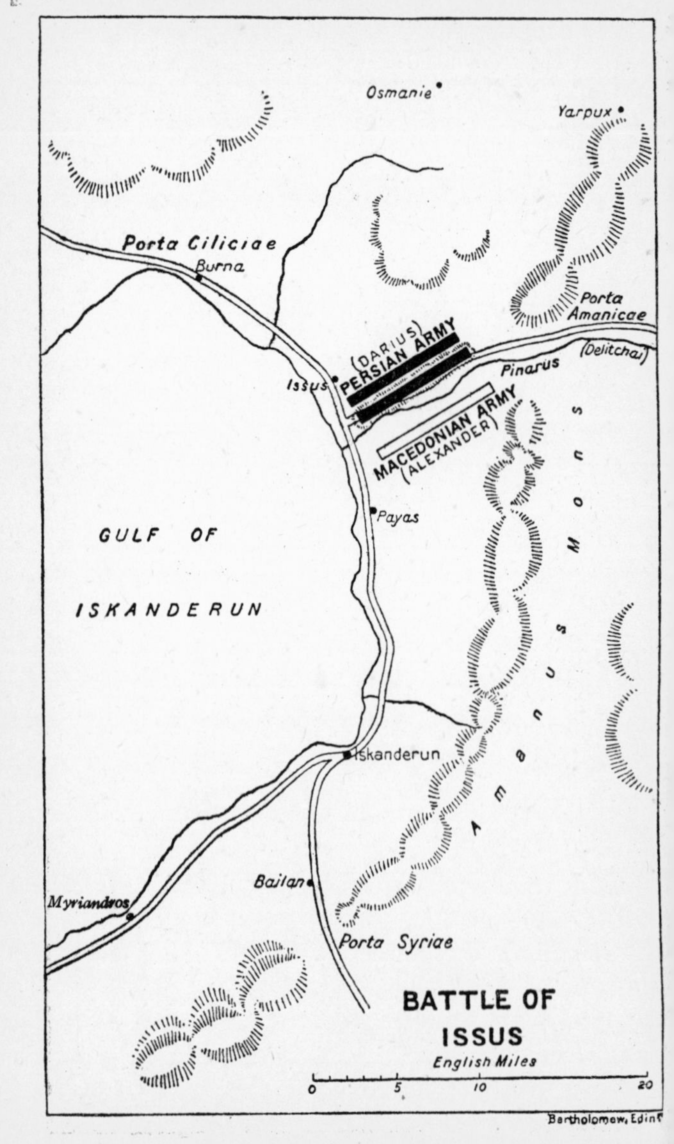
Osmanie
Yarpux
Porta Ciliciae
Burna
Porta
Amanicae
(DARIUS)
PERSIAN ARMY
(Delitchai)
Pinarus
Issus
MACEDONIAN ARMY
(ALEXANDER)
Payas
GULF OF
ISKANDERUN
Amanus Mons
Iskanderun
Bailan
Myriandros
Porta Syriae
BATTLE OF
ISSUS
English Miles
0
5
10
20
Bartholomew, Edin

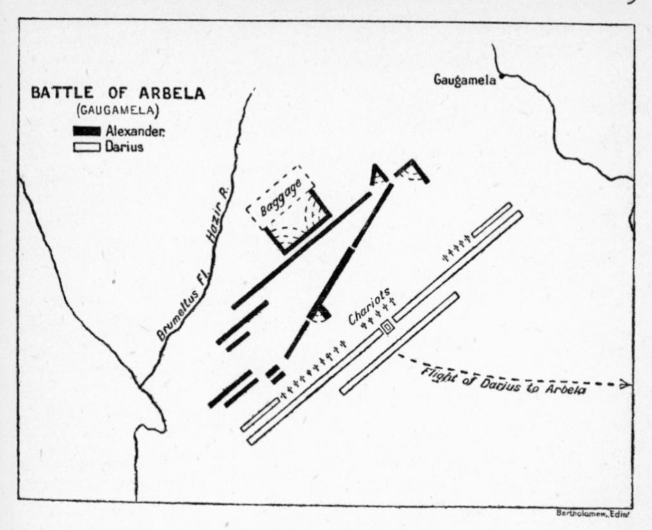
BATTLE OF ARBELA
(GAUGAMELA)
Alexander
Darius
Gaugamela
Baggage
Hazir R.
Brumeltus Fl.
Chariots
Flight of Darius to Arbela
Bartholomew, Edin.

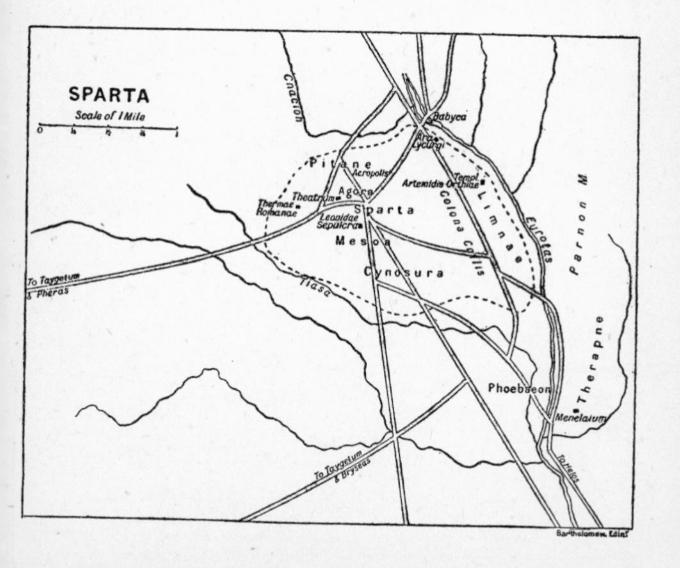
SPARTA
Scale of 1 Mile
0
1
Cnacion
Babyca
Ara Lycurgi
Pitane
Acropolis
Templ. Artemidis Orthiae
Agora
Theatrum
Thermae Romanae
Sparta
Leonidae Sepulcra
Mesoa
Cynosura
Colona Collis
Limnae
Eurotas
Parnon M
To Taygetum & Pheras
Tiasa
Phoebaeon
Therapne
Menelaium
To Taygetum & Bryseas
To Helos
Bartholomew, Edin.

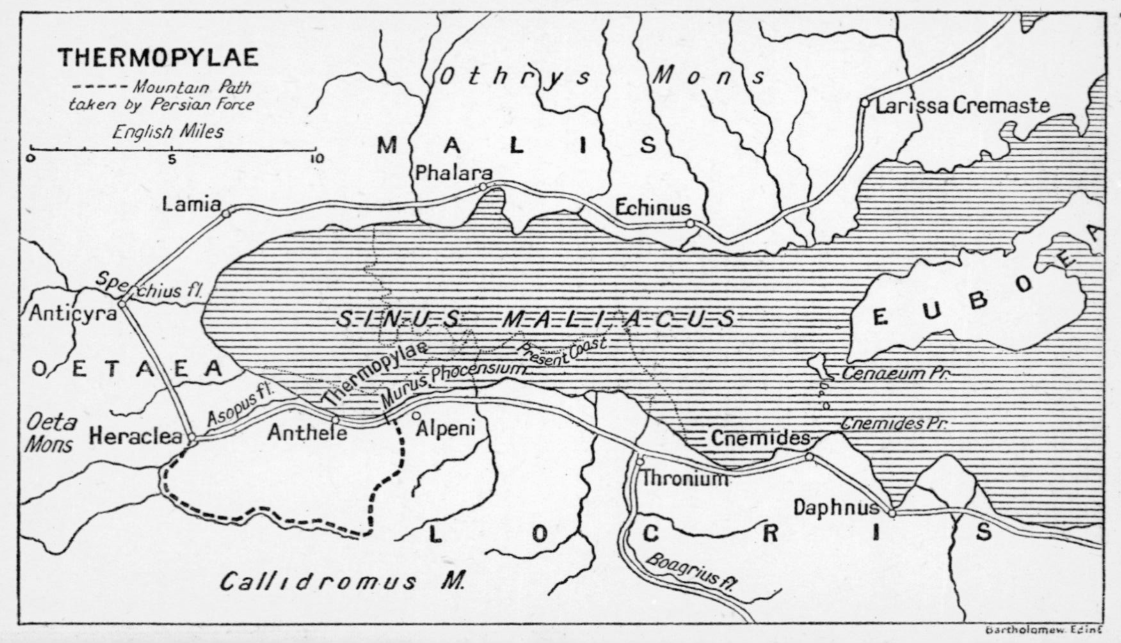
THERMOPYLAE
----- Mountain Path taken by Persian Force
English Miles
0
5
10
Othrys Mons
MALIS
Larissa Cremaste
Phalara
Lamia
Echinus
Sperchius fl.
Anticyra
OETAEA
SINUS MALIACUS
EUBOEA
Present Coast
Thermopylae
Murus Phocensium
Cenaeum Pr.
Asopus fl.
Oeta Mons
Heraclea
Anthele
Alpeni
Cnemides Pr.
Cnemides
Thronium
Daphnus
LOCRIS
Boagrius fl.
Callidromus M.
Bartholomew, Edin.

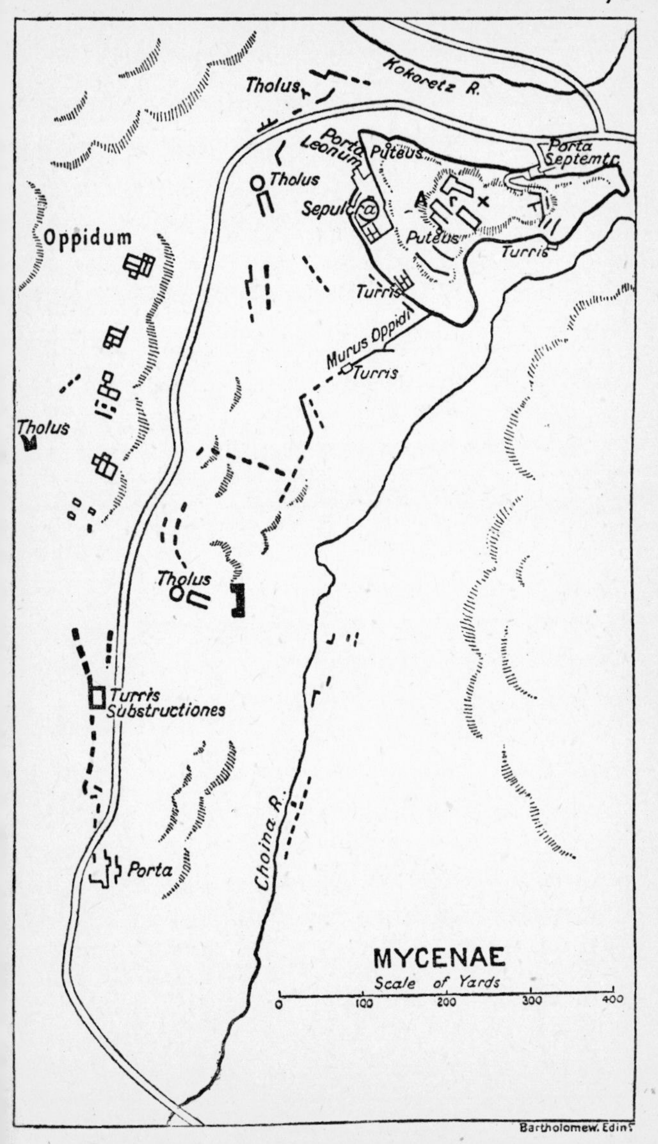
Kokoretz R.
Tholus
Porta Leonum
Puteus
Porta Septemtr.
Tholus
Sepulcr.
A
Puteus
Turris
Oppidum
Turris
Murus Oppidi
Turris
Tholus
Tholus
Turris Substructiones
Porta
Choina R.
MYCENAE
Scale of Yards
0
100
200
300
400
Bartholomew. Edinr.

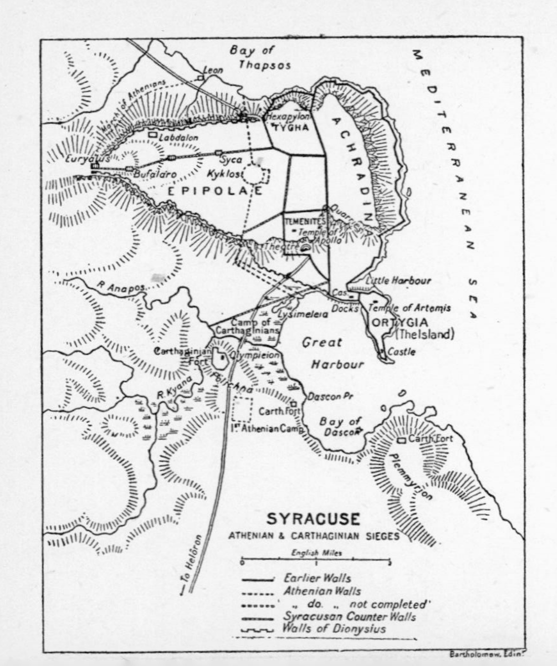
Bay of Thapsos
Leon
March of Athenians
MEDITERRANEAN SEA
Hexapylon
TYCHA
Labdalon
Euryalus
Bufalaro
Syca
Kyklos
EPIPOLAE
ACHRADINA
TEMENITES
Temple of Apollo
Quarries
Theatre
R. Anapos
Little Harbour
Docks
Temple of Artemis
ORTYGIA
(The Island)
Castle
Lysimeleia
Camp of Carthaginians
Great
Harbour
Carthaginian Fort
Olympieion
Polichna
R. Kyana
Dascon Pr
Carth. Fort
1st Athenian Camp
Bay of Dascon
Carth. Fort
Plemmyrion
To Heloron
SYRACUSE
ATHENIAN & CARTHAGINIAN SIEGES
English Miles
Earlier Walls
Athenian Walls
" do. " not completed
Syracusan Counter Walls
Walls of Dionysius
Bartholomew, Edin.

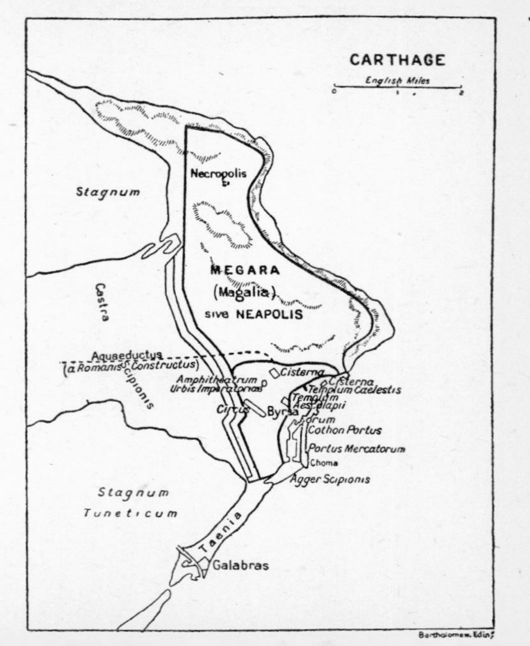
CARTHAGE
English Miles
Stagnum
Necropolis
MEGARA
(Magalia)
sive NEAPOLIS
Castra
Scipionis
Aqueductus
(a Romanis Constructus)
Cisterna
Amphitheatrum
Urbis Imperatorias
Cisterna
Templum Caelestis
Templum Aesculapii
Circus
Byrsa
Forum
Cothon Portus
Portus Mercatorum
Choma
Agger Scipionis
Stagnum
Tuneticum
Taenia
Galabras
Bartholomew, Edin.

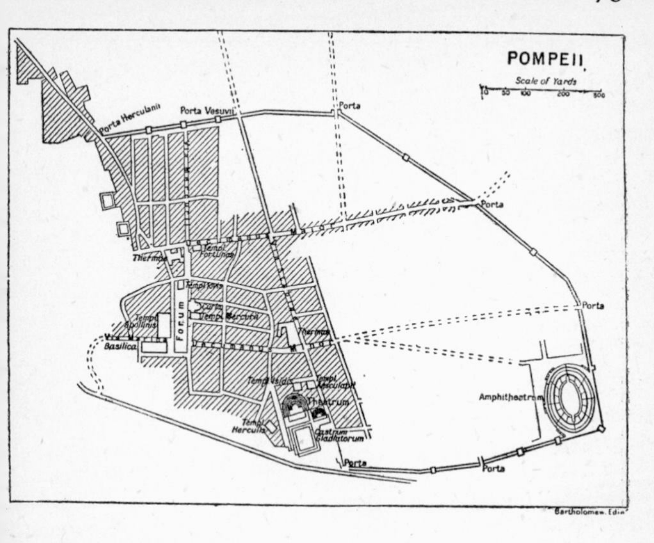
POMPEII
Scale of Yards
Porta Herculanii
Porta Vesuvii
Porta
Porta
Porta
Thermae
Forum
Basilica
Thermae
Amphitheatrum
Theatrum
Porta
Porta
Bartholomew, Edin

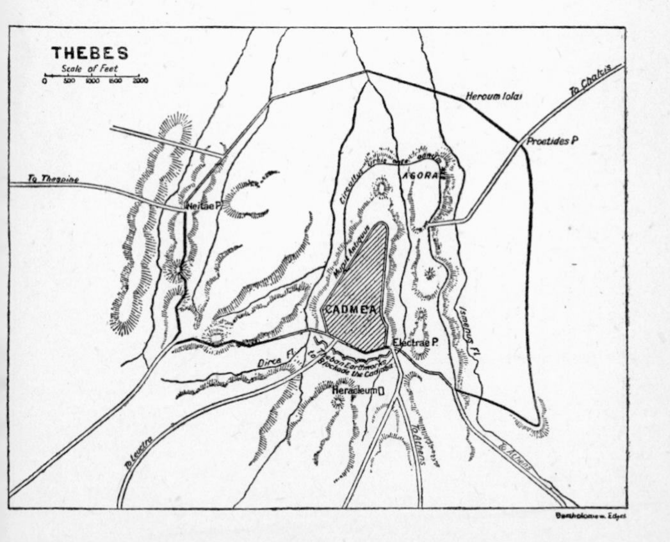
THEBES
Scale of Feet
To Thespiae
Heroum Iolai
To Chalcis
Proetides P
Neitae P
AGORA
Murus Antiquus
CADMEA
Electrae P.
Ismenus Fl.
Dirca Fl.
Theban Earthworks to Blockade the Cadmea
Heracleum
To Leuctra
To Athens
To Athens
Bartholomew, Edin

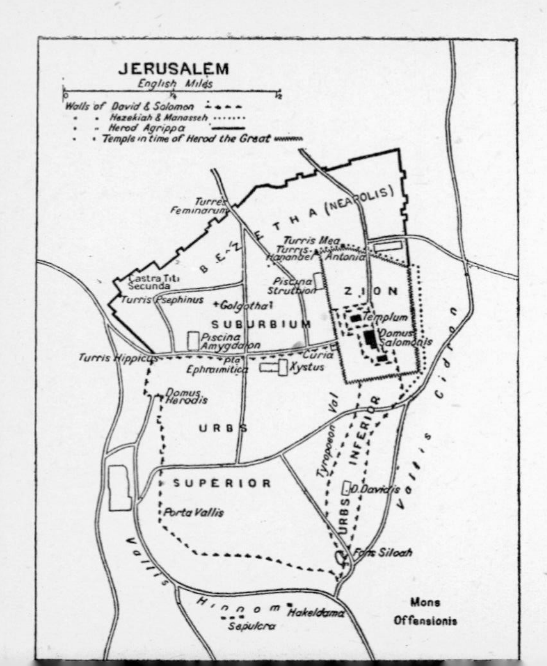
JERUSALEM
English Miles
Walls of David & Solomon
Hezekiah & Manasseh
Herod Agrippa
Temple in time of Herod the Great
BEZETHA (NEAPOLIS)
Turres Feminarum
Castra Titi Secunda
Turris Psephinus
Turris Hippicus
Turris Mea
Turris Hananeel
Antonia
ZION
Templum
Domus Salomonis
Piscina Struthion
+Golgotha
SUBURBIUM
Piscina Amygdalon
Pte Ephraimitica
Curia
Xystus
Domus Herodis
URBS
SUPERIOR
Porta Vallis
Tyropoeon Val
URBS INFERIOR
D. Davidis
Fons Siloah
Vallis Cidron
Vallis Hinnom
Hakeldama
Sepulcra
Mons Offensionis

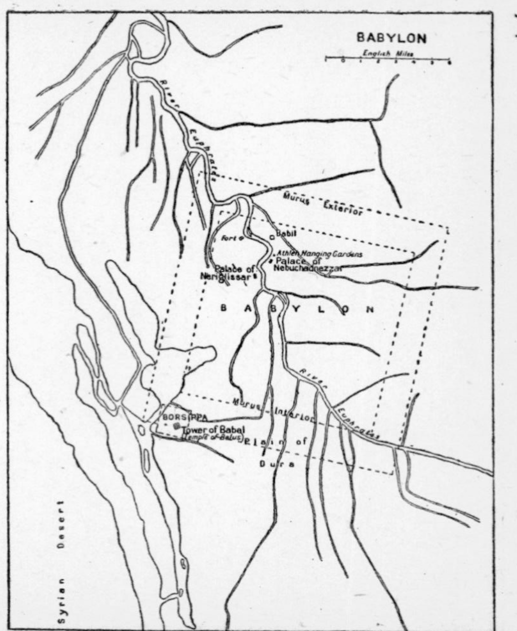
BABYLON
English Miles
River Euphrates
Murus Exterior
Fort
Babil
Palace of Neriglissar
Palace of Nebuchadnezzar
BABYLON
Murus Interior
BORSIPPA
Tower of Babel
Plain of Dura
Syrian Desert

TYRE
Scale of Yards
0
200
400
600
800

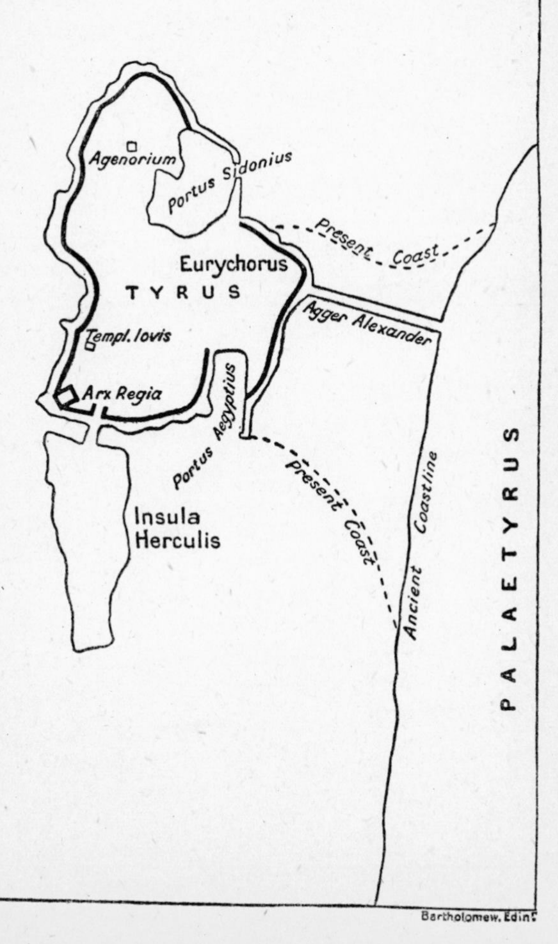
Agenorium
Portus Sidonius
Present Coast
Eurychorus
TYRUS
Agger Alexander
Templ. Iovis
Arx Regia
Portus Aegyptius
Present Coast
Insula
Herculis
Ancient Coastline
PALAETYRUS
Bartholomew, Edinr

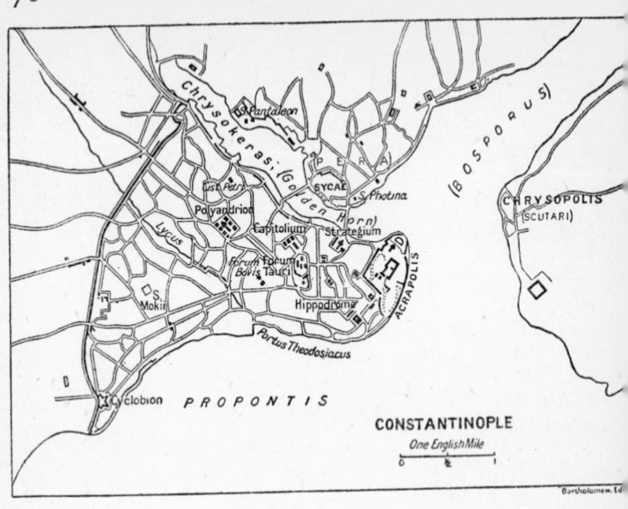
Chrysokeras (Golden Horn)
S. Pantaleon
PERA
SYCAE
S. Photina
(BOSPORUS)
CHRYSOPOLIS
(SCUTARI)
Cist. Petri
Polyandrion
Capitolium
Strategium
Lycus
Forum Bovis
Forum Tauri
S. Mokii
Hippodrome
ACRAPOLIS
Portus Theodosiacus
Cyclobion
PROPONTIS
CONSTANTINOPLE
One English Mile
0
½
1
Bartholomew, Ed

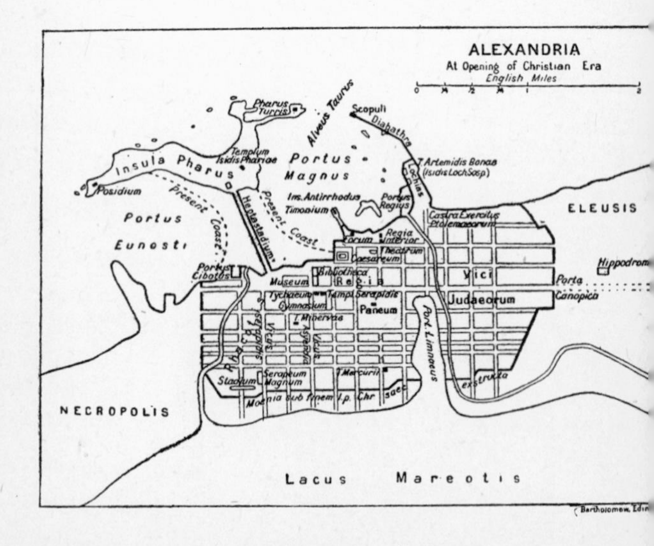
ALEXANDRIA
At Opening of Christian Era
English Miles
0
¼
½
¾
1
2
Pharus Turris
Alveus Taurus
Scopuli
Diabathra
Templum Isidis Phariae
Insula Pharus
Portus Magnus
T. Artemidis Bonae (Isidis Loch Sosp)
Lochias
Posidium
Present Coast
Ins. Antirrhodus
Timonium
Portus Regius
Castra Exercitus Ptolemaeorum
ELEUSIS
Portus Eunosti
Heptastadium
Forum
Regia Interior
Theatrum
Caesareum
Portus Ciboto
Bibliotheca
Museum
Regia
Vici
Judaeorum
Hippodrom
Porta Canopica
Tychaeum
Templ. Serapidis
Gymnasium
Paneum
T. Minervae
Port. Limnaeus
Serapeum Magnum
Stadium
T. Mercurii
exstructa
Moenia sub finem I p. Chr saec
NECROPOLIS
Lacus Mareotis
Bartholomew, Edin

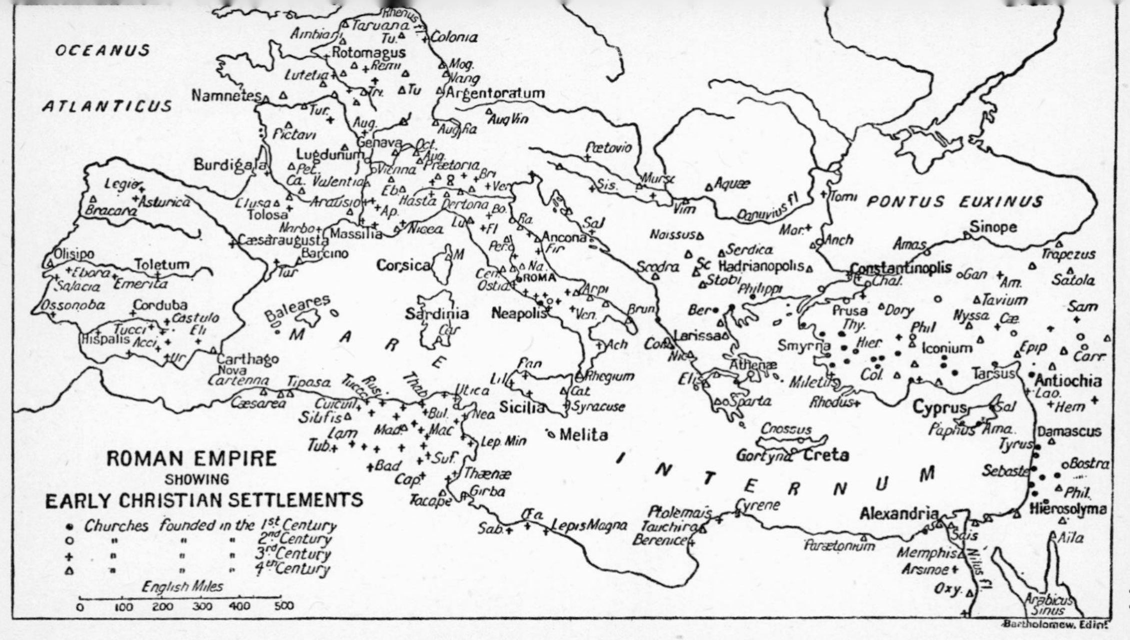
ROMAN EMPIRE
SHOWING
EARLY CHRISTIAN SETTLEMENTS
• Churches founded in the 1st Century
o " " " 2nd Century
+ " " " 3rd Century
Δ " " " 4th Century
English Miles
0 100 200 300 400 500
OCEANUS
ATLANTICUS
PONTUS EUXINUS
MARE INTERNUM
Rhenus fl.
Danuvius fl.
Nilus fl.
Arabicus Sinus
Taruana
Ambiani
Tu.
Colonia
Rotomagus
Remi
Lutetia
Mog.
Vang
Namnetes
Tri.
Tu
Argentoratum
Tur.
Aug.
Aug Vin
Augusta
Pictavi
Genava
Oct.
Lugdunum
Aug. Prætoria
Burdigala
Pet.
Vienna
Bri
Ca. Valentia
Ver
Legio
Eb
Asturica
Bracara
Clusa
Arausio
Hasta
Dertona
Bo.
Tolosa
Ap.
Ra.
Narbo
Massilia
Nicea
Lu
Fl
Ancona
Cæsaraugusta
Barcino
Per.
Fir
Olisipo
Toletum
Corsica
M
Ebora
Tar
Na.
Salacia
Emerita
Cen.
Ostia
ROMA
Arpi
Ossonoba
Corduba
Baleares
Sardinia
Neapolis
Castulo
Car
Ven.
Brun
Tucci
Eli
Hispalis
Acci
Ur
Ach
Carthago Nova
Pan
Cartenna
Tipasa
Lil
Rhegium
Cæsarea
Rusi
Thab
Utica
Cat.
Cuicul
Tuccc
Bul.
Sicilia
Syracuse
Sitifis
Nea
Lam
Mad
Mac
Melita
Tub.
Lep. Min
Suf.
Bad
Cap
Thænæ
Tacape
Girba
Sab.
Oea
Lepis Magna
Ptolemais
Tauchira
Berenice
Cyrene
Pætovio
Mursa
Aquæ
Sis.
Vim
Sal
Naissus
Tomi
Mar.
Anch
Sinope
Serdica
Amas.
Trapezus
Scodra
Sc
Hadrianopolis
Constantinopolis
Chal.
Gan
Am.
Satola
Stobi
Philippi
Tavium
Ber
Prusa
Dory
Nyssa
Cæ.
Sam
Thy.
Phil
Larissa
Smyrna
Hier
Iconium
Epip
Carr
Cor
Nic
Athenæ
Col.
Tarsus
Antiochia
Elis
Miletus
Lao.
Sparta
Rhodus
Cyprus
Sal
Hem
Cnossus
Paphus
Ama.
Damascus
Gortyna
Creta
Tyrus
Sebaste
Bostra
Phil.
Alexandria
Hierosolyma
Sais
Aila
Parætonium
Memphis
Arsinoe
Oxy.
Bartholomew, Edinr.

HISTORICAL GAZETTEER

ALEXANDRIA

Alexandria, the Hellenic capital of Egypt, was founded by Alexander the Great in 332 B.C. It is situated at the western end of the Nile Delta in lat. 31° 11′ N., long. 29° 15′ E. It remained the capital of Egypt for over a thousand years from its foundation. On his journey from Memphis to Canopos, Alexander perceived the natural advantages of the little Egyptian town of Rhacotis. Rhacotis, on the N.E. shore of the Lake Mareotis, was in existence in 1300 B.C. judging by the date of statues which have been found there. The harbour of Rhacotis with the island of Pharos had been from remote times a haven for Greek and Phœnician searovers. The island of Pharos, mentioned by Homer (*Odyssey* IV 355), is now joined to the mainland, being the modern Ras-el-Tin, a promontory, to the N. and N.W. of which the remains of a prehistoric harbour have been found under the sea. Alexander rejected Pharos as the site of his future capital and chose Rhacotis. The site was more favourable then than it is now, as Lake Mareotis was at that time much deeper, being an important inland waterway, connected with the Nile which, by a canal from Memphis, was linked up with the Red Sea. The ground plan was traced by Alexander himself, and building was commenced under the supervision of his architect, Deinocrates. Alexander, however, did not see the city rise, but left Egypt and was only brought back to Alexandria to be buried. After the death of Alexander construction was continued, the plan of

Deinocrates being carried out by another architect, Cleomenes of Naucratis. The city was completed in the reign of Ptolemy II Philadelphus, 285–247 B.C., but continued to receive embellishment and extension throughout the Ptolemaic dynasty. The principal monuments of the Ptolemaic city were the Great Lighthouse, the Royal Palace, the Mouseion, and the Serapeion. Ancient writers—Strabo, Plutarch, and Pliny—compare the shape of Alexandria to the cloak worn by the Macedonian cavalry.

It was of an oblong figure, rounded at the S.E. and S.W. extremities. Its length from E. to W. was nearly 4 miles, its breadth from S. to N. nearly a mile, and its circumference, according to Pliny, was about 15 miles.

The construction of the walls was attributed by Tacitus (*Hist.* IV 83) to Ptolemy I (323–285 B.C.).

The interior was laid out in parallelograms: the streets crossed one another at right angles, and were all wide enough to admit of both wheel carriages and foot-passengers. Beneath each street was a subterranean channel. Two grand thoroughfares nearly bisected the city. The longer of these, 40 stadia (nearly 5 miles) in length, the great Canopic street, ran from the Canopic Gate (in Arabian times the Rosetta Gate) in the E. to the Necropolis in the W. It is believed that the present Rue Rosette and its continuation follows much the same line, and some authorities identify the Rosetta Gate with the Ptolemaic Gate of the Sun. This would place the corresponding Gate of the Moon at the western end of the Canopic street. Other authorities, however, place the 'Moon Gate' on the mainland, at the end of the Heptastadion, where it abuts on to what is now the Grand Square. In this case the main transversal street, 7 to 8 stadia in length, probably began here, running to a point S. of the city, and intersecting the Canopic street at a point close to where rose the Soma of Alexander. On its northern side Alexandria was bounded by the sea; on the S. by the Lake Mareotis; to the W. were the Necropolis and its numerous gardens; to the E. the Eleusinian road and the Great Hippodrome. Alexandria was well situated for a commercial city. The headland of Lochias sheltered its harbours to the E.; the Lake Mareotis was both a wet-dock and the general haven of the inland navigation of the Nile valley, while canals connected the lake with the deltaic branches of the river. The springs of Rhacotis were few and brackish, but a canal, beginning at Schedia on the Canopic branch of the Nile, 18 miles from Alexandria, supplied the city with fresh water, and acted as a navigable waterway. The main stream of this canal emptied itself into the basin, called Kibotos (chest), of the western harbour, and for much of its length must have followed the course of the present Mahmoudieh Canal (completed 1820). A branch of this canal also probably traversed the eastern portion of the city, emptying itself into the Great Harbour. The drinking water drawn from these canals was stored in underground cisterns, fed by subterranean channels. These tanks were very numerous in the time of Julius Cæsar, and further developments to supply the whole town with fresh water were ordered by Augustus Cæsar. The soil, partly sandy and partly calcareous, made a natural drainage, and the periodical coastal fogs were dispersed by the north winds which, in the summer, ventilate the delta, and contribute so much to the healthy climate for which Alexandria is celebrated.

The harbour-line commenced from the E. with the peninsular strip Lochias, which terminated seaward in a fort called Acro-Lochias, the modern Pharillon. The ruins of a pier on the eastern side of it mark an ancient landing-place, probably belonging to the Palace of the Ptolemies which, with its gardens, occupied this peninsula. Like all the principal buildings of Alexandria, it commanded a view of the bay and the Pharos. The Lochias formed, with the island of Antirrhodos, the Closed or Royal Port, which was kept exclusively for the king's galleys, and around the head of which were the royal dockyards. The Lochias, like all the coastline, has almost entirely subsided, and the island of Antirrhodos has disappeared altogether. When the sea is calm, the foundations of ancient buildings are still to be seen near the Pharillon. W. of the Royal Port was the Poseideion or Temple of Neptune where mariners made their vows. The northern point of this temple, situated on a promontory, was called the Timonium, built by Mark Antony, and here he retired after his flight from Actium in 31 B.C. Between Lochias and the Great Mole (Heptastadion) was the Great Harbour, and on the western side of the Mole was the smaller port of Eunostos or Haven of Happy Return, connected by the Kibotos basin with the canal that led, by one arm, to the Lake Mareotis, and by the other to the Canopic arm of the Nile. The Eunostos fronted the quarter of the city called Rhacotis. It was less difficult of access than the Great Harbour, as the reefs lie principally N.E. of the Pharos. From the Poseideion to the Heptastadion the shore was lined with dockyards and warehouses, upon whose granite quays ships discharged their lading without boats. On the western horn of the Eunostos were public granaries.

Fronting the city, and sheltering both the harbours, lay the island of Pharos. It was a white calcareous rock, about a mile from Alexandria, and 150 stadia (about 17 miles) from the Canopic mouth of the Nile. At its eastern point stood the far-famed lighthouse, the work of Sostratos of Cnidos, and, nearer the Heptastadion, was a temple of Ptah or Hephæstus. The lighthouse, itself known as the Pharos, one of the 'Seven Wonders', was begun by Ptolemy I Soter, but was completed by his son, and dedicated by him to 'the gods Soteres', or Soter and Berenice, his parents. There is a double reference here, however, because the 'Saviour Gods' ordinarily meant Castor and Pollux, the gods who protect seamen. The lighthouse consisted of four stories, set in a colonnaded court, the bottom story being square, the second octagonal, and the third circular. In the fourth was the lantern and the celebrated 'mirror'—either a telescope or a metal reflector. The whole was crowned by a statue of Poseidon, and the entire height was over 400 feet. The Pharos continued intact until the Arab Conquest, A.D. 641, shortly after which date the lantern fell. The lower stories were eventually destroyed by an earthquake in the fourteenth century. The Pharos was originally on an islet connected to the mainland by a bridge, but the intervening land formed in the ninth century. The present Fort Kait Bey (built 1480) was erected on the foundations of the lighthouse.

The prehistoric harbour on the N.W. of Pharos island has already been noticed. A theory is that it was Minoan work, but even if its origin is Egyptian, it probably dates back to Rameses II (1300 B.C.). It must be distinguished from a later harbour in existence on the N. side of the island in Julius Cæsar's time.

The island of Pharos was connected with the mainland by the artificial mole, called from its length, the Heptastadion (7 stadia, ¾ of a mile). There were two breaks in the mole to let the water through and prevent the accumulation of silt; over these passages bridges were laid which could be raised at need. The silting up has now obliterated the Heptastadion, and the former Kibotos basin no longer connects with the sea.

Interior of the City.—Alexandria was divided into three regions: (1) The Regio Judæorum; (2) The Brucheion or Pyrucheion, the Royal or Greek Quarter; (3) The Rhacotis or Egyptian Quarter. This division corresponded to the three original constituents of the Alexandrian population. After 31 B.C. the Romans added a fourth element, but this was principally military and financial, and confined to the Brucheion.

1. *Regio Judæorum*, or Jew's Quarter, occupied the N.E. angle of the city, and was encompassed by the sea, the city walls, and the Brucheion. Like the Jewry of modern European cities, it had walls and gates of its own, which were at times highly necessary for its security, since between the Alexandrian Greeks and Jews frequent hostilities raged.

2. *Brucheion*, or *Pyrucheion*, the Royal or Greek Quarter, was bounded to the S. and E. by the city walls, N. by the Greater Harbour, and W. by the region Rhacotis and the main transversal street. It was also surrounded by its own walls, and was the quarter in which Cæsar defended himself against the Alexandrians. The Brucheion was bisected by the High Street, which ran from the Canopic Gate to the Necropolis, and was supplied with water from the Nile by a tunnel or aqueduct, which entered the city on the S., and passed a little to the W. of the Gymnasium. This was the quarter of the Alexandrians proper, or Hellenic

citizens, the royal residence, and the district in which were contained the most conspicuous of the public buildings. It was so much extended by the later Ptolemies that it eventually occupied one-fifth of the entire city. It contained the following remarkable edifices. On the Lochias, the Palace of the Ptolemies, with the smaller palaces appropriated to their children and the adjacent gardens. The library and museum (Mouseion), with its theatre for lectures and public assemblies, connected with one another and with the palaces by long marble colonnades, and adorned with obelisks and sphinxes taken from the Pharaonic cities. The library contained, according to one account, 700,000 volumes, according to another, 400,000; part, however, of this unrivalled collection was lodged in the temple of Serapis, in the quarter Rhacotis. Here were deposited the 200,000 volumes collected by the kings of Pergamus, and presented by Mark Antony to Cleopatra. The library of the museum was destroyed during the blockade of Julius Cæsar; that of the Serapeion was frequently injured by the civil broils of Alexandria, and especially when that temple was sacked by the Christian mob under the Patriarch Theophilus in A.D. 391. With the invasion of the Arabs the last of the library disappeared; the legend grew that it was burnt by Amrou, the lieutenant of the Caliph Omar, A.D. 640. The museum succeeded the once renowned college of Heliopolis as the University of Egypt. It contained a great hall, where the professors dined in common; an exterior peristyle, for exercise and ambulatory lectures; and a theatre where public disputations and scholastic festivals were held.

In the Brucheion also stood the Cæsarium, or Temple of the Cæsars, where divine honours were paid to the emperors, deceased or living. Near the site of the Cæsarium is a tower perhaps not inappropriately named the 'Tower of the Romans', and from here, too, have been removed the two obelisks, known by the misleading name of 'Cleopatra's Needles'. Proceeding westward, we come to the public granaries and the mausoleum of the Ptolemies, which, from its containing the body of Alexander the Great, was denominated Soma. In this quarter also was the High Court of Justice, in which, under the Ptolemies, the senate assembled and where afterwards the Roman Juridicus held his court. A stadium, a gymnasium, palæstra, and an amphitheatre, provided exercise and amusement for the spectacle-loving Alexandrians. The Arsinoëum, on the western side of the Brucheion, was a monument raised by Ptolemy Philadelphus to the memory of his favourite sister, Arsinoë; and the Panium was a stone mount with a spiral ascent on the outside, from whose summit was visible every quarter of the city. The purpose of this structure is, however, not ascertained. The edifices of the Brucheion had been so arranged by Deinocrates as to command a prospect of the Great Harbour and the Pharos. In its centre was a spacious square, surrounded by cloisters and flanked to the N. by the quays—the Emporium, or Alexandrian Exchange. Hither, for nearly eight centuries, every nation of the civilized world sent its representatives.

3. *The Rhacotis*, or Egyptian Quarter, occupied the site of the ancient Rhacotis. Its principal buildings were granaries along the western arm of the Kibotos, a stadium, and the Temple of Serapis. The Serapeion was erected by the first or second of the Ptolemies. The image of the god, which was of wood, was, according to Clemens (*Protrept. c.* 4), plated over with layers of every kind of metal and precious stones: it seems also, either from the smoke

of incense or from varnish, to have been of a black colour. Its origin and import are doubtful. The Serapeion is the most celebrated of all Alexandrian temples, and is placed by Strabo in the W. of the city. Its site is now identified as being in the proximity of the so-called 'Pompey's Pillar'. This pillar was probably erected near the Serapeion in honour of Diocletian, who besieged the city in A.D. 297. It was given the erroneous name of 'Pompey's Pillar' by the crusaders in the fifteenth century. The plan of the Serapeion, according to classical writers, was rectangular, the temple being surrounded by a cloister. Some subterranean galleries and the fragments of a frieze still exist, which may have belonged to the temple. The Alexandria which the Arabs besieged was nearly identical with the Rhacotis. It had suffered calamities both from civil feud and from foreign war. Its Serapeion was twice consumed by fire, once in the reign of Marcus Aurelius, and again in that of Commodus. But this district survived both the Regio Judæorum and the Brucheion.

Of the beauty of Alexandria, we have the testimony of numerous writers. Its dilapidation was the effect not of time but of the hand of man. Its dry atmosphere preserved, for centuries after their erection, the sharp outline and gay colours of its buildings; and when in A.D 120 the Emperor Hadrian surveyed Alexandria he beheld almost the virgin city of the Ptolemies.

ARBELA

A town of Eastern Adiabene, one of the provinces of Assyria, between the Lycos and the Capros. Arbela has been celebrated as the scene of the last conflict between Darius and Alexander the Great. The battle, however, really took place near the village of Gaugamela, on the banks of the Bumodos, a tributary of the Lycos, about 50 miles to the N.W. of Arbela. Darius left his baggage and treasures at Arbela when he advanced to meet Alexander.

ATHENS

Athens is situated between 4 and 5 miles from the sea coast, in the central plain of Attica, which is enclosed by mountains on every side except the S., where it is open to the sea. This plain is bounded on the N.W. by Mt. Parnes, on the N.E. by Mt. Pentelikos, on the S.W. by Mt. Ægaleos. In the southern part of the plain the most prominent mountain is the celebrated Lykabettos, now called the Hill of St. George. This mountain, which was not included within the ancient walls, lies to the N.W. of Athens and forms the most striking feature in the environs of the city. S.W. of the Lykabettos there are four hills which formed part of the city. Of these the nearest to Lykabettos, at a distance of a mile, was the Acropolis, a square, craggy rock, rising abruptly about 150 feet, with a flat summit about 1,000 feet long from E. to W. by 500 feet broad from N. to S. Immediately W. of the

Acropolis is a second hill of irregular form, the Areiopagos. To the S.W. there rises a third hill, the Pnyx, on which the assemblies of citizens were held; and to the S. of the latter is a fourth hill, known as the Mouseion or Hill of the Muses. E. and W. of the city there run two small streams. The Ilissos on the E., joined by the Eridanos, flows in the S.W. direction through the southern quarter of the city. The stream on the W., named the Kephissos, runs due S., at a distance of about a mile and a half from the walls. S. of the city was seen the Saronic Gulf, with the harbours of Athens.

Historical Development.

Primitive.—The original city on the Acropolis was said to have been built by Cecrops, and was called Cecropia even in later times. Among his successors, the name of Erechtheus I is preserved by the buildings of Athens. He dedicated to Athena a temple on the Acropolis and set up in it an image of the goddess, made of olive wood—known in later times as the statue of Athena Polias, the most sacred object in all Athens. Erechtheus is said to have been buried in this temple, henceforth called the Erechtheion. In his reign the inhabitants, originally Pelasgians and called Cranai, afterwards named Cecropidæ, now received the name of Athenians, in consequence of the prominence given by him to the worship of Athena (Herod. VIII 44). Theseus, the national hero of Attica, is still more celebrated. He is said to have united into one political body the twelve independent states into which Cecrops had divided Attica, and to have made Athens the capital of the new state (eighth or tenth century B.C.). To accommodate the increased population Theseus enlarged the city by building on the ground to the

S. of the Acropolis, on the banks of the Ilissos, near the fountain Kalirrhoë. In this neighbourhood was situated the Olympieion, the ancient sanctuary of Ge (Earth) and Olympian Zeus, consecrated according to legend by Deucalion to mark the place where the last waters of the deluge flowed away. Here to the S. of the Acropolis was established the aristocratic quarter, the Asty or City, known either as the Lower City in opposition to the Acropolis, or as the Upper City in opposition to the lower town of Peiræeus. In addition to the Asty suburbs formed on the N. and N.W. of the Acropolis in the districts Kerameikos, Melite, and Kollytos. The agora in the Inner Kerameikos, within the walls, supplanted that of the south districts, which later became more and more isolated. In this agora the democracy of the seventh and sixth centuries placed those erections most vital to the life of the city: the Altar of the Twelve Gods; the Prytaneion, the council-place of all Attica, where the laws of Solon were preserved; the Leocorion or monument of the daughters of Leos, where feasts were held; the Bouleuterion, or Council House of the Five Hundred; and the Metroon, or Temple of the Mother of the Gods, whose statue was made by Pheidias.

Sixth Century.—In the historical age the first attempt to embellish Athens appears to have been made by Peisistratus and his sons (560–514 B.C.). Thus we are told that they founded the Temple of Apollo (Thuc. VI 54), and commenced the gigantic temple of the Olympian Zeus, which remained unfinished for centuries. In 500 B.C. the Dionysiac theatre was commenced on the S.E. slope of the Acropolis, in consequence of the falling of the wooden construction in which the early dramas had been performed; but the new theatre was not completed till 340 B.C., although it must have been used for the representation of plays long before. Stoa Pœcile, erected by his kinsman, Peisianax, was adorned with paintings by Mikon, Polygnotos, and Panænos. Cimon also planted and adorned the agora and the academy. The north wall to the Peiræeus and the wall to Phaleron were begun by Cimon in 461 B.C., and the wall between these two, or the south wall to the Peiræeus, was built by Pericles and Callicrates about 445. The Phaleric wall was rendered unnecessary by the wall built by Pericles, and was not reconstructed by Conon. From the fourth century the north and south walls of the Peiræeus were known as the two 'legs' of Athens. They were 40 stadia, or nearly 5 miles in length (Thuc. II 13).

Fifth Century.—Under the administration of Cimon the Theseion was built and the Stoa. It was to Pericles, however, that Athens was chiefly indebted for her architectural splendour. On the Acropolis he built the Parthenon (447–438), the Erechtheion (completed 407), and the Propylæa (437–432); in the city he erected a new odeion (before 446), and outside the walls he enlarged the Lyceion.

The Peloponnesian War ended any further building in Athens. On the capture of the city in 404 B.C., the long walls and the fortifications of the Peiræeus were destroyed by the Lacedæmonians; but they were again restored by Conon in 393 B.C., after gaining his naval victory over the Lacedæmonians off Cnidos.

Fourth Century and following.—Towards the close of the reign of Philip, the orator Lycurgus, who was entrusted with the management of the finances (338–326), obtained means for defraying expenses of public buildings. The Dionysiac theatre and the Panathenaic stadium were completed, and the Lyceion further improved. Lycurgus also formed a magazine of arms in the Acropolis, and built dock-yards in the Peiræeus.

After the battle of Chæroneia (338 B.C.), Athens, although nominally independent, became a dependency of Macedonia. Athens having sided with the Romans in their war with the last Philip of Macedonia, this monarch destroyed all the beautiful temples in the Attic plain and all the suburbs of the city, 200 B.C. (Liv. XXXI 26). Athens experienced a greater calamity upon its capture by Sulla in 86 B.C. He destroyed the long walls, and the fortifications of the city and the Peiræeus, and permanently ruined the prosperity and importance of the maritime city.

Roman Epoch.—Wherever the Greek language was spoken and Greek literature studied, Athens was held in honour, and the most remarkable buildings erected at Athens, after the decline of her power, were executed at the expense of foreign potentates. In 275 B.C. Ptolemy Philadelphus of Egypt built a gymnasium near the temple of Theseus (Paus. I 17). About 240 B.C. Attalus, King of Pergamus, ornamented the S.E. wall of the Acropolis with four compositions in statuary (Paus. I, 25). About 174 B.C. Antiochus Epiphanes of Syria continued work upon the Olympieion which had been left unfinished by the Peisistratidæ. Soon after Sulla's siege of Athens, Ariobarzanes II of Macedonia repaired the Odeion of Pericles. Julius Cæsar and Augustus contributed to the erection of the portico of Athena Archegetis, which still exists.

Hadrian (A.D. 117–138) was the greatest benefactor of Athens. He completed the Olympieion and adorned the city with other public buildings—two temples, a gymnasium, a library, and a stoa—and gave the name of Hadrianopolis to a new quarter of the city which he supplied with water by an aqueduct. Later, Herodes Atticus, a native of Marathon, built a theatre on the S.W. side of the Acropolis in memory of his wife, Regilla, and also covered with Pentelic marble the seats in the stadium of Lycurgus.

Athens was never more splendid than in the time of the Antonines, and it was at this epoch that the city was visited by Pausanias, to whose account we are chiefly indebted for our knowledge of its topography. After the Antonines, Athens received no further embellishment, but her public buildings appear to have existed in undiminished glory until the fourth century A.D. Their decay was due partly to the declining prosperity of the city, and partly to the fall of paganism.

The Acropolis. Although the site of the original city, the Acropolis had ceased to be inhabited from the time of the Persian wars, and was appropriated to the worship of Athena and the other guardian deities of the city. The summit of the rock was stripped of everything except temples and statues, the whole forming one vast composition in architecture, sculpture, and painting, the dazzling whiteness of the marble relieved by brilliant colours and glittering in the transparent clearness of the Athenian atmosphere.

Walls of the Acropolis.—The ancient fortifications are ascribed to the Pelasgians, who are said to have levelled the summit of the rock, and to have built a wall around it. This Pelasgic wall was over 30 feet high, and the principal entrance was in the N.E. Later, in the tenth(?) century B.C., the fortifications on the western slope were strengthened by an outer system of works, comprehending nine gates, hence called the Enneapylon. These fortifications were strong enough to defy the Spartans when the Peisistratidæ took refuge in the Acropolis;

but after the expulsion of the tyrants (510 B.C.) they were partly dismantled.

After the Persian Wars Themistocles rebuilt the walls on the W. and N. to a height of 16 feet and a thickness of 13 feet. The southern wall was completed by Cimon. At the S.E. angle the Hellenic masonry of the Cimonian wall is still to be seen. Westward of this point the wall has been encased in mediæval and recent times, but the Hellenic masonry can be traced under the casing as far as the Propylæa. The S.W. reach of the Hellenic wall terminates westwards in a solid tower about 30 feet high, which is surrounded by the temple of Nike Apteros ('without wings'). This tower commanded the unshielded side of any troops approaching the gate, which was probably in the same position as the present entrance. After passing through the gate and proceeding northward underneath the west face of the tower we come to the Propylæa. The effect of emerging from the dark gate and narrow passage to the magnificent marble staircase, 70 feet broad, surmounted by the Propylæa, must have been grand. After passing the gateways of the Propylæa we come upon the area of the Acropolis. Upon entering, the colossal statue of Athena Promachos ('in the van of war') was seen to the left and the Parthenon to the right. On the right, as we leave the Propylæa, and on the road itself, are traces of five votive altars, one of which is dedicated to Athena Hygieia. Farther on, to the left, is the site of the statue of Athena Promachos. Northwards of this statue, there is a staircase close to the edge of the rock, partly built, partly cut out, leading to the grotto of Aglauros. The staircase passes downwards through a cleft in the rock, opening out in the face of the cliff a little below the foundations of the wall.

The highest part of the Acropolis is that situated N. of a level platform in front of the eastern portico of the Parthenon. Westwards of this spot is the area between the Parthenon and the Erechtheion, which slopes from the former to the latter. Near the Parthenon is the mouth of a cistern, which may have been supplied with water from the roof of the temple. Close to the S. or caryatid portico of the Erechtheion, is a small levelled area on which was probably placed one of the many altars or statues surrounding that temple.

The Propylæa.—The architect of the Propylæa was Mnesicles, in the time of Pericles. It was commenced in the archonship of Euthymenes, 437 B.C., and completed in 5 years. The building was constructed of Pentelic marble, and covered the W. end of the Acropolis, which was 168 feet in breadth. The central part consisted of two Doric hexastyle porticoes, covered with a roof of white marble. They were divided into two unequal halves by a wall, pierced by five gates, by which the Acropolis was entered. The western portico, facing the city, was 43 feet in depth, and the eastern, facing the Acropolis, about half this depth. The central part of the building was 58 feet in breadth, and consequently did not cover the whole width of the rock: the remainder was occupied by two wings, which projected 26 feet in front of the western portico, each built in the form of a Doric temple. In the N. wing (on the left hand ascending the Acropolis) a porch of 12 feet in depth conducted into a chamber of 35 feet by 30, usually called the *Pinakotheka*, from its walls being covered with paintings. The S. wing (on the right hand ascending the Acropolis) consisted only of a porch 26 feet by 17, not conducting into any chamber behind. On the W. front of this S. wing stood the small temple of Nike Apteros, the Wingless Victory, identified with Athena. This temple, demolished in 1687, consisted of a cella with four Ionic columns at either front, but with none on the sides, being of the class called Amphiprostyle Tetrastyle. It was raised upon a stylobate of 3 feet and was 27 feet in length, and 18 feet in breadth. On the W. front of the N. wing of the Propylæa stands a lofty pedestal, about 12 feet square and 27 high. An inscription, which effaces one much older, dedicates the statue, probably equestrian, to Vipsanius Agrippa, nephew of Augustus.

The Parthenon.—This derived its name from being the temple of Athena Parthenos, or Athena the Virgin. It was also called Hecatompedon, the Temple of One Hundred Feet, from its breadth. It was built under the administration of Pericles, and was completed in 432 B.C., probably after 15 years' work. In 438 the statue by Pheidias was installed in the cella, and by 434 the sculptures were nearly completed. The architects, according to Plutarch, were Ictinos and Callicrates. The superintendence of the work was entrusted to Pheidias.

The Parthenon was probably built on the site of an earlier temple destroyed by the Persians. It stood on the highest part of the Acropolis. Its architecture was of the Doric order. It was built of Pentelic marble and rested upon a rustic basement of limestone, upon which stood the marble stylobate or platform, 5½ feet in height, and composed of three steps. The dimensions of the Parthenon, taken from the upper step of the stylobate, were about 228 feet in length, 101 feet in breadth, and 66 feet in height to the top of the pediment. It consisted of a cella surrounded by a peristyle, which had 8 columns at either front, and

17 at either side (reckoning the corner columns twice), thus containing 46 columns in all. These columns were 6 feet 2 inches in diameter at the base, and 34 feet in height. Within the peristyle at either end, there was an interior range of 6 columns, of 5½ feet in diameter, standing before the end of the cella, and forming, with the prolonged walls of the cella, an apartment before the door. The cella was divided into two chambers of unequal size, of which the E. chamber or *naos* was about 98 feet and the W. chamber or *episthodomos* about 43 feet. In both these chambers the ceiling was supported by inner rows of columns. In the E. chamber there were 23 columns, of the Doric order, in two stories, one over the other, 10 on each side, and 3 on the western return: the diameter of these columns was about 3½ feet at the base. In the W. chamber there were 4 columns, the position of which is marked by four large slabs, symmetrically placed on the pavement. These columns were about 4 feet in diameter, and were probably of the Ionic order, as in the Propylæa. Architecturally, the temple is called Peripteral Octastyle. The whole building was adorned within and without with sculptures, executed under the direction of Pheidias by various artists. The grandest and most celebrated sculpture was the colossal statue of the Virgin Goddess, the work of Pheidias. It stood in the eastern or principal chamber of the cella. It belonged to that kind of work called chryselephantine, ivory being employed for those parts of the statue which were unclothed, while the dress and other ornaments were of solid gold. The goddess was represented standing, clothed with a tunic reaching to the ankles, with her spear in her left hand, and an image of victory, 4 cubits high, in her right. She was girded with the ægis, and had a helmet on her head, and

her shield rested on the ground by her side. The height of the statue was 26 cubits, or nearly 40 feet.

The Erechtheion.—This ancient temple was built upon the place where, according to legend, Athena and Poseidon disputed the possession of Attica, Athena asserting her claim by the olive tree, Poseidon by the imprint of his trident and the well of salt water which he caused to spring forth. Erechtheus, King of Athens, was associated with Poseidon under the name of Poseidon-Erechtheus. The two deities, Athena Polias and Poseidon-Erechtheus, were worshipped in two adjoining sanctuaries, forming one temple. This ancient Erechtheion was burnt down by the Persians, but the rebuilding was begun in 421, interrupted, resumed in 409, under the architect Philocles, and completed in 406.

The Erechtheion differs in form from every other known example of a Greek temple. Although oblong in shape and having a portico at the E. front, it had no portico at its W. end; but from either side of the latter a portico projected to the N. and S., thus forming a kind of transept. Consequently, the temple had three porticoes (*prostaseis*). The E. portico, before the principal entrance, consisted of 6 Ionic columns standing in a single line before the wall of the cella. The N. portico also consisted of 6 Ionic columns, but only 4 of these are in front; the two others are placed, one on either flank. The roof of the S. portico was supported by 6 caryatids, called the *Korai* (maidens), arranged in the same manner as the columns in the N. portico.

The sanctuary of Athena Polias was situated in the eastern half of the building, and next to this was the sanctuary of Poseidon-Erechtheus, which was separated from the western end by a third compartment. The internal arrangement of the building is, however, conjectural. Pausanias states that the temple of Pandrosos, the daughter of Cecrops, was attached to that of Athena Polias. The Pandroseion may have been within the cella of the Erechtheion or, more probably, lay outside its E. end adjoining the W. wall of the Erechtheion. Here in the Pandroseion, in the open air, grew the olive tree of Athena and here was situated the altar of Zeus Herkeios. Another portion of the Erechtheion, situated possibly in the Portico of the Caryatids, was called the Cecropion, Cecrops being traditionally buried there.

The Statue of Athena Promachos, one of the most celebrated works of Pheidias, was a colossal bronze figure, and represented the goddess in the very attitude of battle. It stood in the open air nearly opposite the Propylæa.

The Quadriga, in bronze, dedicated from the spoils of Chalcis, stood before the entrance of the Propylæa (Herod. V 77). Later it was transported into the interior of the Acropolis where it was seen by Pausanias.

The Gigantomachia, a composition in sculpture, stood upon the S. or Cimonian wall, and just above the Dionysiac theatre. It was one of four compositions, each 3 feet in height, dedicated by Attalus.

Temple of Artemis Brauronia, the bear-goddess, stood between the Propylæa and the Parthenon. It contained a statue of the goddess made by Praxiteles.

Temple of Rome and Augustus stood about 90 feet before the E. front of the Parthenon. It was built after 27 B.C., and was probably circular, 23 feet in diameter, with an Ionic colonnade of 9 columns.

The Asty or City. As to the site of the following places and monuments there is little or no doubt.

The Areiopagos, or Hill of Ares, was the rocky height opposite the W. end of the Acropolis, from which it was separated only by some hollow ground. The spot is memorable as the place of meeting of the Council of the Areiopagos, called the Upper Council, to distinguish it from the Council of the Five Hundred, which held its sittings in the valley below the hill.

The Pnyx, or place of assembly of the Athenian people, was a semicircular terrace about 230 feet deep and about 390 feet at its greatest width, situated on the N.E. slope of a hill facing the Acropolis. The open end of the semicircle, on the higher slope, was backed by a rock-cut wall, against which was the celebrated Bema, often called 'the Stone', from whence the orators addressed the multitude in the semicircular area before them. The Bema is 11 feet broad, rising from a graduated basis: the summit is broken, but the present height is about 20 feet. The Pnyx could accommodate 18,000 people sitting, and more than 25,000 standing.

Hill of the Nymphs, which lay a little to the N.W. of the Pnyx, gains its name from a rock-cut inscription on the summit.

The Mouseion was the hill to the S.W. of the Acropolis. It is described by Pausanias (I 25) as a hill within the city walls, where the mythical poet, Mousæos, was buried.

The Dionysiac Theatre.—The stone theatre of Dionysus was commenced in 500 B.C., but was not completely finished till 340 B.C., during the financial administration of Lycurgus. The theatre lay beneath the S. wall of the Acropolis, near its eastern end. The middle of it was excavated out of rock, and its extremities were supported by solid piers of masonry. The rows of seats were in the form of curves, rising one above the other; the diameter increased with the ascent. From the summit to the hollow below, which may, however, be higher than the ancient orchestra, the slope is about 300 feet in length. The theatre was sufficiently large to accommodate the whole Athenian population, as well as the strangers who flocked to the Dionysiac festival. It probably held more than the 14,000 or 17,000 which is the estimated number of the seats. In the sixth century the Assembly of the People found the new theatre a better meeting place than the Pnyx. In Roman times, probably under Nero, the orchestra was reconstructed to allow of numerous actors and even gladiatorial games.

Above the upper seats of the theatre and the Cimonian wall of the Acropolis is a grotto which was converted into a small temple by Thrasyllos, a victorious choragus, to commemorate the victory of his chorus, 320 B.C., as we learn from an inscription. Hence it is called the Choragic Monument of Thrasyllos. Upon the entablature of the temple was a colossal figure of Dionysus.

The Odeion, or Music-Theatre of Regilla, also lay beneath the S. wall of the Acropolis, but at its western end. It was built shortly after A.D. 161 by Herodes Atticus in honour of his deceased wife. According to Pausanias, who does not mention it in his first book as it was not then built, but who describes it later (VII 20), it surpassed all other odeia in Greece; and its roof of cedar wood was also much admired. The length of its diameter within the walls was about 240 feet, and it accommodated probably about 6,000 persons.

Cave of Apollo and Pan, and Fountain of Clepsydra.—The cave lay at the base of the N.W. angle of the Acropolis. The worship of Apollo in the cave was of great antiquity, and the worship of Pan was not introduced till after the battle of Marathon. His statue was dedicated by Miltiades. The cave measures about 18 feet in length, 30 in height, and 15 in depth. The fountain near the cave, of which Pausanias does not mention the name, was called Clepsydra ('Hidden Water'), more anciently Empedo. It derived the former name from being supposed to have a subterraneous connection with the harbour of Phaleron.

The Aglaurion, the sanctuary of Aglauros, one of the three daughters of Cecrops, was a cavern situated in the northern face of the Acropolis. The rocks on the N. side were called the Long Rocks, and evidently from several passages in the *Ion* of Euripides the Aglaurion was in some part of these precipices.

The Theseion is the traditional name of this temple which is the best preserved of all Athenian monuments. It is situated on a height in the N.W. of the city, N. of the Areiopagos, and it was thought to be the Temple of Theseus, by reason of the sculptures which represent the hero's deeds. But its site does not correspond to that of the true sanctuary of Theseus, built by Cimon to receive the bones of the hero, which he brought from Scyros to Athens in 479 B.C. The so-called Theseion is now believed to be a temple for the worship of Hephæstus and Athena Hephæstia: it is, therefore, the Hephæsteion mentioned by Pausanias. It was built of Pentelic marble, and stands upon an artificial limestone foundation. It is a Peripteral Hexastyle, that is, it is surrounded by columns, 34 in number, and has 6 at each front. The length is 104 feet and the breadth 45 feet. The height from the bottom of the stylobate to the top of the pediment is 33½ feet.

The Olympieion, or Temple of Olympian Zeus, is

indicated by 16 gigantic Corinthian columns of white marble, to the S.E. of the Acropolis, and near the right bank of the Ilissos. The temple, the largest in Athens, was commenced by Peisistratus and finished by Hadrian, after many interruptions, the work occupying a period of nearly 700 years. The original founder of the temple is said to have been Deucalion (Paus. I 18). Its size, judging by the existing remains, was 354 feet in length and 171 feet in breadth. The 13 columns standing of the original 120 are 6½ feet in diameter and above 60 feet high.

The Horologium of Andronicus Cyrrhestes, vulgarly called the Temple of the Winds, is situated N. of the Acropolis. It is thought to belong to the period of Alexander the Great. It served as the weathercock and public clock of Athens. It is an octagonal tower with its eight sides facing respectively the direction of the eight winds into which the Athenian compass was divided. On the summit there stood originally a bronze figure of a Triton, turning on a pivot, which served for a windvane.

The Choragic Monument of Lysicrates, vulgarly called the Lantern of Demosthenes, was dedicated by the victorious choragus, Lysicrates, in 335 B.C. It is a small circular building on a square basement of white marble and covered by a cupola, supported by 6 Corinthian columns.

The Fountain of Kallirrhoë, or Enneacrounos, was situated in the S.E. of the city. It was the only source of good drinking water in Athens (Paus. I 14). The fountain was renamed Enneacrounos from being fitted with 9 pipes by the Peisistratidæ.

The Panathenaic Stadium was situated on the S. side of the Ilissos, and is described by Pausanias as 'a hill rising above the Ilissos, of a semicircular form in its upper part, and extending from thence in a double right line to the bank of the river' (Paus. I 19). The stadium was used since early times for the gymnic contests of the Panathenaic games; improvements were made to it by Lycurgus about 350 B.C. The slopes were covered with marble seats by Herodes Atticus, and the stadium could accommodate about 70,000 persons.

The Arch of Hadrian, which is still extant, is opposite the N.W. angle of the Olympieion. It is a paltry structure and was probably erected in Hadrian's honour by the Athenian municipality, rather than by Hadrian himself.

The Agora, named the Agora of the Kerameikos to distinguish it from the Old Agora, the exact position of which cannot be determined. The Agora of the Kerameikos was situated in hollow ground, bounded on the W. by the celebrated hill called Colonos, more usually Colonos Agoraios, or Misthios, on the S. by the Areiopagos, and by the Acropolis in the E. It was quadrilateral in shape, about 650 feet long and 490 feet wide. It was surrounded by colonnades and public buildings. On the N. it opened upon the plain of Eridanos. The remains found on the W. side are probably those of the Stoa Basileios, the portico of Zeus Eleutherios ('the Deliverer'), and the temple of Apollo Patroos. In the S.W. corner are the probable foundations of the Metroon. The S. limits of the agora were marked by the Bouleuterion, the Tholos, and the Theseion. The Tholos was a circular building where the Council of Fifty Deputies (the *Prytaneis*) took their common meals. Near it stood the statues of the *Eponymi*, or heroes from whom were derived the names of the Attic tribes. The agora in the E. was probably bordered by the Portico of Attalus, founded by Attalus II, King of Pergamus (159–138 B.C.). N. of this portico was the Stoa Pœcile and S. of it the Ptolemæon, a gymnasium and library founded by Ptolemy II Philadelphus about A.D. 275. The Agora of the Kerameikos, which was planned to replace the Old Agora probably about the time of Solon, rapidly became the centre of Athenian life.

CARTHAGE

The present remains of Carthage are insufficient to guide us to an understanding of the obscure statements of the ancient writers; and the inquirer often sighs over the loss of that picture, representing the site and size of Carthage, which Mancinus, the commander of the fleet in the Third Punic War (148 B.C.), exhibited to the Roman people in the forum, and won the consulship by his zeal in explaining its details. Appian (*Pun.* 95) is almost the only ancient author who has left any considerable details; and he is very inexact, and in some points evidently quite wrong. We know that the old Punic city grew up round the original Bosra or Byrsa (whether the citadel called Byrsa in historical times even stood on the old site is doubtful), and that it gradually covered the whole peninsula; and we know that it had a large suburb called Megara or Magalia, and also the New City. We also know that the Roman city stood on a part of the ancient site, and was far inferior to the Old City in extent. But, whether the original Punic city with its harbours was on the N. or S. part of the peninsula; on which side of it the suburb of Megara was situated; and whether the Roman city was built on the site of the former, or of the latter; are questions on which scholars hold opposite opinions.

Upon the whole, comparing the statement of the ancient writers with the present state of the locality, it seems probable that the original city was on the S.E. part of the peninsula about the two headlands now called Ras (Cape) Ghamart (300 feet high) and Ras Sidi Bou Said or C. Carthage (400 feet high).

The following are the most important details of the topography:

1. *Tænia.*—This was a tongue of land, of a considerable length, and half a stadium in breadth, mentioned again and again by Appian in such a manner that the determination of its position goes far to settle the chief doubt already referred to. It jutted out from the isthmus towards the W., between the lake and the sea, and in the closest proximity to the harbours, and also at the weaker extremity of the strong landward wall of the city. All the particulars of Appian's description seem to point to the sandy tongue of land which extends S.W. from the S. extremity of the peninsula to the *Goletta*, or mouth of the Lagoon of Tunis, and divides in part this lagoon from the open sea. That this tongue of land is larger than he describes it, is a confirmation of the identity, considering the changes which we know to have been going on; and the slight discrepancy involved in his making the Tænia jut out from the isthmus, whereas it actually proceeds from the peninsula, is surely hardly worthy of discussion. No room would have been left for doubt, had Appian told us what lake he meant; but that he omits to tell us this, seems of itself a strong proof that he meant the Lagoon of Tunis.

2. *Walls.*—These are especially difficult to trace with any certainty. At the time when the city was most flourishing, it is pretty clear that they encom-

passed, as might have been expected, the whole circuit of the peninsula, speaking generally; and Appian informs us that on one side (evidently towards the sea, but the words are wanting) there was only a single wall, because of the precipitous nature of the ground; but that on the S., towards the land side, there was a triple wall. But when we come to particulars, first, as to the sea side, it is not certain whether the two headlands of C. Ghamart and C. Carthage were included within the fortifications, or were left, either wholly or in part, unfortified on account of their natural strength. In the final siege, we find Mancinus attacking from the side of the sea a part of the wall, the defence of which was neglected on account of the almost inaccessible precipices on that side, and establishing himself in a fort adjacent to the walls. On the whole, it seems probable that on both the great heights the walls were drawn along the summit rather than the base, so that they would not include the N. slope of C. Ghamart, nor the E. and S. slopes of C. Carthage.

The land side presents still greater difficulties. The length of the wall which Scipio drew across the isthmus to blockade the city, and which was 25 stadia (nearly 3 miles) from sea to sea, gives us only the measure of the width of the isthmus (probably at its narrowest part), not of the land face of the city, which stood on wider ground. Strabo (XVII p. 832) assigns to the whole walls a circumference of 360 stadia (nearly 42 miles), 60 of which belonged to the wall on the land side, which reached from sea to sea. Explicit as this statement is, it seems impossible to reconcile it with the actual dimensions of the peninsula, for which even the 23 Roman miles assigned to it by Livy would seem too much. The 60 stadia (nearly 7 miles) of

Strabo have been obtained by taking in the walls along the N. and S. sides of the peninsula, as well as that across it on the land side, which is inconsistent with the meaning of the writer; or by supposing that Strabo gives the total length of the triple line of wall, a most improbable assumption. Besides, the language of Strabo seems to refer to the actual width of that part of the isthmus across which the wall was built. The only feasible explanation seems to be, that the wall was not built across the narrowest part of the isthmus, but was thrown back to where it had begun to widen out into the peninsula; and it seems also fair to make some allowance for deviations from a straight line. A confirmation of the length assigned to the wall by Strabo is found in Appian's statement, that Scipio made simultaneous attacks on the land defences of Megara alone at points 20 stadia distant from each other, the whole breadth of the isthmus being, as we have seen, only 25 stadia.

Be this as it may, we know that this land wall formed by far the most important part of the defences of the city. It consisted of three distinct lines, one behind the other, each of them 30 cubits (about 45 feet) high without the parapets. There were towers at the distance of 2 plethra (202 feet), 4 stories high, and 30 feet deep. Within each wall were built two stories of vaulted chambers, or casemates, in the lower range of which were stables for 300 elephants, and in the upper range stables for 4,000 horses, with stores of food for both. In the spaces between the walls there were barracks for 20,000 infantry and 4,000 cavalry, with magazines and stores of proportionate magnitude; forming a vast fortified camp between the city and the isthmus. It would seem from Appian (VIII 95) that this description applied to the S. part of the landward wall, behind which lay Byrsa. The N. part of the landward wall, surrounding the suburb of Megara, seems to have been less strongly fortified, and accordingly we find some of the chief attacks of Scipio directed against it. Appian adds to his description of the triple wall, that its corner which bent round towards the harbours, by the Tænia, was the only part that was weak and low; and on this point also we find the Romans directing their attacks.

The limits of the Roman city can be defined with greater certainty. It remained, indeed, without a fortified enclosure down to the fourteenth year of Theodosius II (424 B.C.), when the increasing dangers of the African province both from the native and foreign barbarians suggested the policy of fortifying its capital. The remains of the wall then built can still be traced, and sufficient ruins of the city are visible to indicate its extent; while the limits are still further marked by the position of the great reservoirs, which we know to have been without the walls.

That Roman Carthage stood on the site of the ancient Punic city, and not on that of the suburb of Megara, seems tolerably clear. Not to lay too much stress on Pliny's phrase 'in vestigiis magnæ Carthaginis', it appears that the new city was supplied from the same aqueduct and reservoirs, and had its citadel and chief temples on the same sites, as of old. The restored temple of Æsculapius was again the chief sanctuary, and that of the goddess Cælestis became more magnificent than ever.

3. *Harbours.*—The double harbour of Carthage must be looked for on the S. side of the peninsula, at the angle which it forms with the Tænia described above, within the Lagoon of Tunis. The fact that Scipio Africanus the Elder could see from Tunis the

Punic fleet sailing out of the harbour seems a decisive proof of the position.

The port consisted of an outer and an inner harbour, with a passage from the one into the other; and the outer had an entrance from the sea 70 feet wide, which was closed with iron chains. The outer harbour was for merchantmen. The inner harbour was reserved for the ships of war. Just within its entrance was an island called Cothon, rising to a considerable elevation above the surrounding banks, and thus serving the double purpose of a mask to conceal the harbour from without, and an observatory for the port-admiral. The shores of the island and of the ports were built up with great quays, in which were constructed docks for 220 ships (one, it would seem, for each), with storehouses for all their equipments. The entrance of each dock was adorned with a pair of Ionic columns, which gave the whole circuit of the island and the harbour the appearance of a magnificent colonnade on each side. So jealously was this inner harbour guarded even from the sight of those frequenting the outer, that, besides a double wall of separation, gates were provided to give access to the city from the outer harbour, without passing through the docks.

4. *Byrsa.*—This name is used in a double sense, for the most ancient part of the city, adjoining to the harbours, and for the citadel or Byrsa, in the stricter sense. When Appian speaks (*Pun.* 95) of the triple land wall on the S., as 'where the Byrsa was upon the isthmus', it may be doubted in which sense he uses the term; but, when he comes to describe the storming of the city (*Pun.* 127), he gives us a minute description of the locality of the citadel.

Close to the harbours stood the Forum, from which three narrow streets of houses six stories high ascended to the Byrsa, which was by far the strongest position in the whole city. There can be little doubt of its identity with the Hill of St. Louis, an eminence rising to the height of 200 feet, and having its summit in the form of an almost regular plateau, sloping a little towards the sea. Its regularity suggests the probability of its being an artificial mound formed of the earth dug up in excavating the harbours; a kind of work which we know to have been common among the old Semitic nations.

On the sides of the hill there are still traces of the ancient walls which enclosed the Byrsa and made it a distinct fortress, and which seem to have risen, terrace above terrace, like those of the citadel of Ecbatana.

On the summit stood the temple of Æsculapius (Esmun), by far the richest in the city, raised on a platform which was ascended by sixty steps. It was in this temple that the senate held in secret their most important meetings.

The Byrsa remained the citadel of Carthage in its later existence; and the temple of Æsculapius was restored by the Romans. On it was the prætorium of the proconsul of Africa, which became successively the palace of the Vandal kings and of the Byzantine governors.

5. *Forum and Streets.*—As we have just seen, the Forum lay at the S. foot of the hill of Byrsa, adjacent to the harbours. It contained the senate house, the tribunal, and the temple of the god whom the Greeks and Romans call Apollo, whose golden image stood in a chapel overlaid with gold to the weight of 1,000 talents. The three streets already mentioned as ascending from the Forum to the Byrsa formed an important outwork to its fortifications; and Scipio had to storm them house by house. The centre street, which probably led straight up

to the temple of Æsculapius, was called, in Roman Carthage, Via Salutaris. The other streets of the city seem to have been for the most part straight and regularly disposed at right angles.

6. *Other Temples.*—On the N. side of the Byrsa, on lower terraces of the hill, are the remains of two temples, which some take for those of Cælestis and Saturn; but the localities are doubtful. We know that the worship of both these deities was continued in the Roman city.

7. On the W. and S.W. side of the Byrsa are ruins of Baths, probably the Thermæ Gargilianæ, a locality famous in the ecclesiastical history of Carthage; of a spacious circus, and of an amphitheatre.

8. *Aqueduct and Reservoirs.*—The great aqueduct 50 miles long, by which Carthage was supplied with water from Jebel Zaghwan, is supposed by some to be a work of the Punic age; but Barth (*Wanderungen*, pp. 100, *sq.*) believes it to be Roman. The reservoirs are among the most interesting remains of Carthage, especially on account of the peculiarly constructed vaulting which covers them. They are probably of Punic workmanship. Besides some smaller ones, there are two principal sets; those on the W. of the city, where the aqueduct terminated, and those on the S., near the Cothon.

9. Besides the above, there are ruins which seem to be those of a theatre, and also the remains of a great building, apparently the largest in the city, which Barth conjectures to be the temple of Cælestis. These ruins consist, like the rest, only of broken foundations (Barth, *Wanderungen*, 105, 106).

10. The suburb of Megara, Magar, or Magalia, afterwards considered as a quarter of the city, under the name of Neapolis (New City), was surrounded by a wall, and adorned with beautiful gardens.

11. *Necropolis.*—From the few graves found in the rocky soil of the hill of C. Ghamart, it seems probable that here was the ancient necropolis, N. of the city, a position in which it is frequently, if not generally, found in other ancient cities. There is, however, some doubt on the matter, which the evidence is insufficient to decide.

CONSTANTINOPLE

The ancient city of Byzantium was founded traditionally by the Megarians in 667 B.C. In 628 a second colony was sent out from Megaris under Zeuxippus.

Ancient Byzantium was situated on the first of the seven hills upon which, rising one above another, the modern city stands; but its area occupied more than the first region of the later town. In all probability it extended over the three regions which lie behind the triangular space later filled by the Seraglio. According to Dionysius of Byzantium, its circumference was 40 stadia. It was on the second hill that Constantine pitched his tent at the siege of Byzantium, and to commemorate his success, he chose this site for the principal forum of the new city. The forum was probably elliptical in shape. The two opposite entrances formed triumphal arches; the porticoes, which enclosed it on every side, were filled with statues of the tutelar deities of Greece.

The foundations of Constantine's city were laid according to imperial edict, in obedience to the commands of Heaven. On foot with a lance in his hand, the Emperor Constantine headed a procession which was to mark the boundaries of the New Rome, the foundations of which were, like those of ancient Rome, to be laid upon seven hills. The rites of inauguration, accompanied by chariot games and a strange medley of religious ceremonial, lasted forty days, but the 11th of May, A.D. 330, is considered the birthday of the city. The name, New Rome, confirmed by a law, engraved on a marble column in a place called the Strategion, was soon superseded by that of Constantinople in honour of the founder.

The walls of Constantine across the enlarged breadth of the triangle were begun at a distance of 15 stadia (nearly 2 miles) from the old fortifications, and stretching from the port to the Propontis, enclosed five out of the seven hills upon which the city stood, but were not finished before the reign of Constantius. In 401, Arcadius repaired these walls which had fallen in the earthquake that had taken place in that year. In 413, during the minority of Theodosius II, Anthemius, the Prætorian prefect, razed the old fortifications and built a new enclosure of walls. These walls included in the city the district outside the Constantine walls, called *Exokionion*—the territory beyond the column of Constantine. Here as a defence to the city the Gothic legionaries were stationed. The triumphal arch in the S.W. of this district was built, according to the inscription on the headstone, now dislodged, by Theodosius the Great to commemorate his suppression of the rebellion of Maximus in A.D. 388. This archway, together with the smaller arch, was incorporated by Anthemius in the Theodosian walls, and was, therefore, no longer an isolated monument. It became the chief gate of the city, known as the Golden Gate. The Theodosian walls were thrown down by an earthquake in 447 and were rebuilt in three months by the prefect Cyrus. This double line of strong and lofty stone walls has, except on the land side, almost disappeared, but in a dilapidated state still exists and extends from the port to the Sea of Marmora for about 4 miles, presenting magnificent specimens of mural ruins. The walls were flanked at short intervals by towers, mostly rectangular. The extreme length of the city at this period, and it never greatly exceeded these limits, was under 3 miles, and the circuit about 12½ miles. The Sycæ, or fig trees, formed the thirteenth region beyond the harbour, which was much embellished by Justinian. The suburb of Blachernæ was not taken into the city till the reign of Heraclius.

In the new capital of Constantine, emancipated from the restraint of Pagan associations and art, the Byzantine builders founded an architecture peculiarly their own. Of this the cupola was the great characteristic, to which every other feature was subordinate. That which at Athens was straight, angular, and square, became in Constantinople curved and rounded, concave within, and convex without. Thus the old architecture of Greece owed its destruction to the same nation from which it had taken its first birth.

At each end of the principal forum were two shrines, one of which held the statue of Cybele, which was said to have been placed by the Argonauts upon Mt. Dindymon, but deprived of her lions and with her hands from the attitude of command distorted into that of a suppliant for the city; in the other was the Fortune of Byzantium. The centre of the forum was occupied by a lofty pillar, which, formed of marble and porphyry, rose to the height of 120 feet. On this column Constantine placed his own statue with the attributes of Christ and Apollo, and substituted the nails of the Passion for the rays of the sun; Constantine was replaced by Julian, Julian by Theodosius. In A.D. 1412 the keystone was loosened by an earthquake. The statue fell under Alexius Comnenus, and was replaced by the Cross. The Palladium was said to be buried under the pillar. Besides the principal fourm there was a second one, which has been sometimes confounded with the other; it was square, with porticoes surrounding it, consisting of two ranks of columns; in this the Augusteum, or court of the palace, stood the Golden Miliarium, which was an elevated arcade embellished with statues.

The Miliarium did not therefore resemble its namesake at Rome, but it served the same purpose, being the milestone from which all distances from Constantinople were measured.

The circus, or hippodrome, situated S.W. of the Augusteum, was a stately building, begun by Severus, but completed by Constantine. The space between the *metæ* or goals was filled with statues and obelisks. The Turks retain the translated name of the horse-course (*Atmeidan*), but the ancient splendour of the place has disappeared. It was once not only the scene of sport and recreation, but also of political activity, the centre of the life of the Byzantine world. It is now no longer a circus, but an oblong space.

At the upper end is a granite obelisk, covered with hieroglyphics of poor workmanship. It is called after Theodosius. Near this stands the wreathed column of bronze, which, according to legend, bore the golden tripod of Delphi, and was shattered by the iron mace of Mohammed II. Fourteen churches, fourteen palaces, several triumphal arches, and eight public baths are assigned to the founder of the city. Constantine, and in this his example was followed by his successors, imitated ancient Rome in the construction of sewers. Two large subterranean cisterns, constructed by the Greek emperors in case of a siege, still remain; one, called by the Turks the palace of the 'Thousand and One Pillars', is now perfectly dry. The other, still existing as a cistern, and called the 'Subterranean Palace', may be described as an underground lake, with an arched roof to cover it, supported on 336 marble pillars.

From the throne, seated upon which the emperor viewed the games of the circus, a winding staircase called *cochlea* descended to the palace. This was a magnificent building, covering a great extent of ground, on the banks of the Propontis, between the hippodrome and the church of St. Sophia, later the Seraglio. The Empress Eudoxia, wife of Arcadius, ornamented the city with a palace and baths. Theodosius II encouraged architecture, and executed considerable works; in his reign the walls of Constantinople were in great measure rebuilt, and the city adorned with *thermæ*, a forum, and two palaces for the sisters of Pulcheria. The baths of Zeuxippus—the site of which it is difficult to fix, as, while history seems to connect them with St. Sophia and the palace, the original plan places them on the other side of the city, near the harbour—were so embellished by Constantine with statues of marble and bronze that they became famed as the most beautiful in the world.

While private houses and public buildings for business, for convenience, for amusement, and splendour rose with the rapidity of enchantment, one class of edifices was wanting. A few temples, such as those of the Sun, the Moon, and Aphrodite, were permitted to stand in the Heropolis, though deprived of their revenues. But few churches were built; of these one was dedicated to the Supreme Wisdom. The ancient Temple of Peace, which afterwards formed part of St. Sophia, was appropriately transformed into a church. The Church of the Twelve Apostles appears from Eusebius to have been finished a few days before the death of Constantine; it fell to ruin 20 years afterwards, was repaired by Constantius, rebuilt by Justinian, and demolished by Mohammed II.

The main thoroughfare of Constantinople, called the Mese, as it crossed the centre of the city, began at the Miliarium in the Augusteum. It linked up the Forum of Constantine on the second hill, the Forum Tauri, or of Theodosius after the column of that emperor, on the third hill, the Forum Amastrianon, and the Forum Bovis, outside which stood the Golden Gate of the Constantine wall. From this point the road crossed the Exokionion, passing the Forum of Arcadius, and turned S. to the Golden Gate, where all triumphal processions began, following this route back to the city. A branch of the road at the Forum Amastrianon led past the Church of the Apostles and past the Cistern of Aspar, chief of the Gothic militia under Leo I (457–474), to the other great gate of the city—the Charisius Gate (now known as the Adrianople Gate). From the Forum Bovis an imperial road led to St. Romanus's Gate, following the seventh hill. These were the main streets—of which there were over 400, covering the 14 Regions into which the city was divided for administrative purposes.

In 447, after the great earthquake, the edifices of Constantinople were restored with renewed splendour. Marcian turned his attention chiefly to the aqueducts; Leo I Thrax to the churches of Constantinople. Justin I contributed to the embellishment, or rather restoration, of Constantinople. The reign of Justinian is the most brilliant epoch of the Neo-Greek or Byzantine architecture; and, like Hadrian, this emperor was entitled to the proud distinction of being called by his contemporaries 'reparator orbis'. The great ornament of Constantinople was the temple reared by Justinian in honour of the Eternal Wisdom (St. Sophia). This, the principal church of Constantinople, had been originally constructed by Constantine in 325 and enlarged by his son, Constantius. It had been destroyed by fire in 404 after the exile of St. John Chrysostom, reconstructed by Theodosius in 415, and again destroyed by fire in 532 in the riots against Justinian during the *Nika* of the Blue and Green factions. Justinian planned an ambitious reconstruction and employed the architects Anthemius of Tralles and Isidorus of Miletus. Disregarding the cardinal rule that all architectural artifice is inconsistent with good taste, they endeavoured to make it appear entirely hovering in air without the least earthly resting-place. The attempt was unsuccessful, for, in A.D. 558, twenty-one years after the dedication, an earthquake nearly destroyed it. Another Isidorus, nephew of the former, was employed to restore it; an elevation of 20 feet more than it had before its fall was given to the dome, and the originally circular form was changed to an elliptical. Though such was the lightness of the dome that it appeared suspended 'by a chain from Heaven', the circle which encompasses the dome rested on four strong arches, supported on four massive piles, assisted on the N. and S. sides by four columns of granite, the shaft of each 40 feet long. Two larger and six smaller semi-domes sprouted out and encircled the central cupola. The ground-plan describes the figure of a Greek cross within a quadrangle. Besides this great model of Eastern architecture, Justinian erected more than twenty-five churches in Constantinople and its suburbs. In honour of himself a colossal statue, representing the emperor mounted on horseback and in an attitude of defiance, was placed upon a column in the Augusteum before St. Sophia. The palace was also restored by Justinian, and magnificently adorned with bronze, many-coloured marbles, and mosaics representing the glories of the African and Italian triumphs. From the time of Heraclius to the hour of her fall, the outward glories of Constantinople shared the same fate as her renown and greatness.

ISSUS

A town of Cilicia, on the gulf of Issus. Herodotus calls the gulf of Issus the gulf of Myriandros (IV 38), from the town of Myriandros, which was on it.

The gulf of Issus is now named the gulf of Iskenderun, or Scanderoon, from the town of Scanderoon, formerly Alexandria ad Issum, on the E. side. It is the only large gulf on the southern side of Asia Minor and on the Syrian coast, and it is an important place in the systems of the Greek geographers. This gulf runs in a N.E. direction into the land to the distance of 47 miles. Issus is the remotest city in this part of Cilicia which Ptolemy mentions. Xenophon also speaks of it as the last city of Cilicia on the road to Syria.

Xenophon says that Cyrus marched 15 parasangs (nearly 52 miles) from the Pyramos 'to Issi, the uttermost city of Cilicia, on the sea, great and prosperous'. From Issus to the Pylæ of Cilicia and

Syria, the boundary between Syria and Cilicia, was 5 parasangs (Xen. *Anab.* I 4). The next stage was 5 parasangs to Myriandros, occupied by Phœnicians, a trading place, where many merchant ships were lying.

The nearest road to Susa from Sardis was through the Cilician plains. The difficulties were the passage into the plains by the Cilician Pylæ, or pass, and the way out of the plains along the gulf of Issus into Syria. The great road to Susa, which Herodotus describes (V 49, 52), went N. of the Taurus to the Euphrates. The land forces in the expedition of Datis and Artaphernes, 490 B.C., crossed the Syrian Amanus, and went as far as the Aleian plain in Cilicia; and there they embarked. They did not march by land through the Cilician Pylæ over the Taurus into the interior of the peninsula; but Mardonius in the previous expedition had led his troops into Cilicia, and sent them on by land to the Hellespontus, while he took ship and sailed to Ionia. The land force of Mardonius must have passed out to Cilicia by the difficult pass in the Taurus.

Shortly before the battle of Issus (333 B.C.), Alexander was at Mallos, when he heard that Darius with all his force was at Sochi in Assyria; which place was distant two marches from the Assyrian Pylæ (Arrian, *Anab.* II 6). 'Assyria' and 'Assyrian' here mean 'Syria' and 'Syrian'. Darius had crossed the Euphrates, probably at Thapsacus, and was encamped in an open country in Syria, which was well suited for his cavalry. Curtius (III 8) says that Alexander only reached Castabala on the second day from Mallos; that he went through Issus, and there deliberated whether he should go on or halt. Darius crossed the Amanus, which separates Syria from the bay of Issus, by a pass called the Amanicæ Pylæ, and advancing to Issus, was in the rear of Alexander, who had passed through the Cilician and Syrian Pylæ. Darius came to the pass in the Amanus, says Curtius, on the same night that Alexander came to the pass by which Syria is entered. The place where Darius crossed the Amanus was so situated that he came to Issus first, where he shamefully treated the sick of the Macedonians who had been left there. The next day he moved from Issus to pursue Alexander, that is, he moved towards the pylæ, and he came to the banks of the river Pinarus, where he halted. Issus was, therefore, N. of the Pinarus, and some little distance from it.

Alexander, hearing that the Persians were in his rear, turned back to the pylæ, which he reached at midnight, and halted till daybreak, when he moved on. When he came to where the pass widened, he arranged his army in order of battle. Darius was posted on the N. side of the Pinarus. It is plain, from this description, that Alexander did not march very far from the pylæ before he reached the wider part of the valley, and the river. Polybius (XII 17), who criticizes the description of the battle by Callisthenes, states, on his authority, that Darius descended into Cilicia through the Pylæ Amanides, and encamped on the Pinarus, at a place where the distance between the mountains and the sea was not more than 14 stadia (1½ miles). Callisthenes said, that when Alexander, after having passed the defile, heard of Darius being in Cilicia, he was 100 stadia (11½ miles) from him, and accordingly he marched back through the defile. It is not clear, from Polybius, whether the 100 stadia are to be reckoned to Issus or to the Pinarus. According to Arrian, when Alexander heard of Darius being behind him, he sent some men in a galley back to Issus, to see if it was so; and it is most consistent with the narrative to suppose that the men saw the Persians at Issus before they had advanced to the river; but this is not quite certain. The Persian army was visible, being near the coast, where it would be, if it were seen at Issus.

Strabo, following the historians of Alexander, adds nothing to what Arrian has taken from them. Alexander, he says, led his infantry from Soli along the coast and through the Mallotis to Issus and the forces of Darius; an expression which might mislead, if we had no other narrative. He also says, after Mallos is Ægæ, a small town with a harbour, then the Amanides Pylæ, where there is a harbour; and after Ægæ is Issus, a small town with a harbour, and the river Pinarus, where the fight was between Alexander and Darius. Accordingly he places Issus N. of the Pinarus. Cicero, during his proconsulship of Cilicia, led his forces against the mountaineers of the Amanus, and he was saluted as imperator at Issus, 'where', he says (*Ad Fam.* II 10), 'as I have often heard from you, Clitarchus told you that Darius was defeated by Alexander'. In another passage (*Ad Att.* V 20) he says that he occupied for a few days the same camp that Alexander had occupied at Issus against Darius. And again (*Ad Fam.* XIV 20), he says that 'he encamped for four days at the roots of the Amanus, at the Aræ Alexandri.' If this is the same fact that he mentions in his letter to Atticus, the Aræ were at Issus, and Issus was near the foot of the Amanus.

JERUSALEM

Jerusalem is situated in the heart of the mountain district which commences at the S. of the great plain of Esdraelon and is continued throughout the whole of Samaria and Judæa quite to the southern extremity of the Promised Land. It is almost equidistant from the Mediterranean and from the river Jordan, being about 30 miles from each, and situated at an elevation of 2,000 feet above the level of the Mediterranean. Its site is well defined by its circumjacent valleys.

Valleys.—1. In the N.W. quarter of the city is a shallow depression, occupied by an ancient pool. This is the head of the Valley of Hinnom, which from this point takes a southern course, confining the city on the western side, until it makes a sharp angle to the E., and forms the southern boundary of the city to its S.E. quarter, where it is met by another considerable valley from the N., which must be next described.

2. At the distance of somewhat less than 1,500 yards from the 'upper pool' at the head of the Valley of Hinnom, are the 'Tombs of the Kings', situated at the head of the Valley of Jehoshaphat, which runs at first in an eastern course at some distance N. of the modern city, until, turning sharply to the S., it skirts the eastern side of the town, and meets the Valley of Hinnom at the S.E. angle, as already described, from whence both valleys run in a southerly direction to the Dead Sea.

The space between the basin at the head of the Valley of Hinnom and the head of the Valley of Jehoshaphat is occupied by a high rocky ridge or swell of land, which attains its highest elevation a little without the N.W. angle of the present town.

The city, then, occupied the termination of this broad swell of land, being isolated, except on the N., by the two great valleys already described, towards which the ground declined rapidly from all parts of the city. This rocky promontory is, however, broken by one or two subordinate valleys.

3. There is, for example, another valley, very inferior in magnitude to those which encircle the city, but of great importance in a topographical view, as being the main geographical feature mentioned by Josephus in his description of the city. This Valley of the Tyropœon (Cheesemakers) meets the Valley of Hinnom at the Pool of Siloam, very near its junction with the Valley of Jehoshaphat, and can be distinctly traced through the city, along the W. side of the Temple enclosure, to the Damascus gate, where it opens into a small plain.

Hills.—The ancient Jebusite city was probably situated on the eastern hill between the Kidron and the Tyropœon valleys, and dependant for its water upon the Virgin's Fountain. This spring, the only natural source of water near Jerusalem, rises in a cave in the Kidron Valley, a little to the south of the present city. Traditionally, however, the ancient city was placed on the western hill between the Tyropœon and the Hinnom valleys. The determination of the former site is favoured by the discovery of an artificially dug trench to protect the city in the north. Evidence of potsherds shows that the trench was filled up about 1600 B.C., and probably ceased to be a defence about that date. There are evidences of a community having been in existence on the eastern hill as early as 2000 B.C. The city was not extended to include the third hill on the N.E., called the Temple Mount, until the time of Solomon. When in process of time the city overflowed its old boundaries, the hill, Bezetha, or New City, was added to the ancient hills, as is thus described by Josephus: 'The city, being over-abundant in population, began gradually to creep beyond its old walls, and the people joining to the city the region which lay to the N. of the Temple and close to the hill (of Acra), advanced considerably, so that even a fourth eminence was surrounded with habitations, viz. that which is called Bezetha, situated opposite to the Antonia, and divided from it by a deep ditch; for the ground had been cut through on purpose, that the foundations of the Antonia might not, by joining the eminence, be easy of approach, and of inferior height'.

The Antonia was a castle situated at the N.W. angle of the outer enclosure of the Temple, occupying a precipitous rock 50 cubits high (75 feet).

Walls. 1. *Upper City and Old Wall.*—'Of the three walls, the old one was difficult to be taken, both on account of the ravines, and of the eminence above them on which it was situated. But, in addition to the advantage of the position, it was also strongly built, as David and Solomon, and the kings after them, were very zealous about the work. Beginning towards the N., from the tower called Hippicus, and passing through the place called Xystus, then joining the council chamber, it was united to the western cloister of the Temple. In the other direction, towards the W., commencing from the same place, and extending through a place called Bethso to the gate of the Essenes, and then turning towards the S. above the fountain Siloam, thence again bending toward the E. to the Pool of Solomon, and running through a place which they called Ophla, it was joined to the eastern cloister of the Temple.' To understand this description by

Josephus, it is only necessary to remark that the walls are described, not by the direction in which they run, but by the quarter which they face, i.e. the wall 'turning towards the S.' is the S. wall; so that the Hippic Tower evidently lay at the N.W. angle of the Upper City.

The Hippic Tower is mentioned in connection with two neighbouring towers on the same N. wall, the Tower Phasælus and the Tower Mariamne, all three built by Herod the Great, and connected with his splendid palace that occupied the N.W. angle of the Upper City. 'These towers,' says Josephus, 'surpassed all in the world in extent, beauty, and strength, and were dedicated to the memory of his brother, his friend, and his best loved wife.'

The Royal Palace adjoining these towers was, according to Josephus, 'entirely surrounded by a wall 30 cubits high (45 feet), with decorated towers at equal intervals, and contained enormous banqueting halls, besides numerous chambers richly adorned. There were also many porticoes encircling one another, with different columns to each, surrounding green courts, planted with a variety of trees, having long avenues through them; and deep channels and reservoirs everywhere around, filled with bronze statues, through which the water flowed; and many towers of tame pigeons about the fountains.'

As the Xystus is mentioned next to the Hippicus by Josephus, in his description of the N. wall of the Upper City, it may be well to proceed at once to that. The xystus is properly a covered portico attached to the Greek gymnasium, which commonly had uncovered walks connected with it. As the Jerusalem Xystus was a place where public meetings were occasionally convened, it must be understood to be a wide public promenade, though not necessarily connected with a gymnasium, but perhaps rather with another palace which occupied 'this extremity of the Upper City'.

The House of the Asmonæans was above the Xystus, and was apparently occupied as a palace by the Younger Agrippa; for, when he addressed the multitude assembled in the Xystus, he placed his sister Berenice in the house of the Asmonæans, that she might be visible to them.

At the Xystus, we are told, a causeway joined the Temple to the Upper City, and one of the Temple gates opened on to this causeway.

It is highly probable that the Xystus was nothing else than the wide promenade over this mound, adorned with a covered cloister between the trees, with which the Rabbinical traditions assure us that Solomon's causeway was shaded. It is clear that the N. wall of the Upper City must have crossed the valley by this causeway to the Gate Shallecheth, which is explained to mean the Gate of the Embankment (1 Chron. xxvi 16).

The Council Chamber is the next place mentioned on the northern line of wall, as the point where it joined the western portico of the Temple.

We have now to trace the wall of the Upper City in the opposite direction from the same point, viz. the Hippic Tower at the N.W. angle. The points noticed are comparatively few. 'It first ran southward (i.e. with a western aspect), through a place called Bethso, to the Gate of the Essenes; then, turning E., it ran (with a southern aspect) above the fountain of Siloam; thence it bent northward, and ran (with an eastern aspect) to the Pool of Solomon, and extending as far as a place called Ophla, was joined to the eastern cloister of the Temple.'

Along the S. face of the Upper City the old wall

may still be traced, partly by scarped rock and partly by foundations of the ancient wall. As it is clear that the Upper City was entirely encompassed with a wall of its own, nowhere noticed by Josephus, except so far as it was coincident with the outer wall, it may be safely conjectured that this E. wall of the Upper City followed the brow of the ridge from the S.E. angle of the Hill Sion, along a line nearly coincident with the aqueduct; while the main wall continued its easterly course down the steep slope of Sion, across the valley of the Tyropœon, not far from its mouth—a little above the Pool of Siloam—and then up the ridge Ophel, until it reached the brow of the eastern valley.

The further course of the wall to the eastern cloister of the Temple is equally obscure, as the several points specified in the description are not capable of identification by any other notices. These are the Pool of Solomon and a place called Ophla, in the description already cited, to which may be added, from an incidental notice, the Basilica of Grapte or Monobazus.

The Pool of Solomon has been sometimes identified with the Fountain of the Virgin, from which the Pool of Siloam is supplied, and sometimes with that very pool. Both solutions are unsatisfactory, for Siloam would scarcely be mentioned a second time in the same passage under another name, and the fountain in question cannot, with any propriety, be called a pool.

The place called Ophla—in Scripture Ophel—is commonly supposed to be the southern spur of the Temple Mount, a narrow rocky ridge extending down to Siloam. But it is more certain that it is used in a restricted sense in this passage, than that it is ever extended to the whole ridge. It was apparently a large fortified building, to the S. of the Temple, connected with an outlying tower, and probably situated near the southern extremity of the present area of the Mosque of Omar.

2. *The Second Wall, and the Lower City.*—The account of the second wall in Josephus is very meagre. He merely says that it began at the Gate Gennath, a place in the old wall; and, after encompassing the Lower City, had its termination at the Fortress Antonia. There is here no clue to the position of the Gate Gennath. It is, however, certain that it was between the Hippic Tower and the Xystus.

There is the head of an old archway still existing above a heap of ruins, at a point about half-way between the Hippic Tower and the N.W. angle of Mount Sion, where a slight depression in that hill brings it nearly to a level with the declivity to the N. This would afford a good starting-point for the second wall, traces of which may still be discovered in a line N. of this, quite to the Damascus Gate, where are two chambers of ancient and very massive masonry, which appear to have flanked an old gate of the second wall at its weakest part, where it crossed the Valley of the Cheesemakers. From this gate, the second wall probably followed the line of the present city wall to a point near the Gate of Herod, now blocked up; whence it was carried along the brow of the hill to the N.E. angle of the Fortress Antonia, which occupied a considerable space on the N.W. of the Temple area.

3. *The Third Wall, and the New City.*—The third wall, which enclosed a very considerable space to the N. of the Old City, was the work of Herod Agrippa the Elder, and was only commenced about thirty years before the destruction of Jerusalem, and never completed according to the original design, in consequence of the jealousy of the Roman

government. The following is Josephus's account: 'This third wall Agrippa drew round the super-added city, which was all exposed. It commenced at the Tower Hippicus, from whence it extended to the northern quarter, as far as the Tower Psephinus; then, passing opposite to the Monuments of Helena, and being produced through the Royal Caves, it bent, at the angular tower, by the monument called the Fuller's, and, joining the old wall, terminated at the valley of the Kidron.'

As the site of the Hippic Tower has been already fixed, the first point to be noticed in this third wall is the Psephine Tower, which, Josephus informs us, was the most wonderful part of this great work, situated at its N.W. quarter, over against Hippicus, octagonal in form, 70 cubits in height, commanding a view of Arabia towards the E., of the Mediterranean towards the W., and of the utmost limits of the Hebrew possessions.

The next point mentioned is the Monuments of Helena, which, we are elsewhere told, were three pyramids, situated at a distance of 3 stadia (606¾ yards) from the city. Notwithstanding repeated monuments of the Queen of Adiabene, it is not now possible to fix their position with any degree of certainty, some archæologists assigning them to the Tombs of the Kings, others to the Tombs of the Martyrs, about three-quarters of a mile to the W. of the former. A point half-way between these two monuments would seem to answer better to the incidental notices of the monuments. Opposite the Monuments of Helena was the Gate of the Women in the third wall, which is mentioned more than once, and must have been between the Nablus road and the Psephine Tower.

The Royal Caves are the next point mentioned on the third wall. They are, doubtless, identical with the remarkable and extensive excavations still called the Tombs of the Kings, most probably the same which are elsewhere called the Monument of Herod, and, from the character of their decorations, may very well be ascribed to the Herodian period.

The Fuller's monument is the last-mentioned point on the new wall, and as an angular tower occupied this site, the monument must have been at the N.E. angle of the New City; probably one of the many rock graves cut in the perpendicular face of the Valley of Jehoshaphat. From this N.E. angle the third wall followed the brow of the Valley of Jehoshaphat until it reached the wall of the Outer Temple at its N.E. angle.

The Temple Mount.—The Temple Mount, called in Scripture the Mountain of the Lord's House, and Moriah, is situated at the S.E. of the city, and is easily identified with the site of the Dome of the Mosque in modern Jerusalem. It was originally a third hill of the Old City, over against Acra, but separated from it by a broad ravine, which, however, was filled up by the Asmonæan princes, so that these two hills became one, and are generally so reckoned by Josephus.

1. *The Outer Court.*—The Temple, in the widest signification of the word, consisted of two courts, one within the other, though the inner one is sometimes subdivided, and distributed into four other courts. The area of the Outer Court was in great part artificial, for the natural level space on the summit of the mount, being found too confined for the Temple, with its surrounding chambers, courts, and cloisters, was gradually increased by mechanical expedients. This extension was commenced by Solomon, who raised from the depth of the eastern valley a wall of enormous stones, bound together with lead, within which he raised a bank of earth,

to a level with the native rock. On this was erected a cloister, which, with its successors, always retained the name of 'Solomon's Porch'. This process of enlarging the court by artificial embankments was continued by successive kings; but particularly by Herod the Great, who, when he reconstructed the Temple proper, enlarged the Outer Court to double its former size, and adorned it with stately cloisters.

2. *The Inner Court.*—The Inner Temple was separated from the Outer by a stone wall 3 cubits (nearly 5 feet) in height, on which stood pillars at equal distances, with inscriptions, in Greek and Latin, prohibiting aliens from access. To this court there was an ascent of fourteen steps, then a level space of 10 cubits, and then a farther ascent of five steps to the gates, of which there were four on the N. and S. sides, and two on the E., but none on the W., where stood the Sanctuary.

The place of the Altar is determined with precision by the existence in the Sacred Rock of the Moslems, under their venerated dome, of the cesspool and drain of the Jewish altar, which furnishes a key to the restoration of the whole Temple.

The Altar was 32 cubits square (48 feet) at its base, but gradually contracted, so that its hearth was only 234 cubits square (36 feet). It was 15 cubits high, and had an ascent by an inclined plane on the S. side, 32 cubits long and 16 wide.

Between the Altar and the porch of the Temple was a space of 22 cubits (33 feet), rising in a gentle ascent by steps to the vestibule, the door of which was 40 cubits high and 20 wide. The total length of the Holy House itself was only 100 cubits (150 feet), and this was subdivided into three parts: the Pronaos 11, the Sanctuary 40, the Holy of Holies 20, allowing 29 cubits for the partition walls and a small chamber behind (i.e. W. of) the Most Holy place. The total width of the building was 70 cubits (105 feet); of which the Sanctuary only occupied 20, the remainder being taken up by side chambers, in three stories assigned to various uses. The Pronaos was, however, 30 cubits wider, 15 on the N. and 15 on the S., giving it a total length of 100 cubits, which, with a width of only 11 cubits (16½ feet), must have presented the proportions of a Narthex in a Byzantine church. Its interior height was 90 cubits (135 feet), and, while the chambers on the sides of the Temple rose only to the height of 60 cubits, there was an additional story of 40 cubits above the Sanctuary, also occupied by chambers, rising into a clerestory of the same elevation as the vestibule.

The front of the Temple was plated with gold, and reflected back the beams of the rising sun with dazzling effect; and, where it was not encrusted with gold, it was exceedingly white. Some of the stones of which it was constructed were 45 cubits long, 5 deep, and 6 wide (67½ by 7½ by 9 feet).

E. of the Altar was the Court of the Priests, 135 cubits long and 11 wide, (202½ by 16½ feet); and, E. of that again, was the Court of Israel, of the same dimensions. E. of this was the Court of the Women, 135 cubits square, considerably below the level of the former, to which there was an ascent of 15 semicircular steps to the magnificent gates of Corinthian brass, 50 cubits in height, with doors of 40 cubits, so ponderous that they could with difficulty be shut by twenty men. The spontaneous opening of these gates was one of the portents of the approaching destruction of the Temple, mentioned by Josephus and repeated by Tacitus.

We must now notice the Acropolis, which occupied the N.W. angle of the Temple enclosure, and which was, says the historian, the fortress of the Temple, as the Temple was of the city. Its original name was Baris, until Herod the Great, having greatly enlarged and beautified it, changed its name to Antonia, in honour of his friend Mark Antony. It combined the strength of a castle with the magnificence of a palace, and was like a city in extent—comprehending within its walls not only spacious apartments, but courts and camping ground for soldiers. It was situated on an elevated rock, faced with slabs of smooth stone, upon which was raised a breastwork of 3 cubits high, within which was the building, rising to a height of 40 cubits (60 feet). It had turrets at its four corners, three of them 50 cubits high, but that at the S.E. angle was 70 cubits, and commanded a view of the whole Temple. The fortress was protected toward Bezetha by an artificial fosse.

It is certain, from several passages, that the Fortress Antonia did not cover the whole of the northern front of the Temple area; and, as the second wall, that encircled the Lower City, ended at the fortress, it is clear that this wall could not have coincided with the modern wall at the N.E. quarter of the modern city. It is demonstrable, from several allusions and historical notices, that there must have been a considerable space between the second and third wall on the northern front of the Temple area.

MARATHON

The plain of Marathon in the N.E. of Attica contained four places, named Marathon, Probalinthos, Tricorythos, and Œnoë, which originally formed the Tetrapolis, one of the twelve districts into which Attica was divided before the time of Theseus. Few places have obtained such celebrity as Marathon, on account of the victory which the Athenians here gained over the Persians in 490 B.C.

The plain is open to a bay of the sea on the E. and is shut in on the opposite side by the heights of Brilessos (subsequently called Pentelikos) and Diacria, which send forth spurs extending to the sea and bounding the plain to the N. and S. The principal shelter of the bay is afforded by a long rocky promontory to the N., anciently called Kynosura and now Stómi. The plain is about 6 miles in length and 3 in width in its broadest part. It is somewhat in the form of a half-moon, the inner curve of which is bounded by the bay and the outer by the range of mountains already described. At its N. and S. extremities the plain is bounded by two marshes, of which the northern offers several parts which are at all seasons impassable. There are four roads leading out of the plain. 1. The first runs along the coast by the S.W. extremity of the plain. Here the plain of Marathon reduces to a narrow maritime strip, 3 miles in length, where the mountains fall so gradually towards the sea as to present no very defensible impediment to the communication between the districts of Marathóna and Mesogæa. The road afterwards passes through the valley between Pentelikos and Hymettos through the ancient demos of Pallene. This is the most level road to Athens and the only one practicable for carriages. It was the one by which Peisistratus marched to Athens after landing at Marathon. 2. The second road runs through the pass of Vraná, so called from a small village of this name, situated in the southern of the two valleys, which branch off from the interior of the plain. This road leads through Kephissia into the northern part of the plain of Athens. 3. The third road follows the vale of Marathóna, the northern of the two valleys already named, in which lies the village of the same name, the largest in the district. The two valleys are separated from one another by a hill called Kotróni, very rugged, but of no great height. This third road leads to Aphidna, from which the plain of Athens may also be reached. 4. The fourth road leaves the plain on the N.E. by a narrow pass between the northern marsh and a round naked rocky height now called Mt. Koráki or Stavrokoráki. It leads to Rhamnus; and at the entrance of the pass stands the village of Lower Súli.

Three places in the Marathonian district retain vestiges of ancient demes. 1. Vraná, which Leake supposes to be the site of the demos of Marathon. It lies upon a height fortified by the ravine of a torrent, which descends into the plain after flowing between Mts. Argalíki and Aforismó, which are parts of Mt. Pentelikos. A little below Vraná are four tumuli of earth, one larger than the others; and in a pass at the back of the hill of Kotróni, which leads from the vale of Vraná into that of Marathóna, there are some remains of an ancient gate. Three-quarters of a mile to the S.E. of the tumuli of Vraná, there is a rising ground, upon which are traces of a Hellenic wall, apparently the peribolus of a temple. This was probably the temple of Heracles, in whose sacred enclosure the Athenians were encamped before the battle (Herod.

VI 108). 2. There are several fragments of antiquity situated at the head of the valley of Marathóna at a spot called Inói, which is no doubt the site of the ancient Œnoë, one of the four demes of the district. 3. There are also evident remains of an ancient demos situated upon an insulated height in the plain of Súli, near the entrance of the pass leading out of the Marathonian plain to Súli. These ruins are probably those of Tricorythos, the situation of which agrees with the order of the maritime demes in Strabo, where Tricorythos immediately precedes Rhamnus.

The site of Probalinthos is uncertain, but it should probably be placed at the S.W. extremity of the Marathonian plain. This might be inferred from Strabo's enumeration, who mentions first Probalinthos, then Marathon, and lastly Tricorythos. Between the southern marsh and Mt. Argalíki there are foundations of buildings at a place called Valarí, which is, perhaps, a corruption of Probalinthos.

The principal monument in the Marathonian plain was the tumulus erected to the 192 Athenians who were slain in the battle, and whose names were inscribed upon ten pillars, one for each tribe, placed upon the tomb. There was also a second tumulus for the Platæans and slaves, and a separate monument to Miltiades. All these monuments were seen by Pausanias 600 years after the battle. The tumulus of the Athenians still exists. It stands in the centre of the plain, about half a mile from the sea-shore.

The exact ground occupied by the Greek and Persian armies at the battle of Marathon can only be a matter of conjecture. It is probable that the Athenian camp was in the valley of Vraná near its opening into the plain, and that on the day of battle the Athenian line extended from a little in front of the Heracleion at the foot of Mt. Argalíki, to the bend of the river of Marathóna, below the village of Seféri; also that the Persians, who were 8 stadia (nearly a mile) in front of them, had their right resting on Mt. Koráki, and their left extending to the southern marsh, which prevented them from having a front much greater than that of the Athenians. When the Persians defeated the Athenian centre, they pursued the latter up one or both of the two valleys on either side of Mt. Kotróni since Herodotus says that the pursuit continued quite into the interior. Nearly at the same time the Persian left and right were defeated; but instead of pursuing them, the Athenians returned towards the field to the aid of their own centre. The Persian right fled towards the narrow pass leading into the plain of Tricorythos; and here numbers were forced into the marsh, as Pausanias relates.

MYCENÆ (sometimes MYCENE)

One of the most ancient towns in Greece, and celebrated as the residence of Agamemnon. It is situated at the N.E. extremity of the plain of Argos upon a rugged height, which is shut in by two commanding summits of the range of mountains which borders this side of the Argeian plain. From its retired position it is described by Homer as situated in a recess of the Argeian land. The position was one of great importance. In the first place it commanded the upper part of the great Argeian plain, which spread out under its walls towards the W. and S.; and secondly the most important roads from the Corinthian gulf, the roads from Phlius, Nemea, Cleonæ, and Corinth, unite in the mountains above Mycenæ, and pass under the height upon which the city stands. It was said to have been built by Perseus, the son of Danaë and the grandson of Acrisios, and its massive walls were believed to have been the work of the Cyclopes. The Danaan dynasty of Perseus disappeared when the Achæans, under the leadership of Pelops, settled in the Peloponnesus. Mycenæ became the favourite residence of the Pelopidæ, and under Agamemnon was regarded as the first city in Greece. Excavations show the strong influence of Crete upon Mycenæ in the seventeenth century B.C., and from the sixteenth to the fourteenth centuries the Cretan civilization was predominant in the Peloponnesus and in N. Greece. The Achæans eventually overcame this supremacy, and in the fourteenth century a powerful king on the throne of Mycenæ erected a palace with greater splendour than formerly. The Mycenæan civilization spread over the whole of Greece, into Asia Minor in the E. and Sicily in the W. Mycenæ was at the height of its power in the time of the Trojan War (? 1180 B.C.). Its greatness, however, belongs only to the heroic age, and it ceased to be a place of importance after the return of the Heracleidæ, and the settlement of the Dorians in Argos, which then became the first city in the plain. Mycenæ, however, maintained its independence and sent some of its citizens to the assistance of the Greeks against Xerxes, although the Argives kept aloof from the common cause. Eighty Mycenæans were present at Thermopylæ (Herod. VII 202). In 468 B.C. the Dorians of Argos, resolving to bring the whole district under their sway, laid siege to Mycenæ; but the massive walls resisted their attacks, and they were obliged to have recourse to a blockade. Famine compelled the inhabitants to abandon the city, more than half taking refuge in Macedonia. From this time Mycenæ remained desolate, although an inscription of the time of the tyrant Nabis, third century B.C., shows that it was then inhabited.

Mycenæ consisted of an Acropolis and a lower town, each defended by a wall. The Acropolis was situated on the summit of a steep hill, projecting from a higher mountain behind it. The lower town lay on the south-western slope of the hill, on either side of which runs a torrent from E. to W. The Acropolis is in the form of an irregular triangle, of which the base fronts the S.W., and the apex the E. On the southern side the cliffs are almost precipitous, overhanging a deep gorge; but on the northern side the descent is less steep and rugged. The summit of the hill is rather more than 1,000 feet in length, and around the edge the ruined walls of the Acropolis still exist in their entire circuit, with the exception of a small open space above the cliff on the southern side, which perhaps was never defended by a wall. The walls are more perfect than those of any other fortress in Greece; in some places they are 15 or 20 feet high. They are built of the dark-coloured limestone of the surrounding mountains. Some parts of the walls are built, like those of Tiryns, of huge blocks of stone of irregular shape, no attempt being made to fit them into one another, and the gaps being filled up with smaller stones. But the greater part of the walls consists of polygonal stones, skilfully hewn and fitted to one another, and their faces cut so as to give the masonry a smooth appearance. In other parts, especially in the approach to the Gate of Lions, the walls are constructed of blocks of nearly quadrangular shape.

The chief gate of the Acropolis is at the N.W.

angle of the wall. It stands at right angles to the adjoining wall of the fortress, and is approached by a passage 50 feet long and 30 wide, formed by that wall and by another wall exterior to it. The opening of the gateway widens from the top downwards; but at least two-thirds of its height is now buried in ruins. The width at the top of the door is 9½ feet. This door was formed of two massive uprights, covered with a third block, 15 feet long, 4 feet wide, and 6 feet 7 inches high in the middle, but diminishing at the two ends. Above this block is a triangular gap in the masonry of the wall, formed by an oblique approximation of the side courses of stone, continued from each extremity of the lintel to an apex above its centre. The vacant space is occupied by a block of stone, 10 feet high, 12 broad, and 2 thick, upon the face of which are sculptured two lions in low relief, standing on their hind legs, upon either side of a covered pillar, upon which they rest their forefeet. The column becomes broader towards the top, and is surmounted with a capital, formed of a row of four circles, enclosed between two parallel fillets. The heads of the animals are gone, together with the apex of the cone that surmounted the column.

In a walled area in the W. of the Acropolis is a circular space, the entrance of which faces the Gate of Lions. It was in this circular space that Schliemann in 1886 made his celebrated discovery of the Mycenæan tombs. Six rectangular tombs, containing 19 skeletons, had been cut into the rock to a depth of 25 feet, an altar was erected on the surface and 10 sculptured stelæ marked the places of the tombs. It was here that tradition placed the tombs of Atreus, of his charioteer Eurymedon, of Electra, Cassandra, and others, while Ægisthus and Clytæmnestra were buried outside the walls.

E. of the royal burial-place are traces of the royal road conducting to the palace of the Mycenæan age, on the summit of the Acropolis (910 feet). On the foundations of the Mycenæan palace are the remains of a Doric temple of the seventh century. In the N.E. corner of the Acropolis is a subterranean stairway which follows a natural fissure in the rock, and, at a depth of 40 feet, ends in a deep well, fed from an outside source. This is the fountain Perseia, mentioned by Pausanias (II 15). In this corner of the Acropolis is a second gate. It is constructed of three stones and is 5 feet 4 inches wide at the top.

Near the Gate of Lions the wall of the lower city may be traced, extending from N. to S. In the lower town are four subterraneous buildings, which are evidently the same as those described by Pausanias, in which the Atreidæ deposited their treasures. Of these the largest, called the 'Treasury of Atreus', is in nearly a perfect state of preservation. It is approached by a passage now in ruins, and contains two chambers. The passage leads into a large chamber of a conical form, about 50 feet in width and 40 in height; and in this chamber there is a doorway leading into a small interior apartment. The remains of the second subterraneous building are near the Gate of Lions; and those of the two others are lower down the hill towards the W.

OLYMPIA

The Temple and Sacred Grove of Olympian Zeus, situated at a small distance W. of Pisæ in Peloponnesus. It originally belonged to Pisæ, and the plain in which it stood was called in more ancient times the plain of Pisæ; but after the destruction of this city by the Eleians in 572 B.C., the name of Olympia was extended to the whole district. Besides the Temple of Olympian Zeus, there were several other sacred edifices and public buildings in the Sacred Grove and its immediate neighbourhood; but there was no distinct town of Olympia.

The plain of Olympia is open towards the sea on the W., but is surrounded on every other side by hills of no great height, yet in many places abrupt and precipitous. Nearly isolated on the N. of the level plain there rises the bold, cone-like mountain, 410 feet in height, called Mt. Kronion, or the Hill of Kronos, frequently noticed by Pindar and other writers. The hills which bound the plain on the S. are higher than the Kronian ridge, and, with the exception of one bare summit, are distant about half a mile from the river Alpheus. This isolated peak was the Typæan Rock, from which married women who frequented the Olympic games, or who crossed the river on forbidden days, were condemned to be hurled headlong. Another range of hills closes the vale of Olympia to the E., at the foot of which runs the rivulet of Miráka. On the W. the vale was bounded by the Kladeos which flowed from N. to S. along the side of the Sacred Grove and fell into the Alpheus. This river rises at Lala in Mt. Pholoë. The Alpheus, which flows along the southern edge of the plain, constantly changes its course, and all the remains of buildings and monuments which stood in the southern part of the Sacred Grove have been either buried beneath the new alluvial plain or swept away by the river.

Olympia lay partly within and partly outside of the Sacred Grove. This Sacred Grove bore from the most ancient times the name of Altis. It was adorned with trees, and in its centre there was a grove of planes. On the W. it ran along the Kladeos; on the S. its direction may be traced by a terrace raised above the Alpheus; on the E. it was bounded by the Stadium. There were several gates in the wall, but the principal one, through which all the processions passed, was situated in the middle of the western side, and was called the Pompic Entrance. From this gate, a road, called the Pompic Way, ran across the Altis, and entered the Stadium by a gateway on the eastern side.

1. *The Olympieion*, or Temple of Olympian Zeus. An oracle of the Olympian god existed on this spot from the most ancient times, and here a temple was doubtless built even before the Olympic games became a Pan-Hellenic festival. The Eleians, following their conquest of Pisæ in 572 B.C., devoted the spoils of the conquered cities to the erection of a new temple of the Olympian god. The architect was Libon of Elis. The temple was not, however, finished till nearly a century afterwards, at the period when the Attic school of art was supreme in Greece, and the Parthenon on the Athenian Acropolis had surpassed all previous works of art. Shortly after the dedication of the Parthenon, the Eleians invited Pheidias and his school of artists to remove to Elis, and adorn the Olympian temple in a manner worthy of the king of the gods. Pheidias probably remained at Olympia for four or five years from about 437 B.C. to 434 or 433. The colossal statue of Zeus in the cella and the figures in the pediments of the temple

were executed by Pheidias and his associates. The pictorial embellishments were the work of his relative Panænos. The temple stood in the south-western portion of the Altis, to the right hand of the Pompic Entrance. It was a Doric hexastyle temple, with 6 columns at each end and 13 at the side. The height of the columns was 35 feet. Nothing remains of the statue and throne of Zeus. The pedestal was 3 feet high and 22 feet broad. The throne was of gold. The cella of the temple, in which the statue was placed, was amphiprostyle, and was twice as long as it was broad, the length being 93 feet 9 inches.

2. *The Pelopion*, or Sanctuary of Pelops. This, one of the most ancient monuments of the Altis, was dedicated by the Achæans of Pisæ in honour of their hero. Its position is defined by Pausanias, who says that it stood to the right of the entrance into the temple of Zeus and to the north of that building. It was an enclosure, containing trees and statues, having an opening to the W. A Doric propylæa in stone, dating probably from the fifth century, replaced the ancient wooden entrance.

3. *The Heræon*. This long low Doric building was originally dedicated to Zeus and Hera, but after the erection of the Olympieion it became the temple solely of Hera. It was probably the earliest large temple in Greece, built originally of wood and stone. It is situated to the N. of the Pelopion. The two most remarkable monuments in the Heræon were the table, on which were placed the garlands prepared for the victors in the Olympic contests, and the celebrated chest of Kypselos, a work of the sixth century, covered with figures in relief.

4. *The Great Altar of Zeus* is described by Pausanias as equidistant from the Pelopion and the Heræon, and as being in front of them both. The

total height of the altar was 22 feet. It had two platforms, of which the upper was made of the cinders of the thighs sacrificed on this and other altars.

5. *The Metroon*, or temple of the Mother of the Gods. This is a small, badly preserved temple, although Pausanias describes it as a large Doric temple. Its roof was of terra cotta, and its erection was later than that of the Olympieion.

6. *The Prytaneion*, a building of the fifth century B.C., many times renovated. It was the centre of the political and priestly government of Olympia. The S. extremity of the building contained the shrine of Hestia, where the sacrificial fires were maintained day and night, and were transported from there to the Altar of Zeus. The northern half of the building contained the Hestiatorion, a large rectangular banqueting hall where the Olympian victors were feasted.

7. *The Philippeion*, a circular Ionic building, erected by Philip after the battle of Chæroneia, to the S.W. of the Heræon. The steps and roof were of Parian marble, and the building contained statues by Leochares, representing Philip, his father, Amyntas, his mother, Eurydice, his wife, Olympias, and his son, Alexander.

8. *The Hippodameion*, named from Hippodameia, who was buried here, was near the Pompic Way.

9. *The Temples of the Olympian Eileithyia* (Lucina) and of the *Olympian Aphrodite* stood on the outskirts of Mt. Kronion (Paus. VI 20).

10. *The Treasuries*, small temples, situated within the N. wall of the Altis. They were built by the peoples of various Greek cities, especially of Sicily and Greater Greece, for the purpose of housing their offerings to the Olympian Zeus. They did not contain an altar to the god. Pausanias

enumerates eleven treasuries. Fourteen such buildings have been excavated, but of these one contains an altar of Heracles, another an altar of Gæa, and two more were probably not treasuries.

11. *Zanes*, statues of Zeus, erected from the produce of the fines levied upon athletes who had violated the regulations of the games. They stood upon a stone platform at the foot of Mt. Kronion to the E. of the Metroon.

12. *The Stadium*, on the slopes of Mt. Kronion, to the E. of the Altis. It is described by Pausanias as a mound of earth, upon which there was a seat for the Hellanodicæ, and over against it an altar of marble, on which sat the priestess of Demeter Chamyne, the only woman to witness the games. There were two entrances into the Stadium, the Pompic and the Secret. The latter, through which the Hellanodicæ and the agonistæ entered, was near the Zanes; the former probably entered the area in front of the rectilinear extremity of the Stadium.

The course measured 696 feet 10 inches by 105 feet 10 inches. The distance between the starting and finishing posts at either end of the course was 1 stade (606¾ feet).

13. *The Hippodrome.*—S. of the Stadium and parallel to it was the Hippodrome.

One side of the Hippodrome was longer than the other, and was formed by a mound of earth. There was a passage through this side leading out of the Hippodrome; and near the passage was a kind of circular altar, called Taraxippos, or the terrifier of horses, because the horses were frequently seized with terror in passing it, so that chariots were broken. Beyond the Taraxippos were the terminal pillars, round which the chariots turned. On one of them stood a brazen statue of Hippodameia about to bind the tænia on Pelops after his victory. The other side of the Hippodrome was a natural height of no great elevation. On its extremity stood the temple of Demeter Chamyne. The course of the Hippodrome appears to have been 2 diauli, or 4 stadia (809 yards). No trace of the Hippodrome remains to-day, but from a manuscript, found at Constantinople, the dimensions were 3 stadia and 1 plethron (640½ yards) in length and 1 stadion and 4 plethra (303¾ yards) in breadth.

14. *The Portico of the Echoes* or *Pœcile.*—This long colonnade, lying in the E. of the Altis, consisted of a stylobate supporting 44 Doric columns and of an interior promenade divided by a row of 21 Ionic columns. The building was erected in the fourth century at the same time as the Philippeion. It measured half a stade (303 feet 4½ inches) in length and was 32 feet in depth. Previous to the fourth century an ancient portico stood in the rear of the present building. It was demolished when the embankment of the Stadium was enlarged.

15. *The Theatre.*—The empty space between the Pœcile and the Altar of Zeus may have been the site of the theatre, mentioned by Xenophon. This later disappeared, probably when musical contests were discontinued. Pausanias does not mention a theatre.

The undermentioned buildings were situated outside the Altis:

1. *The Bouleuterion,* or Council Chamber.—This building consisted of an Ionic portico (second century) on the E. façade, and of a square central chamber, flanked on the N. and S. by two long wings. The entrance was at the N. end of the portico upon the Pompic Way. The N. and S. wings (sixth and fifth centuries respectively) were of the same plan,

having an interior division of 7 Doric columns, supporting the roof. The central chamber was unroofed and contained the statue of Zeus Horkios ('Zeus invoked in oaths'). It was here that competitors took their oath, before the games, in the presence of the Hellanodicæ.

2. *The Leonidæon.*—The N.E. corner of this huge quadrilateral building abutted upon the W. end of the Pompic Way, where there was a Roman arch. The original building was erected by Leonidas of Naxos in the fourth century, and was twice enlarged in Roman times. It was the largest building in Olympia, measuring 266½ feet by 241½ feet. It was probably used for the reception of honoured guests to the Olympic Games and in later times became the residence of the Roman governors.

3. *The Studio of Pheidias,* situated to the N. of the Leonidæon. It was here that Pheidias worked upon the statue of Zeus for the Olympieion. The dimensions of the studio corresponded to the cella of the temple.

4. *The Theokoleon.*—Originally a fourth century building, 63 feet square, situated to the N. of the Studio of Pheidias and used as a residence for the priestly officers.

5. *The Gymnasium.*—In the N.W. corner of Olympia, on the banks of the Kladeos, was the Gymnasium, bordered on the S. and the E. by two xysti with a propylæa in the S.E. corner. Attached to the Gymnasium and between the S. xystus and the Theokoleon was the Palæstra. This was a square building (216 feet 8 inches) of the third century B.C., and contained rooms for the competitors and baths, also rooms for wrestling and indoor training.

Besides the buildings which have been mentioned, there was a large number of statues in every part of the Sacred Grove, many of which were made by the greatest masters of Greek art, and of which Pausanias has given a description.

POMPEII

An ancient city of Campania, situated on the coast of the beautiful gulf called the Crater or Bay of Naples, at the mouth of the river Sarnus, and immediately at the foot of Mt. Vesuvius. It was intermediate between Herculaneum and Stabiæ.

The founders of Pompeii were the Oscans, and the city is believed to have been in existence by the sixth century B.C. To this date is ascribed the Doric temple in the Forum Triangulare. The Campanian Oscans, whose language was allied to Latin, were succeeded in Pompeii according to Strabo (V 4, 8), by the Tyrrhenians (Etruscans) and Pelasgians. In 420 B.C. the kindred race of the Oscans, the Samnites, took Pompeii and became the dominating race in S. Italy, although the influence of Greek culture is seen in the remains of the city. As a result of the Samnite Wars (343–290 B.C.). Pompeii and other Campanian cities lost their independence to Rome, although Campania was not completely romanized until the time of the Social War (90–88 B.C.). In 89 B.C. Pompeii was besieged by Sulla, but without success. In 83 B.C. Sulla, returning victorious from Asia, settled his army in winter quarters in Campania. Later, in 80 B.C., Pompeii became a colony for Roman veterans, Publius Sulla, a nephew of the Dictator, being governor. From this period until its destruction in A.D. 79, Pompeii was a summer pleasure resort of the Roman aristocracy. The city was also prosperous industrially. Vesuvius was believed to be extinct until Pompeii, with Herculaneum and Nuceria, suffered severely in a violent earthquake on 5th February, A.D. 63. Pompeii was for some time deserted, but was largely rebuilt before the final catastrophe on 24th August, A.D. 79. The course of the eruption of Vesuvius can be gauged only from the two contemporary letters of the Younger Pliny to Tacitus, from the account by Dion Cassius, written 150 years later, and from excavations. Pompeii and Herculaneum were buried beneath a rain of pumice stone to the depth of ten feet and of volcanic dust, in descending mixed to a mud by rain, to a depth of six or seven feet. The sky was completely blackened, and with the dust came earthquake shocks. Fires were local, but the charred condition of all the woodwork, since excavated, was probably due to the gradual effect of moisture, as happens with coal. The plan to rebuild the city came to nothing. Judging by the records kept since the first systematic excavations of 1763, about 2,000 of the inhabitants perished. The total population is believed to have been about 20,000 at the time of the earthquake.

The area occupied by the ancient city was an irregular oval, about 2 miles in circumference. It was surrounded by a wall, which is still preserved round the whole of the city, except on the side towards the sea. There were eight gates, the most considerable of which was that which formed the entrance to the city by the high road from Herculaneum. The order of the gates, placed at intervals in the wall on the landward side, was as follows: the Herculaneum Gate in the N.W. corner, then the Gates of Vesuvius, of Capua, of Nola, of the Sarnus, of Nuceria, of Stabiæ, and on the seaward side, the

Porta Marina. All these names are modern, but are convenient in assisting us to describe the city. The walls were strengthened with an *agger* or rampart, faced with masonry, and having a parapet or outer wall on its external front: they were further fortified at intervals with square towers, which in some parts occur regularly at about 100 yards from each other, in other parts are added more sparingly.

The general plan of the city is very regular, and most of the streets are straight; but the principal street, which runs from the Gate of Herculaneum to the Forum, is an exception, being irregular and crooked as well as narrow. Though it must have been one of the chief thoroughfares of the city, and the line followed by the high road from Capua, Neapolis, and Rome itself, it does not exceed 12 or 14 feet in width, including the raised footpaths on each side, so that the carriage-way could only have admitted the passage of one vehicle at a time. Some of the other streets are broader; but few of them exceed 20 feet in width, and the widest yet found is only about 30. They are uniformly paved with large polygonal blocks of hard lava or basalt. The principal street was crossed, a little before it reached the Forum, by a long straight line of street which, passing by the Temple of Fortune, led direct to the Gate of Nola. In the angle formed by the two stood the public baths or Thermæ, and between these and the Temple of Fortune a short broad street led direct to the Forum, to which it seems to have formed the principal entrance. From the Forum two other parallel streets struck off in an easterly direction, which have been followed till they cross another main line of street that leads from the Gate of Vesuvius directly across the city to the gate adjoining the theatres. This last line crosses the street already noticed, leading from the Gate of Nola westward, and the two divide the whole city into four quarters, though of irregular size.

The Forum was situated in the S.W. quarter of the city, and was distant about 400 yards from the Gate of Herculaneum. It was surrounded by the principal public buildings, and was the centre of the life and movement of the city. The extent of it was not, however, great; the actual open space (exclusive of the porticoes which surrounded it) did not exceed 160 yards in length by 42 in breadth, and a part of this space was occupied by the Temple of Jupiter. It was surrounded on three sides by a Grecian-Doric portico, which appears to have been surmounted by a gallery or upper story, though no part of this is now preserved. This portico had replaced an older arcade on the eastern side of the Forum, a portion of which still remains, so that this alteration was not yet completed when the catastrophe took place. At the N. end of the Forum, and projecting out into the open area, are the remains of the Temple of Jupiter. The temple stands on a podium 10 feet high and, with the steps, 125 feet long. It had a portico of six Corinthian columns in front, and three on each side of the vestibule. The head of a colossal statue of the Capitoline Jupiter was found in the cella, where the pedestal of the statue still rests. Juno and Minerva were also worshipped here, and the temple probably dates from the pre-Roman period. It was left in ruins by the earthquake of A.D. 63. At the N.E. angle of the Forum, adjoining the temple, stands a triumphal arch, once faced with marble, though now only the brickwork remains. It was the chief entrance to the Forum and was dedicated to Nero Cæsar, the son of Germanicus. On the E. side of the Forum were four public buildings. The first (towards the N.) was once thought to be a Pantheon, but it is now established that the building was a macellum or provision market. It consisted of a court in the shape of a rectangle, surrounded by deep colonnades on the four sides. At one time a street opened into the Forum, S. of the Macellum, but later in the time of Augustus, it was closed, and the space occupied by a building, measuring 60 by 70 feet. The walls and floors were once covered with marble, and an altar was placed in the middle of the main room. The building was probably the Sanctuary of the City Lares. S. of this building is situated a temple built after the earthquake of 63. Once thought to be the Temple of Mercury, it was really erected in honour of an emperor, probably Vespasian. Between this and the street known as the Street of the Silversmiths, which issued from the Forum near its S.E. angle, was a large building which, as we learn from an inscription still existing, was erected by a city priestess named Eumachia. It consists of a large and spacious area (about 130 feet by 65) surrounded by a colonnade, and having a raised platform at the end with a semicircular recess. It is possible that the building was a cloth market. The last building on the E. side of the Forum, being probably unroofed, was originally more of an open extension of the Forum. It was once separated from the Forum and the street of the Silversmiths by a row of pillars, but in the rebuilding after the earthquake of 63, much of this space opening on to the Forum and the street was walled up. It is possible that the building was originally a comitium or voting place.

The S. end of the Forum was occupied by three buildings of very similar character, standing side by side, each consisting of a single hall with an apse or semicircular recess at the farther extremity.

The most probable opinion is that these were the courts of justice, in which the tribunals held their sittings. The western side of the Forum was principally occupied by a Basilica, and a large temple called the Temple of Apollo. The former is the largest building in Pompeii; it is of an oblong form, 220 feet in length by 80 in breadth, and abutted endwise on the Forum, from which it was entered by a vestibule with five doorways. The roof was supported by a peristyle of 28 Ionic columns of large size, but built of brick, coated with stucco. There is a raised tribunal at the farther end, but no apse, which is usually found in buildings of this class. Numerous inscriptions are found scratched on the walls, one of which gives the date of the consulship of M. Lepidus and Q. Catulus (78 B.C.), and thus proves the temple to have been erected before that time. Between this edifice and the Temple of Apollo is the Via Marina, a wide street extending from the Forum in a westerly direction, and communicating with the port. It is now established that the temple on the N. side of this street was dedicated to the worship of Apollo, not of Venus as was once believed. The temple was probably erected in very early times, and may have once been surrounded by an open colonnade. It was an extensive building consisting of a peripteral temple with a small cella, elevated on a podium or basement, surrounded by a much more extensive portico, and the whole again enclosed by a wall, forming the peribolus or sacred enclosure. All parts of the building are profusely decorated with painting. The temple itself is Corinthian, but the columns of the portico seem to have been originally Doric, though afterwards clumsily transformed into Corinthian, or rather an awkward imitation of Corinthian. The buildings at the N.W. corner of the Forum seem to have served as the public granaries and prisons.

The open area of the Forum was paved with broad marble slabs, thus showing that it was never designed for the traffic of any kind of vehicles. It was adorned with numerous statues, the pedestals of which still remain: they are all of white marble, but the statues themselves have uniformly disappeared.

Besides the temples which surrounded the Forum, the remains of four others have been discovered; three of which are situated in the immediate vicinity of the theatres. Of these the most interesting is one which stood a little to the S.W. of the great theatre, near the wall of the city, and which is evidently more ancient than any of the other temples at Pompeii: it is of the Doric order and of pure Greek style, but of very ancient character. Unfortunately only the basement and a few capitals remain.

It was commonly called the Temple of Hercules, but originally Apollo and Artemis were worshipped here. An Oscan inscription also assigns the temple to the worship of Minerva. The temple stood in an open area of considerable extent, and of a triangular form, surrounded on two sides by porticoes: but this area, which is commonly called the Forum Triangulare, has been evidently constructed at a much later period, and with no reference to the temple, which is placed very awkwardly in relation to it. Another temple in the same quarter of the town, immediately adjoining the great theatre, is interesting because we learn with certainty from an inscription that it was consecrated to Isis, and had been rebuilt by N. Popidius Celsinus 'from the foundations' after its overthrow in the great earthquake of A.D. 63. It is built chiefly of brick covered with stucco (only the capitals and shafts of the columns being of a soft stone), and is of small size. Like most of the temples at Pompeii, it consists of a cella, raised on an elevated podium, and surrounded externally by a portico. Adjoining this temple was another, the smallest yet found at Pompeii, and in no way remarkable. It was dedicated to Zeus Milichius, as we learn from an Oscan inscription on the Stabian Gate. This inscription commemorates two architects and refers to the temple as the one to which led the Via Pompeiana. The temple became the home of the Capitoline deities, Jupiter and Juno, after the destruction of the Forum in 63.

The only temple which remains to be noticed is one situated about 60 yards N. of the Forum at the angle formed by the long main street leading to the Gate of Nola with a short broad street which led from it direct to the Forum. This was the Temple of Fortune, as we learn from an inscription.

Pompeii possessed two Theatres and an Amphitheatre. The former were situated close together; the larger one being intended and adapted for theatrical performances properly so called; the smaller one serving as an odeum, or theatre for music. Both are unquestionably of Roman date.

Adjoining the two theatres, and arranged so as to have a direct communication with both, is a large quadrangular court or area (183 feet long by 148 feet wide), surrounded on all sides by a Doric portico. It has been called a provision market, but is more generally regarded as having served as a barrack for the gladiators. On the W. of this, as well as of the great theatre, is the Forum Triangulare already mentioned. The opening of this on the N., where it communicated with the street, was ornamented by a portico or propylæum composed of eight Ionic columns of very elegant style, but consisting of the common volcanic tufa, cased with stucco.

The Amphitheatre is situated at the distance of above 500 yards from the theatres, at the extreme S.E. angle of the city. It offers no very remarkable differences from other edifices of the same kind; its dimensions are 460 feet by 345; and from being excavated out of the soil, it has not the imposing architectural character of other provincial amphitheatres such as those of Verona, Nemausus, or Pola. It had 24 rows of seats and about 20,000 feet of sitting-room, so that it was adapted to receive at least 10,000 spectators.

The Thermæ or Baths were situated in the neighbourhood of the Forum, adjoining the short street which led into it from the Temple of Fortune.

The houses of Pompeii were low, seldom exceeding two stories in height; and even of these the upper story seems to have consisted only of garrets, probably serving for the sleeping-rooms of slaves. It is only on the W. side of the city, where the ground slopes steeply towards the sea, that houses are found which consisted of three stories or more. Externally the houses had little or nothing of an ornamental character; not a single instance has been found of a portico before a private house; and towards the street they presented either dead walls, with here and there a few small and scanty openings as windows, or ranges of shops, for the most part low and mean in character.

The style of decoration of these houses is uniform. The walls are almost invariably ornamented with painting, the atrium and peristyle being decorated with columns; but these are composed only of volcanic tufa, covered with stucco. The floors are generally enriched with mosaics, some of which possess a very high degree of merit as works of art. The most beautiful yet discovered adorned the house known as the House of the Faun, from a bronze statue of a dancing Faun which was also found in it.

Outside the gate leading to Herculaneum stands a house of a different description, being a suburban villa of considerable extent, and evidently the residence of a person of wealth. This villa, being larger, comprises much that is not found in the houses within the town; for instance, a large court (xystus), a complete suite of private baths, etc. Between this villa and the gate of the city are the remains of another villa, said to be on a larger scale and more richly decorated than the one just described; but its ruins, which were excavated in 1764, were filled up again. The approach to the Gate of Herculaneum is bounded on both sides by rows of tombs, extending with only occasional interruptions for above 400 yards. Many of them are remarkable both for size and architectural character.

Besides the Street of Tombs and the two villas already noticed, there have been found the remains of shops and small houses outside the Gate of Herculaneum, and there would appear to have been on this side of the city a considerable suburb.

ROME

Rome, the capital of Italy and at one time of the world, is situated on the left bank of the River Tiber, about 16 miles from the sea; in ancient times on the N.W. confines of Latium.

Historical Development. Rome is said to have been a colony from Alba Longa, and to have been founded by Romulus about 753 B.C. All traditions agree that the original city comprised only the Mons Palatinus or Palatium and some portion of the ground immediately below it. It was surrounded by walls, which followed the line of the Pomœrium, and was built in a square form, whence it was called Roma Quadrata. This city on the Palatine was inhabited only by Latins. On the neighbouring hills there also existed from the earliest times settlements of Sabines and Etruscans. The Sabine town, probably called Quirium, and inhabited by Quirites, was situated on the hills to the N. of the Palatine, that is, the Quirinalis and Capitolinus, or Capitolium, on the latter of which hills was the Sabine Arx or citadel. These Latin and Sabine towns afterwards became united, according to tradition, in the reign of Romulus, and the two peoples formed one collective body, known under the name of 'Populus Romanus (et) Quirites'. The Etruscans were settled on Mons Cælius, and extended over Mons Cispius and Mons Oppius, which are part of the Esquiline. These Etruscans were at an early period incorporated in the Roman state, but were compelled to abandon their seat on the hills, and to take up their abode in the plains between the Cælius and the Esquiline, whence the Vicus Tuscus derived its name. Under the kings the city rapidly grew in population and in size. Ancus Martius added the Mons Aventinus to the city. The same king also built a fortress on the Janiculus, a hill on the other side of the Tiber, as a protection against the Etruscans, and connected it with the city by means of the Pons Sublicius. Rome was still further improved and enlarged by Tarquinius Priscus and Servius Tullius. The former of these kings laid out the Circus Maximus and the Forum, and, according to some traditions, commenced the erection of the Capitoline temple, which was finished by Tarquinius Superbus. The completion of the city, however, was ascribed to Servius Tullius. This king added the Mons Viminalis and Mons Esquilinus, and surrounded the whole city with a line of fortifications, which comprised all the seven hills of Rome (Palatinus, Capitolinus, Quirinalis, Cælius, Aventinus, Viminalis, Esquilinus). Hence Rome was called Urbs Septicollis. These fortifications were about 7 miles in circumference. At the same time Servius extended the pomœrium so as to make the sacred enclosure of the city identical with its walls. In 390 B.C. Rome was entirely destroyed by the Gauls, with the exception of a few houses on the Palatine. On the departure of the barbarians it was rebuilt in great haste and confusion, without any attention to regularity, and with narrow and crooked streets. After the conquest of the Carthaginians and of the monarchs of Macedonia and Syria, the city began to be adorned with many public buildings and handsome private houses; and it was still further embellished by Augustus. So greatly had the appearance of the city improved during his long and prosperous reign that he used to boast that he had found the city of brick, and had left it of marble. Still the main features of the city remained the same; and the narrow streets and mean houses formed a striking and disagreeable contrast to the splendid public buildings and magnificent palaces which had been recently erected. The great fire at Rome in the reign of Nero (A.D. 64) destroyed two-thirds of the city. Nero availed himself of this opportunity to indulge his passion for building; and the city now assumed a more regular and stately appearance. The new streets were made both wide and straight; the height of the houses was restricted; and a certain part of each was required to be built of Gabian or Alban stone, which was proof against fire. Rome had long since extended beyond the walls of Servius Tullius; but down to the third century of the Christian era the walls of this monarch continued to mark the limits of the city properly so called. These walls, however, had long since been rendered useless, and the city was left without any fortifications. Accordingly, the Emperor Aurelian determined to surround Rome with new walls, which embraced the city of Servius Tullius and all the suburbs which had subsequently grown up around it, such as the Mons Janiculus on the right bank of the Tiber, and the Collis Hortulorum, or Mons Pincianus, on the left bank of the river to the N. of the Quirinalis. The walls of Aurelian were commenced by this emperor before he set out on his expedition against Zenobia (A.D. 271), and were terminated by his successor Probus. They were about 11 miles in circumference. They were restored by Honorius, and were also partly rebuilt by Belisarius.

Divisions of the City. Rome was divided by Servius Tullius into 4 Regiones or districts, corresponding to the 4 city tribes. Their names were: 1. *Suburana*, comprehending the space from the

Subura to the Cælius, both inclusive. 2. *Esquilina*, comprehending the Esquiline hill. 3. *Collina*, extending over the Quirinal and Viminal. 4. *Palatina* comprehending the Palatine hill. The Capitoline, as the seat of the gods, and the Aventine, were not included in these Regiones. These Regiones were again subdivided into 27 Sacella Argeorum, which were probably erected where two streets (*compita*) crossed each other. It is probable that each of the 4 Regiones contained 6 of these sacella, and that the remaining 3 belonged to the Capitoline. The division of Servius Tullius into 4 Regiones remained unchanged till the time of Augustus; but this emperor made a fresh division of the city into 14 Regiones, which comprised both the ancient city of Servius Tullius and all the suburbs which had been subsequently added. This division was made by Augustus to facilitate the internal government of the city. The names of the Regiones were: 1. *Porta Capena*, at the S.E. corner of the city by the Porta Capena. 2. *Cælimontium*, N.E. of the preceding, embracing Mons Clæius. 3. *Isis et Serapis*, N.W. of No. 2, in the valley between the Cælius, the Palatine and Esquiline. 4. *Templum Pacis* or *Via Sacra*, N.W. of No. 3, embracing the valley between the Esquiline, Viminal, and Quirinal towards the Palatine. 5. *Esquiline*, the eastern district, including the N. portion of the Esquiline and the Viminal, besides a vast tract of suburbs lying E. of the Servian wall. 6. *Alta Semita*, N. and N.E. of No. 4, comprising the Quirinal. 7. *Via Lata*, N.W. of No. 6, between the Quirinal and the Campus Martius. 8. *Forum Romanum*, S. of No. 7, comprehending the Capitoline and the valley between it and the Palatine. 9. *Circus Flaminius*, N.W. of No. 8, extending as far as the Tiber, and comprehending the whole of the Campus Martius.

10. *Palatium*, S.E. of No. 8, containing the Palatine. 11. *Circus Maximus*, S.W. of No. 10, comprehending the plain between the Palatine, Aventine, and Tiber. 12. *Piscina Publica*, S.E. of No. 11. 13. *Aventinus*, N.W. of No. 12, embracing the Aventine. 14. *Trans Tiberim*, the only region on the right bank of the river, containing the *Insula Tiberina*, the valley between the river and the Janiculus, and a part of this mountain. Each of these Regiones was subdivided into a certain number of *Vici*, analogous to the sacella of Servius Tullius. The houses were divided into 2 different classes, called respectively *domi* and *insulæ*. The former were the dwellings of the Roman nobles, corresponding to the modern palazzi; the latter were the habitations of the middle and lower classes. Each insula contained several apartments or sets of apartments, which were let to different families, and it was frequently surrounded with shops. The insulæ contained several stories; and as the value of ground increased in Rome, they were frequently built of a dangerous height. Hence Augustus restricted the height of all new houses to 70 feet, and Trajan to 60 feet. No houses of any description were allowed to be built close together at Rome, and it was provided by the 12 Tables that a space of at least 5 feet should be left between every house. The number of insulæ, of course, greatly exceeded that of the domi. It is stated that there were 46,603 insulæ at Rome, but only 1,790 domi.

Walls and Gates. I. Wall of Romulus.—The direction of this wall is described by Tacitus. Commencing at the Forum Boarium, the site of which is marked by the arch erected there to Septimius Severus, it ran along the foot of the Palatine, having the valley afterwards occupied by the Circus

Maximus on the right, as far as the altar of Consus, nearly opposite to the extremity of the Circus; thence it turned round the southern angle of the Palatine, followed the foot of the hill nearly in a straight line to the Curiæ Veteres, which stood not far from the site of the Arch of Constantine; thence ascended the steep slope, at the summit of which stands the Arch of Titus, and descended again on the other side to the angle of the Forum, which was then a morass. In this wall there were 3 gates, the number prescribed by the rules of the Etruscan religion. 1. *Porta Mugonia* or *Mugionis*, also called *Porta vetus Palatii*, at the northern slope of the Palatine, at the point where the Via Sacra and the Via Nova met. 2. *Porta Romanula*, at the western angle of the hill near the temple of Victory. 3. The name and position of the third gate is not mentioned, for the *Porta Janualis* appears to be identical with the *Janus* or archway, commonly known as the temple of Janus, which stood on the other side of the Forum, and could have had no connection with the original city of Romulus.

II. Walls of Servius Tullius. It is stated that this king surrounded the whole city with a wall of hewn stone; but there are many reasons for questioning this statement. The 7 hills on which Rome was built were most of them of great natural strength. Instead, therefore, of building a wall around the whole circuit of the city, Servius Tullius appears only to have connected the several hills by walls or trenches drawn across the narrow valleys which separated them. The most formidable part of these fortifications was the Agger or mound, which extended across the broad table-land formed by the junction of the Quirinal, Esquiline, and Viminal, since it was on this side that the city was most open to the attacks of the enemy. The agger was a great rampart or mound of earth, 50 feet wide and above 60 high, faced with flagstones and flanked with towers, and at its foot was a moat 100 feet broad and 30 deep. There are still traces of this work. Starting from the southern extremity of this mound at the Porta Esquilina, the fortifications of Servius ran along the outside edge of the Cælian and Aventine hills to the River Tiber by the Porta Trigemina. From this point to the Porta Flumentana near the S.W. extremity of the Capitoline hill, there appears to have been no wall, the river itself being considered a sufficient defence. At the Porta Flumentana the fortifications again commenced; and ran along the outside edge of the Capitoline and Quirinal hills, till they reached the northern extremity of the agger at the Porta Collina. The number of the gates in the walls of Servius is uncertain, and the position of many of them is doubtful. Pliny, indeed, states that their number was 37; but it is almost certain that this number includes many mere openings made through the walls to connect different parts of the city with the suburbs, since the walls of Servius had long since ceased to be regarded. The following is a list of the gates as far as they can be ascertained: —1. *Porta Collina,* at the N. extremity of the agger, and the most northerly of all the gates, stood at the point of junction of the Via Salaria and Via Nomentana, just above the N. angle of the Vigna dei Certosini. 2. *P. Viminalis,* S. of No. 1, and in the centre of the agger. 3. *P. Esquilina,* S. of No. 2, on the site of the arch of Gallienus, which probably replaced it; the Via Prænestina and Labicana began here. 4. *P. Querquetulana,* S. of No. 3. 5. *P. Cælimontana,* S. of No. 4, on the heights of Mons Cælius, behind the hospital of S. Giovanni in Laterano, at the point of junction of the 2 modern streets which bear the names of S. Stefano Rotondo and the SS. Quattro Coronati. 6. *P. Capena*, one of the most celebrated of all the Roman gates, from which issued the Via Appia. It stood S.W. of No. 5, and at the S.W. foot of the Cælian, on the spot now occupied by the grounds of the Villa Mattei. 7, 8, 9. *P. Lavernalis*, *P. Raudusculana*, and *P. Nævia*, 3 of the most southerly gates of Rome, lying between the Cælian and the Aventine. The walls of Servius probably here took a great bend to the S., enclosing the heights of Sta Balbina and Sta Saba. 10. *P. Minucia*, probably W. of the 3 preceding, and on the S. of the Aventine. 11. *P. Trigemina*, on the N.W. of the Aventine, near the Tiber and the great salt-magazines. 12. *P. Flumentana*, N. of the preceding, near the S.W. slope of the Capitol and close to the Tiber. 13. *P. Carmentalis*, N. of No. 12, and at the foot of the S.W. slope of the Capitoline, near the altar of Carmenta, and leading to the Forum Olitorium and the Theatre of Marcellus. This gate contained 2 passages ,of which the right hand one was called Porta Scelerata from the time that the 300 Fabii passed through it, and was always avoided. 14. *P. Ratumenalis*, N. of No. 13, and at the N.W. slope of the Capitoline, leading from the Forum of Trajan to the Campus Martius. 15. *P. Fontinalis*, N. of No. 4 on the W. slope of the Quirinal, also leading to the Campus Martius. 16. *P. Sanqualis*, N. of No. 15, also on the W. slope of the same hill. 17. *P. Salutaris*, N. of No. 16, on the N.W. slope of the same hill, near the temple of Salus. 18. *P. Triumphalis*. The position of this gate is quite uncertain, except that it led, more or less directly, to the Campus Martius.

III. Walls of Aurelian. These walls are essentially the same as those which surround the modern city of Rome, with the exception of the part beyond the Tiber. The Janiculus and the adjacent suburb was the only portion beyond the Tiber which was included within the fortifications of Aurelian; for the Vatican was not surrounded with walls till the time of Leo IV in the ninth century. On the left bank of the Tiber the walls of Aurelian embraced on the N. the Collis Hortulorum or Pincianus, on the W. the Campus Martius, on the E. the Campus Esquilinus, and on the S. the Mons Testaceus. There were 14 gates in the Aurelian walls, most of which derived their names from the roads issuing from them. These were, on the N. side: 1. *P. Aurelia,* on the Tiber in front of the Pons Ælius. 2. *P. Pinciana,* on the hill of the same name. 3. *P. Salaria,* extant under the same name, but restored in modern times. 4. *P. Nomentana,* leading to the ancient P. Collina. On the E. side: 5. *P. Tiburtina,* leading to the old P. Esquilina, now Porta S. Lorenzo. 6. *P. Prænestina,* now Porta Maggiore. On the S. side: 7. *P. Asinaria,* just S.W. of the modern Porta S. Giovanni. 8. *P. Metronis,* or *Metronii,* or *Metrovia,* which has now disappeared, probably at the entrance to the Caelian, between S. Stefano Rotondo and the Villa Mattei. 9. *P. Latina,* through which passed the Via Latina, a branch of the Via Appia. 10. *P. Appia,* now Porta S. Sebastiano. The roads through this gate and through No. 9, both led to the old Porta Capena. 11. *P. Ostiensis,* leading to Ostia, now Porta S. Paolo. On the W. side: 12. *P. Portuensis,* on the other side of the Tiber near the river, from which issued the road to Portus. 13. A second *P. Aurelia,* on the W. slope of the Janiculus, now Porta S. Pancrazio. 14. *P. Septimiana,* near the Tiber, which was destroyed by Alexander VI.

Bridges. There were 8 bridges across the Tiber, which probably ran in the following order from N. to S.: 1. *Pons Ælius*, which was built by Hadrian, and led from the city to the mausoleum of that emperor, now the bridge and castle of S. Angelo. 2. *Pons Neronianus*, or *Vaticanus*, which led from the Campus Martius to the Vatican and the gardens of Caligula and Nero. The remains of its piers may still be seen, when the waters of the Tiber are low, at the back of the Hospital of San Spirito. *P. Agrippæ*, a bridge, built by Augustus, above the P. Aurelius, where the Aurelian wall meets the Tiber. 4. *P. Aurelius*, sometimes, but erroneously, called *Janiculensis*, which led to the Janiculus and the Porta Aurelia. It occupied the site of the present Ponte Sisto, which was built by Sixtus IV upon the ruins of the old bridge. 5, 6. *P. Fabricius* and *P. Cestius*, the two bridges which connected the Insula Tiberina with the opposite sides of the river, the former with the city, the latter with the Janiculus. Both are still remaining. The P. Fabricius, which was built by one L. Fabricius, curator viarum, a short time before the conspiracy of Catiline, now bears the name of Ponte Quattro Capi. The P. Cestius, which was built at a much later age, is now called Ponte S. Bartolommeo. 7. *P. Æmilius*, below the island of the Tiber, formed the communication between the Palatine and its neighbourhood and the Janiculus. 8. *P. Sublicius*, the oldest of the Roman bridges, said to have been built by Ancus Martius, when he erected a fort on the Janiculus. It was built of wood, whence its name, which comes from *sublices*, 'wooden beams'. It was carried away several times by the river, but from a feeling of religious respect was always rebuilt of wood down to the latest times. 9. *P. Probi*, built by the

Emperor Probus (276–82), crossed the Tiber S. of the N. corner of the Aventine. 10. *P. Milvius*, or *Mulvius*, now Ponte Molle, was situated outside the city, N. of the P. Ælius, and was built by Æmilius Scaurus the censor.

Interior of the City. I. Fora. The Fora were open spaces of ground, paved with stones and surrounded by buildings. In the *fora civilia* justice was administered and public business transacted; in the *fora venalia* provisions were sold. The latter were distinguished as the *forum boarium*, the cattle market, situated between the Circus Maximus and the Pons Sublicius; the *forum olitorium*, the vegetable market which lay outside the Porta Carmentalis; the *forum suarium*, *piscarium*, etc. The principal fora were: 1. *Forum Romanum*, also called simply the Forum, and at a later time distinguished by the epithets *vetus* or *magnum*. It lay between the Capitoline and the Velian ridge, which was a hill opposite the Palatine. It ran lengthwise from the foot of the Capitol in the direction of the Arch of Titus, but not as far as the latter. Its shape was that of an irregular quadrangle, of which the two longer sides were not parallel, but were wider near the Capitol. Its length was 820 feet, and its breadth varied from 160 to 180 feet: a small extent, since the limits of the Forum were fixed in the early days of Rome, and never underwent any alteration. The origin of the Forum is ascribed to Romulus and Tatius, who are said to have filled up the swamp which occupied its site and to have set it apart for the administration of justice. The Forum in its widest sense occupied the Forum proper and the Comitium. The Comitium occupied the narrow or upper end of the Forum, and was the place where the patricians met in their comitia curiata. At a later time the Forum proper was the place of meeting for the plebeians in their comitia tributa, and was separated from the Comitium by the Rostra or platform, from which the orators addressed the people. An important public building in early times, standing on the N. side of the Comitium, was the Curia Hostilia, the place of meeting of the Senate, which was said to have been erected by Tullus Hostilius. 2. *Forum Julium* or *Forum Cæsaris,* built by Julius Cæsar, because the old forum was found too small for the transaction of public business. It was close to the old forum, behind the present church of S. Martino. Cæsar built here a magnificent temple of Venus Genetrix. 3. *Forum Augusti,* built by Augustus. It stood behind the Forum Julium, and its entrance at the other end was an arch, now called Arco de' Pantani. Augustus adorned it with a temple of Mars Ultor, and the forum was used for *causæ publicæ* and *sortitiones judicum.* 4. *Forum Pacis,* commenced by Vespasian, to the N. of the Forum Romanum. The Temple of Peace was situated in this forum. 5. *Forum Nervæ* or *Transitorium,* a small forum between the Temple of Peace and the fora of Julius Cæsar and Augustus. Domitian resolved to pull down the buildings intervening between these fora and the temple, forming an open space serving as a passageway, hence the forum was called Transitorium. The plan was carried out by Nerva, by whose name the forum was also called. 6. *Forum Trajani,* built by Trajan, who employed the architect Apollodorus. It lay between the Forum Augusti and the Campus Martius. It was the most splendid of all the fora, and considerable remains of it still exist. Here are the Basilica Ulpia and the Bibliotheca Ulpia, the celebrated Column of Trajan, an equestrian statue and triumphal arch of Trajan, and a temple of Trajan built by Hadrian.

II. Campi. The Campi were open spaces of ground, covered with grass and planted with trees, and adorned with works of art: 1. *Campus Martius*, the open plain lying between the city walls and the Tiber, of which the southern part, in the neighbourhood of the Circus Flaminius, was called Campus Flaminius, or Prata Flaminia. The Campus Martius is said to have belonged originally to the Tarquins, and to have become the property of the state, and to have been consecrated to Mars upon the expulsion of the kings. Here the Roman youths were accustomed to perform their gymnastic and warlike exercises, and here the comitia of the centuries were held. At a later time, it was surrounded by porticoes, temples, and other public buildings. 2. *Campus Sceleratus*, close to the Porta Collina and within the walls of Servius, where the vestals who had broken their vows of chastity were entombed alive. 3. *Campus Agrippæ*, probably on the S.W. slope of the Pincian hill, E. of the Campus Martius, on the right of the Corso, and N. of the Piazza degli Apostoli. 4. *Campus Esquilinus*, outside of the agger of Servius and near the Porta Esquilina, where criminals were executed, and the lower classes were buried. The greater part of this plain was afterwards converted into pleasure grounds belonging to the palace of Mæcenas. 5. *Campus Viminalis*, on the E. slope of the Viminal near the Villa Negroni.

III. Streets and Districts. There are said to have been in all 215 streets in Rome. The broad streets were called *Viæ* and *Vici*; the narrow streets *Angiportus*. The chief streets were: 1. *Via Sacra*, the principal street in Rome. It began near the Sacellum Streniæ, in the valley between the Cælian and the Esquiline, and leaving the Flavian Amphitheatre (Colosseum) on the left ran along the N. slope of the Palatine, passing under the arch of Titus, and past the Forum Romanum, till it reached the Capitol. 2. *Via Lata*, led from the N. side of the Capitol and the Porta Ratumena to the Porta Flaminia, whence the N. part of it was called *Via Flaminia*. 3. *Via Nova*, by the side of the W. slope of the Palatine, led from the ancient Porta Romanula and the Velabrum to the Forum, and was connected by a side street with the Via Sacra. 4. *Vicus Jugarius*, led from the Porta Carmentalis under the Capitol to the Forum Romanum, which it entered near the Basilica Julia and the Lacus Servilius. 5. *Vicus Tuscus*, connected the Velabrum with the Forum, running W. of, and nearly parallel with, the Via Nova. It contained a great number of shops, where articles of luxury were sold. 6. *Vicus Cyprius*, ran from the Forum to the Esquiline. The upper part of it, turning on the right to the Urbius Clivus, was called *Sceleratus Vicus*, because Tullia here drove her chariot over the corpse of her father Servius. 7. *Vicus Patricius*, in the valley between the Esquiline and the Viminal in the direction of the modern Via Urbana and Via di S. Pudenziana. 8. *Vicus Africus*, in the district of Esquiline, but the exact situation of which cannot be determined, said to have been so called, because African hostages were kept here during the first Punic war. 9. *Vicus Sandalarius*, also in the district of the Esquiline, extending as far as the heights of the Carinæ. Besides the shops of the shoemakers, from whom it derived its name, it contained several booksellers' shops. 10. *Vicus Vitrearius* or *Vitrarius*, in the S.E. part of the city, near the Porta Capena. 11. *Vicus Longus*, in the Vallis Quirini between the Quirinal and Viminal, now S. Vitale. 12. *Caput Africæ*, near the Colosseum, the modern Via de' SS. Quattro Coronati. 13. *Subura* or *Suburra*, a district, through which a street of the same name ran, was the whole valley between the Esquiline, Quirinal, and Viminal. It was one of the most frequented parts of the town and contained a great number of shops and brothels. 14. *Velia*, a height near the Forum, which extended from the Palatine, near the Arch of Titus, to the Esquiline, and which separated the valley of the Forum from that of the Colosseum. On the Velia were situated the Basilica of Constantine and the temple of Venus and Rome. 15. *Carinæ*, a district on the S.W. part of the Esquiline, or the modern height of S. Pietro in Vincoli, where Pompey, Cicero, and many other distinguished Romans lived. 16. *Velabrum*, a district on the W. slope of the Palatine between the Vicus Tuscus and the Forum Boarium, was originally a morass. 17. *Æquimelium*, a place at the E. foot of the Capitol and by the side of the Vicus Jugarius, where the house of Sp. Mælius once stood. 18. *Argiletum*, a district of uncertain site, but probably at the S. extremity of the Quirinal between the Subura, the Forum of Nerva, and the Temple of Peace. 19. *Lautumiæ*, a district near the Argiletum and the Forum Piscatorium, on which subsequently the Basilica Porcia was built. In this district was one of the state prisons, called *Lautumiæ* or *Carcer Lautumiarum*.

IV. Temples. There are said to have been four hundred temples in Rome. Of these the following, enumerated for the most part in chronological order, were the principal: 1. *Templum Jovis Feretrii*, on the Capitoline, the oldest of all the Roman temples, built, according to tradition, by Romulus, and restored by Augustus. 2. *T. Fidei*, likewise on the Capitoline, built by Numa, and restored successively by A. Atilius Collatinus and M. Æmilius Scaurus. 3. *T. Jani*, also called *Janus Bifrons* or *Biformis*, *Janus Geminus*, and *Janus Quirinus*, also built by Numa, was, properly speaking, not a temple, but a passage with an entrance at each end, the gates of which were opened during war and closed in time of peace. It was situated N.E. of the Forum towards the Quirinal. 4. *Ædes Vestæ*, a round temple built by Numa, in the S. part of the forum or on the slope of the Palatine, adjoining the Regia Numæ, probably near Sta Maria Liberatrice. The *Atrium Vestæ*, also called *Atrium Regium*, probably formed a part of the Regia Numæ, which may be regarded as forming a portion of the building sacred to Vesta. 5. *T. Dianæ*, on the Aventine, which hill is hence called by Martial *Collis Dianæ*, built by Servius Tullius, as the place of meeting for the Romans and the members of the Latin league, and restored by Augustus, probably near the modern church of S. Prisca. 6. *T. Lunæ*, frequently confounded with the preceding, also built by Servius Tullius, and on the Aventine, probably on the side adjoining the Circus. 7. *T. Jovis*, usually called the Capitolium, the temple of Jupiter Optimus Maximus, was situated on the Capitoline which derived its name from the temple. The temple is said to have been called the Capitolium as a human head (*caput*) was found in digging the foundations. The building was commenced by Tarquinius Priscus, and was finished by Tarquinius Superbus, but was not dedicated until the third year of the Republic, 507 B.C., by the consul M. Horatius. It was burnt down in the civil wars, 83 B.C., but was rebuilt by Sulla and dedicated by Q. Catulus, 69 B.C. It was burnt down by the soldiers of Vitellius, A.D. 69, and was rebuilt by Vespasian; but it was burnt down a third time in the reign of Titus, A.D. 80, and was again rebuilt by Domitian with greater splendour than before. The Capitol contained three cellæ under the same roof: the middle cella was the temple of Jupiter, and on either side were the cellæ of his attendant deities, Juno and Minerva. The temple was in the form of a square, 200 feet on each side, and was approached by a flight of 100 steps. The gates were of bronze and the ceilings and tiles gilt. In the Capitol were kept the Sibylline books. Here the consuls on entering office offered sacrifices and took their vows; and hither the victorious general, who entered the city in triumph, was carried in his triumphal car to return thanks to the Father of the Gods. 8. *T. Saturni*, which was also used as the Ærarium, on the Clivus Capitolinus and by the Forum, to which it is supposed that the 3 pillars in the Forum belong. It was built by Tarquinius Superbus and restored successively by L. Munatius Plancus and Septimius Severus. 9. *Ædes Castoris* or *T. Castoris et Pollucis*, by the Forum, near the fountain of Juturna, in which the senate frequently assembled. It was vowed (499 B.C.) by the dictator A. Postumius in the great battle with the Latins near the lake Regillus, and was successively restored by L. Metellus Dalmaticus, Tiberius, Caligula, and Claudius. 10. *T. Mercurii*, between the Circus Maximus and the Aventine. 11. *T. Cereris*, on the slope of the Aventine near the Circus. 12. *T. Apollinis*, between the Circus Maximus and the Theatre of Marcellus near the Porticus Octaviæ, where the senate often assembled. 13. *T. Junonis Reginæ*, on the Aventine. 14. *T. Martis*, before the Porta Capena on the Via Appia. 15. *T. Junonis Monetæ*, on the area of the Capitoline, where the house of M. Manlius had stood. 16. *T. Junonis Lucinæ*, on the W. summit of the Esquiline. 17. *T. Concordiæ*, on the slope of the Capitoline above the Forum, in which the senate frequently assembled. There were probably two temples of Concordia, both by the Forum, of which the more ancient was consecrated by Camillus, and the other by L. Opimius after the death of C. Gracchus. The remains of the ancient temple of Concordia are to be seen behind the arch of Septimius Severus. 18. *T. Salutis*, on the slope of the Quirinal near the Porta Salutaris, adorned with paintings by Fabius Pictor, burnt down in the reign of Claudius. 19. *T. Bellonæ*, before the Circus Flaminius, and near the confines of the Campus Martius, in which the senate assembled, in order to give audience to foreign ambassadors and to receive applications from generals who solicited the honour of a triumph. 20. *T. Jovis Victoris*, on the Palatine, between the Domus Augusti and the Curia Vetus. 21. *T. Victoriæ*, on the summit of the Palatine, or the Clivus Victoriæ above the Porta Romanula and the circus, in which the statue of the Mother of the Gods was at first preserved. 22. *T. Magnæ Matris Idææ*, near the preceding and the Casa Romuli, in which the above named statue of the goddess was placed 13 years after its arrival in Rome. 23. *T. Jovis Statoris*, near the arch of Titus on the Via Sacra, where the senate frequently assembled. 24. *T. Quirini*, on the Quirinal, where also the senate frequently assembled, enlarged and adorned by Augustus. 25. *T. Fortunæ*, built by Servius Tullius in the Forum Boarium. 26. *T. Æsculapii* in the island of the Tiber, which was called after it Insula Æsculapii. 27. *T. Mentis* and *Veneris Erycinæ*, both of which were built at the same time (215 B.C.), and close to one another on the Capitoline. There was also another temple of Venus Erycina before the Porta Collina. 28. *T. Honoris et Virtutis*, a double shrine, of which the first part to Honos was built in 234 B.C., and converted into a double shrine by M. Claudius Marcellus in 208. Restored by Vespasian. 29. *T. Fauni*, in the island of the Tiber. 30. *T. Spei*, in the Forum Olitorium. 31. *T. Junonis Sospitæ*, in the Forum Olitorium near the theatre of Marcellus. 32. *T. Pietatis*, in the Forum Olitorium, which was pulled down in order to make room for the theatre of Marcellus. 33. *Ædes Fortunæ Equestris*, in the Campus Flaminius near the theatre of Pompey, built by Fulvius Flaccus, the roof of which, made of marble, was brought from a temple of Juno Lucina in Bruttium. It was probably burnt down in the reign of Augustus or Tiberius, since in A.D. 22 we are told there was no temple of Fortuna Equestris at Rome. There were other temples of Fortuna on the Palatine, Quirinal, etc. 34. *Ædes Herculis Musarum*, close to the Porticus Octaviæ, and between the theatre of Marcellus and the Circus Flaminius, built by M. Fulvius Nobilior (187 B.C.), and adorned with the statues of the Muses brought from Ambracia. 35. *T. Honoris et Virtutis*, built by Marius, but of uncertain site: some modern writers suppose it to have been on the Capitoline. 36. *T. Martis*, in the Campus Martius near the Circus Flaminius, built by D. Brutus Callaicus (138 B.C.), and adorned with a colossal statue of the god. 37. *T. Veneris Genetricis*, in the forum of Cæsar, before which Cæsar's equestrian statue was placed. 38. *T. Martis Ultoris*, in the forum of Augustus, to which belong the 3 splendid Corinthian pillars near the convent of S. Annunziata. 39. *T. Apollinis*, on the Palatine, surrounded by a porticus in which was the celebrated Palatine library. 40. *Pantheon*, the celebrated temple in the Campus Martius, which is still extant and used as a Christian church. It is a circular building, surmounted by a dome, and contains a noble Corinthian portico of 16 pillars. It was built by M. Agrippa in his third consulship, 27 B.C. The name is commonly derived from its being supposed to be sacred to all the gods; but Dion Cassius expressly states that it was dedicated to Mars and Venus. There were statues of Agrippa and Augustus in the pronaos. The Pantheon was burnt down in A.D. 80, and restored by Domitian, again restored by Hadrian, and finally by Septimius Severus, A.D. 202. The Pantheon is the largest circular building of antiquity; the interior diameter of the rotunda is 142 feet, and the height from the pavement to the summit about 148 feet. The portico is 104 feet wide, and the columns 47 feet high. 41. *T. Augusti*, founded by Tiberius and completed by Caligula, on the slope of the Palatine towards the Via Nova. It stood before the temple of Minerva, from which it was probably separated by the Via Nova. 42. *T. Pacis*, one of the most splendid temples in the city, built by Vespasian on the Velia. 43. *T. Isidis et Serapidis* in the 3rd Regio, which was named after the temple. 44. *T. Vespasiani et Titi*, in the Forum, alongside of the temple of Concordia. 45. *T. Antonini et Faustinæ*, at the farther end of the N. side of the Forum under the Velia. The remains of this temple are in the modern church of S. Lorenzo in Miranda. 46. *T. Minervæ*, on the S. side of the Forum, behind the temple of Augustus, built by Domitian. 47. *T. Bonæ Deæ*, a very ancient temple on a spot of the Aventine, which was called Saxum Sacrum, but removed by Hadrian, undoubtedly on the S.E. side of the hill, opposite the heights of S. Sabba and S. Balbina. 48. *T. Romæ et Veneris*, subsequently called *T. Urbis*, a large and splendid temple, built by Hadrian, between the Esquiline and Palatine, N.E. of the Colosseum. It was burnt down in the reign of Maxentius, but was subsequently restored. Its remains are between the Colosseum and the church of S. Maria Nuova or S. Francesca Romana. 49. *T. Solis*, at the upper end of the Circus Maximus. 50. *T. Herculis*, in the Forum Boarium, probably the round temple still extant of S. Maria del Sole, which used to be erroneously regarded as the temple of Vesta. There was another temple of Hercules by the Circus Maximus, near the Porta Trigemina. 51. *T. Solis*, a splendid temple built by Aurelian, E. of the Quirinal. 52. *T. Floræ*, an ancient temple on the S. point of the Quirinal; but the time of its foundation is not recorded. 53. *Vulcanale*, was not a temple, but only an Area dedicated to the god with an altar, on the N. side of the Forum above the Comitium; it was so large that not only were the Curia Hostilia and the Ædes Concordiæ built there, but also a fishmarket was held in the place.

V. Circi. The Circi were places for chariot-races and horse-races. 1. *Circus Maximus*, frequently called simply *the Circus*, was founded by Tarquinius Priscus, in the plain between the Palatine and Aventine, and was successively enlarged by Julius Cæsar and Trajan. Under the emperors it contained seats for 385,000 persons. It was restored by Constantine the Great, and games were celebrated in it as late as the sixth century. 2. *C. Flaminius*, erected by Flaminius in 221 B.C. in the Prata Flaminia before the Porta Carmentalis; it was not sufficiently large for the population of Rome, and was therefore seldom used. 3. *C. Gai et Neronis*, erected by Caligula in the gardens of Agrippina on the other side of the Tiber. There was also another *C. Neronis*, on the other side of the Tiber, near the Moles Hadriani, in the gardens of Domitia. 4. *C. Palatinus*, on the Palatine, in which the Ludi Palatini were celebrated. There are traces of it in the Orto Roncioni on the S. part of the hill. 5. *C. Maxentii*, commonly called Circo di Caracalla, before the Porta Appia in the S. part of the city. Among the Circi we may also reckon: 6. The *Stadium*, likewise called *C. Agonalis* and *C. Alexandri*, in the Campus Martius, erected by Domitian in place of the wooden Stadium built by Augustus. It contained seats for 15,000 persons. Its remains still exist in the Piazza Navona.

VI. Theatres. Theatres were not built at Rome till a comparatively late period, and long after the Circi. At first they were only made of wood for temporary purposes, and were afterwards broken up; but many of these wooden theatres were notwithstanding constructed with great magnificence. The splendid wooden theatre of M. Æmilius Scaurus was capable of containing 80,000 spectators. 1. *Theatrum Pompeii*, the first permanent stone theatre, was erected by Cn. Pompey, 55 B.C., in the Campus Martius, N.E. of the Circus Flaminius, after the model of the theatre of Mytilene. It contained, according to ancient accounts, seats for 40,000 spectators, but the number was probably nearer 10,000. At the top of the cavea a temple of Venus Victrix was built, and the whole building was dedicated as a temple to avoid the impropriety of dedicating a permanent theatre. It was restored successively by Augustus, Tiberius, Caligula, Diocletian, and Theodoric. Its ruins are by the Palazzo Pio, not far from the Campo di Fiore. 2. *Th. Cornelii Balbi*, S.E. of the preceding, near the Tiber, on the site of the Palazzo Cenci. It was dedicated by Cornelius Balbus in 13 B.C., was partly burnt down under Titus, but was subsequently restored. It contained seats for 11,600 persons. 3. *Th. Marcelli*, in the Forum Olitorium, W. of the preceding, between the slope of the Capitoline and the island of the Tiber, on the site of the temple of Pietas. It was begun by Julius Cæsar, and dedicated by Augustus in 13 B.C., to the memory of his nephew Marcellus. It was restored by Vespasian, and perhaps also by Alexander Severus. It contained 20,500 loca, usually interpreted to mean running feet of seating, and would, therefore, accommodate between 10,000 and 14,000 spectators. The remains of its Cavea exist near the Piazza Montanara. These were the only 3 theatres at Rome, whence Ovid speaks of *terna theatra*. There was, however, an Odeum or concert-house, which may be classed among the theatres. 4. *Odeum*, in the Campus Martius, built by Domitian and restored by Apollodorus in the reign of Trajan. It contained 10,600 loca or seats for about 5,000.

VII. Amphitheatres. The amphitheatres, like the theatres, were originally made of wood for temporary purposes. They were used for the shows of gladiators and wild beasts. The first wooden amphitheatre was built by C. Scribonius Curio (the celebrated partisan of Cæsar), and the next by Julius Cæsar during his perpetual dictatorship, 46 B.C. 1. *Amph. Statilii Tauri*, in the Campus Martius, was the first stone amphitheatre in Rome, and was built by Statilius Taurus, 29 B.C. This edifice was the only one of the kind until the building of the Flavian amphitheatre. It did not satisfy Caligula, who commenced an amphitheatre near the Sæpta; but the work was not continued by Claudius. Nero, too, A.D. 57, erected a vast amphitheatre of wood, but this was only a temporary building. The amphitheatre of Taurus was destroyed in the burning of Rome, A.D. 64, and was probably never restored, as it is not again mentioned. 2. *Amph. Flavium*, or, as it has been called since the time of Bede, the *Colosseum* or *Colisæum*, a name said to be derived from the Colossus of Nero, which stood close by. It was situated in the valley between the Cælius, the Esquiline, and the Velia on the marshy ground which was previously the pond of Nero's palace. It was commenced by Vespasian, and was completed by Titus, who dedicated it in A.D. 80, when 5,000 animals of different kinds were slaughtered. This wonderful building, of which there are still extensive remains, covered nearly 6 acres of ground, and furnished seats for 87,000 spectators. In A.D. 217 it was struck by lightning, and so much damage was done to it that the games were for some years celebrated in the Stadium. Its restoration was commenced by Elagabalus and completed by Alexander Severus. 3. *Amph. Castrense*, at the S.E. of the Aurelian walls.

VIII. Thermæ. The Thermæ were among the most magnificent buildings of imperial Rome. They were distinct from the *Balnæ*, or common baths, of which there were a great number at Rome. In the Thermæ the baths constituted a small part of the building. They were, properly speaking, a Roman adaptation of the Greek gymnasia; and besides the baths they contained places for athletic games and youthful sports, exedræ or public halls, porticoes and vestibules for the idle, and libraries for the learned. They were decorated with the finest objects of art, and adorned with fountains, and shaded walks and plantations. 1. *Thermæ Agrippæ*, in the Campus Martius, originally a hot-air bath built by Agrippa in 25 B.C., and adorned with works of art. Later, they became public baths, supplied with water from the Aqua Virgo, completed in 19 B.C. The thermæ were burnt in A.D. 80, restored by Titus or Domitian, and again later by Hadrian, who connected the thermæ with the Pantheon by a series of halls. 2. *Th. Neronis*, erected by Nero in the Campus Martius alongside of the Thermæ of Agrippa: they were restored by Alexander Severus, and were from that time called *Th. Alexandrinæ.* 3. *Th. Titi,* on the Esquiline, near the amphitheatre of this emperor, of which there are still considerable remains. 4. *Th. Trajani,* also on the Esquiline, immediately behind the two preceding, towards the N.E. 5. *Th. Commodianæ* and *Th. Severianæ,* close to one another, near S. Balbina, in the S.E. part of the city. 6. *Th. Antoninianæ,* also in the S.E. part of the city, behind the two preceding, one of the most magnificent of all the Thermæ, in which 2,300 men could bathe at the same time. The greater part of it was built by Caracalla, and it was completed by Heliogabalus and Alexander Severus. There are still extensive remains of this immense building below S. Balbina. 7. *Th. Diocletiani,* in the N.E. part of the Viminal. It was the most extensive of all the Thermæ, containing a library, picture gallery, Odeum, etc., and such immense baths that 3,000 men could bathe in them at the same time. There are still extensive remains of this building near S. Maria delgi Angeli. 8. *Th. Constantini,* on the Quirinal, on the site of the modern Palazzo Rospigliosi, but of which all traces have disappeared. The following Thermæ were smaller and less celebrated. 9. *Th. Decianæ,* on the Aventine. 10. *Th. Suranæ,* erected by Trajan to the memory of his friend Sulpicius Sura, also in the neighbourhood of the Aventine, probably the same as the *Th. Varianæ.*

IX. Basilicæ. The Basilicæ were buildings which served as courts of law, and exchanges or places of meeting for merchants and men of business. 1. *Basilica Porcia,* erected by M. Porcius Cato, in the Forum adjoining the Curia, 184 B.C. It was burnt down along with the Curia in the riots which followed the death of Clodius, 52 B.C. 2. *B. Fulvia*, also called *Æmilia et Fulvia*, because it was built by the censors L. Æmilius Lepidus and M. Fulvius Nobilior in 179 B.C. It was situated in the Forum near the preceding one. It was restored by Æmilius Paulus in the time of Cæsar, and was hence called *B. Æmilia* or *Pauli*. It was dedicated by his son Paulus Æmilius Lepidus in his consulship, 34 B.C. It was burnt down 20 years afterwards (14), and was rebuilt nominally by Paulus Lepidus, but in reality by Augustus and the friends of Paulus. The new building was a most magnificent one; its columns of Phrygian marble were especially celebrated. It was repaired by another Lepidus in the reign of Tiberius, A.D. 22. 3. *B. Sempronia*, built by Ti. Sempronius Gracchus, 171 B.C., in the Forum at the end of the Vicus Tuscus. 4. *B. Opimia*, in the Forum near the Temple of Concordia, built by the consul L. Opimius, 121 B.C. 5. *B. Julia*, the most beautiful of Roman basilicas, was begun in 54 B.C. by Julius Cæsar on the site of the B. Sempronia and completed by Augustus. Destroyed by fire, it was rebuilt by Augustus and dedicated, A.D. 12. Destroyed again by fire in 283, it was rebuilt by Diocletian. 6. *B. Argentaria*, situated in the 8th Regio, was the headquarters for the sale of bronze vessels. 7. *B. Ulpia*, built by Trajan and occupied the centre of the Forum Trajani. It was a rectangular building, 292 feet by 177, and served as a hall of justice. 8. *B. Constantini*, situated in the Forum between the Templum Pacis and the Templum Romæ et Veneris. It was commenced by Maxentius, completed by Domitian, but burnt down in 191. It was rebuilt by Constantine.

X. Porticoes. The Porticoes (*Porticus*) were covered walks, supported by columns, and open on one side. There were several public porticoes at Rome, many of them of great size, which were used as places of recreation, and for the transaction of business. 1. *Porticus Pompeii*, adjoining the theatre of Pompey, and erected to afford shelter to the spectators in the theatre during a shower of rain. It was restored by Diocletian, and was hence called *P. Jovia*. 2. *P. Argonautarum*, or *Neptuni*, or *Agrippæ*, erected by Agrippa in 25 B.C. in the Campus Martius around the temple of Neptune, and adorned with a celebrated painting of the Argonauts. 3. *P. Philippi*, by the side of the T. Herculis Musarum and the Porticus Octaviæ, built by M. Philippus the step-father of Augustus, and adorned with splendid works of art. 4. *P. Minucii* in the Campus Martius, near the Circus Flaminius, built by Q. Minucius Rufus in 109 B.C., to commemorate his victories over the Scordisci and Triballi in the preceding year, There appear to have been 2 porticoes of this name, since we find mention of a *Minucia Vetus et Frumentaria*. It appears that the tesseræ, or tickets, which entitled persons to a share in the public distributions of corn were given to them in the P. Minucia. 5. *P. Metelli*, built by Q. Metellus, after his triumph over Perseus, king of Macedonia, 146 B.C. It was situated in the Campus Martius between the Circus Flaminius and the theatre of Marcellus, and surrounded the 2 temples of Jupiter Stator and Juno Regina. 6. *P. Octaviæ*, built by Augustus on the site of the P. Metelli just mentioned, in honour of his sister Octavia. It was a magnificent building, containing a vast number of works of art, and a public library, in which the senate frequently assembled; hence it is sometimes called *Curia Octavia*. It was burnt down in the reign of Titus. Its ruins are near the church of S. Angelo in Pescaria.

7. *P. Octavia*, which must be carefully distinguished from the P. Octaviæ just mentioned, was built in 168 B.C. by Cn. Octavius, who commanded the Roman fleet in the war against Perseus, king of Macedonia. It was situated in the Campus Martius between the theatre of Pompey and the Circus Flaminius. It was rebuilt by Augustus, and contained 2 rows of columns of the Corinthian order, with brazen capitals, whence it was also called *P. Corinthia*. 8. *P. Europæ*, probably at the foot of the Pincius, in which foot-races took place. 9. *P. Vipsana*, built by Pola, the sister of Agrippa, and finished by Augustus. It was situated in the Campus Agrippæ. 10. *P. Liviæ*, built by Augustus and dedicated to Livia in 7 B.C. It was a magnificent portico surrounding the Templum Concordiæ on the Esquiline.

XI. Triumphal Arches. The Triumphal Arches (*Arcus*) were structures peculiar to the Romans, and were erected by victorious generals in commemoration of their victories. They were built across the principal streets of the city, and, according to the space of their respective localities, consisted either of a single archway or of a central one for carriages, with 2 smaller ones on each side for foot passengers. Ancient writers mention 21 arches in the city of Rome. Of these the most important were: 1. *Arcus Fabianus*, also called *Fornix Fabianus*, near the beginning of the Via Sacra, built by Fabius Maximus in 121 B.C., in commemoration of his victory over the Allobroges. 2. *A. Drusi*, erected by the senate in A.D. 23 in honour of Nero Claudius Drusus. It was situated on the Via Appia, and still exists, forming the inner gate of the Porta di S. Sebastiano. 3. *A. Augusti*, two arches erected in honour of Augustus in the Forum, one in 29 B.C. to commemorate Actium, the other in 19 B.C. to note the return of the standards once captured by the Parthians. 4. *A. Tiberii*, near the temple of Saturn on the Clivus Capitolinus, erected by Tiberius, A.D. 16, in honour of the victories of Germanicus in Germany. 5. *A. Claudii*, in the plain E. of the Quirinal, erected A.D. 51, to commemorate the victories of Claudius in Britain. 6. *A. Titi*, in the middle of the Via Sacra at the foot of the Palatine, which still exists. It was erected to the honour of Titus, after his conquest of Judæa, but was not finished till after his death; since in the inscription upon it he is called 'Divus', and he is also represented as being carried up to heaven upon an eagle. The bas-reliefs of this arch represent the spoils from the temples of Jerusalem carried in triumphal procession. 7. *A. Trajani*, in the forum of this emperor, at the point where it connected with the forum of Augustus. 8. *A. Veri*, on the Via Appia, erected to the honour of Verus after his victory over the Parthians. 9. *A. Marci Aurelii*, in the 7th Regio, probably erected to commemorate the victory of this emperor over the Marcomanni. 10. *A. Septimii Severi*, in the Forum Boarium, was erected by the senate, A.D. 203, in honour of Septimius Severus and his two sons, Caracalla and Geta, on account of his victories over the Parthians and Arabians. 11. *A. Gordiani*, on the Esquiline. 12. *A. Gallieni*, erected to the honour of Gallienus by a private individual, M. Aurelius Victor, also on the Esquiline, S.E. of the Porta Esquilina. It is still extant near the church of S. Vito. 13. *A. Diocletiani*, probably identical with the *A. Novus*, a marble arch spanning the Via Lata in the 7th Regio. 14. *A. Constantini*, at the entrance to the valley between the Palatine and the Cælius, is still extant. It was erected in honour of Constantine after his victory over Maxentius,

A.D. 312. It is profusely ornamented, and many of the bas-reliefs were taken from one of the arches erected in the time of Trajan. 15. *A. Gratiani, Valentiniani, et Theodosii*, erected in honour of these three emperors between A.D. 379 and 383. It was opposite the Pons Neronianus.

XII. Curiæ or Senate Houses. 1. *Curia Hostilia*, frequently called *Curia* simply, was built by Tullus Hostilius, and was used as the ordinary place of assembly for the senate down to the time of Julius Cæsar. It stood in the Forum on the N. side of the Comitium. It was burnt to the ground in the riots which followed the death of Clodius, 52 B.C. It was, however, soon rebuilt, the direction of the work being entrusted to Faustus, the son of the dictator Sulla; but scarcely had it been finished, when the senate, at the suggestion of Cæsar, decreed that it should be destroyed, and a temple of Fortune erected on its site, while a new Curia should be erected, which should bear the name of Julia. (See below.) 2. *C. Pompeia* or *Pompeii*, attached to the Portico of Pompey in the Campus Martius. It was in this Curia that Cæsar was assassinated on the Ides of March. 3. *C. Julia*, built by Julius Cæsar in 44 B.C., situated in the S.E. corner of the Forum Julium, near the Basilica Æmilia, not on the site of the ancient C. Hostilia. It was burnt down and rebuilt by Augustus in 29 B.C. After the fire of Rome in 64, it was rebuilt by Domitian and burnt down a third time in 283, and restored by Diocletian. It was sometimes called the C. Pompilia.

XIII. Castra or Barracks. 1. *Castra Prætoria*, in the N.E corner of the city on the slope of the Quirinal and Viminal, and beyond the Thermæ of Diocletian, were built by the emperor Tiberius in the form of a Roman camp. Here the Prætorian troops or imperial guards were always quartered.

2. *Castra Peregrina*, on the Cælius, probably built by Septimius Severus for the use of the foreign troops, who might serve as a counterpoise against the Prætorians.

XIV. Aqueducts. The Aqueducts (*Aquæductus*) supplied Rome with an abundance of pure water from the hills which surround the Campagna. The Romans at first had recourse to the Tiber and to wells sunk in the city. It was not till 313 B.C. that the first aqueduct was constructed, but their number was gradually increased till they amounted to 14 in the time of Procopius, that is, the sixth century of the Christian era. 1. *Aqua Appia*, was begun by the censor Appius Claudius Cæcus in 313 B.C. Its sources were near the Via Prænestina, between the seventh and eighth milestones, and its termination was at the Salinæ by the Porta Trigemina. Its length was 11,190 passus (nearly 11 English miles); for 11,130 of which it was carried underground, and for the 60 passus within the city, from the Porta Capena to the Porta Trigemina, it was on arches. Its daily supply of water was 1,825 quinariæ or 75,737 cubic metres No traces of it remain. 2. *Anio Vetus*, commenced 272 B.C. by the censor M. Curius Dentatus and finished by M. Fulvius Flaccus. The water was derived from the River Anio, above Tiber, at a distance of 19 miles from the city; but on account of its windings its actual length was about 40 miles (43,000 passus), of which length only 335 yards (221 passus) were above ground. 3. *Aqua Marcia*, which brought the coldest and most wholesome water to Rome, was built by the prætor Q. Marcius Rex, by command of the senate, in 144 B.C. It commenced at the side of the Via Valeria, 36 miles from Rome; its length was 61,710½ passus, of which only

7,463 were above ground; namely, 528 on solid substructions, and 6,935 on arches. It was high enough to supply water to the summit of the Capitoline mount. It was repaired by Agrippa in his ædileship, 33 B.C. (see below, No. 5), and the volume of its water was increased by Augustus, by means of the water of a spring 800 passus from it: the short aqueduct which conveyed this water was called *Aqua Augusta*, but is never enumerated as a distinct aqueduct. Several arches of the Aqua Marcia are still standing. 4. *Aqua Tepula*, which was built by the censors Cn. Servilius Cæpio and L. Cassius Longinus in 125 B.C., began in a spot in the Lucullan or Tusculan land, 2 miles to the right of the tenth milestone on the Via Latina. It was afterwards connected with—5. *Aqua Julia*. Among the splendid public works executed by Agrippa in his ædileship, 33 B.C., was the formation of a new aqueduct, and the restoration of all the old ones. From a source 2 miles to the right of the twelfth milestone of the Via Latina, he constructed his aqueduct (the *Aqua Julia*) first to the Aqua Tepula, in which it was merged as far as the reservoir (*piscina*) on the Via Latina, 7 miles from Rome. From the reservoir, the water was carried along 2 distinct channels, on the same substructions (which were probably the original substructions of the Aqua Tepula newly restored), the lower channel being called the *Aqua Tepula*, and the upper the *Aqua Julia*; and this double aqueduct again was united with the *Aqua Marcia*, over the watercourse of which the other two were carried. The monument erected at the junction of these 3 aqueducts is still to be seen close to the Porta S. Lorenzo. It bears an inscription referring to the repairs under Caracalla. The whole course of the Aqua Julia, from its source, amounted

:o 15,426 passus, partly on massive substructions ınd partly on arches. 6. *Aqua Virgo*, built by Agrippa, 19 B.C., to supply his baths. Its water was as highly esteemed for bathing as that of the Aqua Marcia was for drinking. It commenced by the eighth milestone on the Via Collatina, and was conducted by a very circuitous route, chiefly under the ground, to the M. Pincius, whence it was carried on arches to the Campus Martius: its length was 14,105 passus (13 miles), of which 12,865 were underground. 7. *Aqua Alsietina*, sometimes called also *Aqua Augusta*, on the other side of the Tiber, was constructed by Augustus from the Lacus Alsietinus (Lago di Martignano) which lay 6,500 passus (6 miles) to the right of the fourteenth milestone, on the Via Claudia, and was brought to the part of the Regio Transtiberina below the Janiculus. Its length was 22,172 passus (21 miles), of which only 358 were on arches; and its water was so bad that it could only have been intended for the supply of Augustus's Naumachia, and for watering gardens. 8, 9. *Aqua Claudia* and *Anio Novus* (or *Aqua Aniena Nova*), the 2 most magnificent of all the aqueducts, both commenced by Caligula in A.D. 36, and finished by Claudius in A.D. 50. The *Aqua Claudia* commenced near the thirty-eighth milestone on the Via Sublacensis. Its water was reckoned the best after the Marcia. Its length was 46,406 passus (nearly 44 miles), of which 9,567 were on arches. The *Anio Novus* began at the forty-second milestone on the Via Sublacensis. Its length was 58,700 passus (nearly 56 miles) and some of its arches were 109 feet high. In the neighbourhood of the city, these two aqueducts were united, forming two channels on the same arches, the Claudia below and the Anio Novus above. An interesting monument connected with these aqueducts is the gate now called Porta Maggiore, which was originally a magnificent double arch, by means of which the aqueduct was carried over the Via Labicana and the Via Prænestina. 10. *Aqua Trajana*, was brought by Trajan from the Lacus Sabatinus (now Bracciano) to supply the Janiculus and the Regio Transtiberina. 11. *Aqua Alexandrina*, constructed by Alexander Severus; its source was in the lands of Tusculum, about 14 miles from Rome, between Gabii and the lake Regillus. Its small height shows that it was intended for the baths of Severus, which were in one of the valleys of Rome.

XV. Sewers. Of these the most celebrated was the *Cloaca Maxima*, constructed by Tarquinius Priscus, which was formed to carry off the waters brought down from the adjacent hills into the Velabrum and valley of the Forum. It empties itself into the Tiber nearly opposite one extremity of the Insula Tiberina. This cloaca was formed by 3 arches, one within the other, the innermost of which is a semicircular vault about 14 feet in diameter. It is still extant in its original state.

XVI. Palaces. 1. *Palatium*, or the imperial palace, was situated on the N.E. side of the Palatine between the Arch of Titus and the sanctuary of Vesta; its front was turned towards the Forum, and the approach to it was from the Via Sacra close by the Arch of Titus. It was originally the house of the orator Hortensius, and was enlarged by Augustus, who made it the imperial residence. A part of the Palatium was called *Domus Tiberiana*, which was originally a separate house of Tiberius on the Palatine, and was afterwards united to the palace of Augustus. It was on the side of the hill turned towards the Circus and the Velabrum, and is sometimes called *Postica Pars Palatii.* We read of the Domus Tiberiana even after the imperial palace had been burnt to the ground in the reign of Nero; whence it follows that when the palace was rebuilt a portion of it still continued to bear this name. The Palatium was considerably enlarged by Caligula; but it did not satisfy Nero's love of pomp and splendour. Nero built 2 magnificent palaces which must be distinguished from one another. The first, called the *Domus Transitoria Neronis,* covered the whole of the Palatine, and extended as far as the Esquiline to the gardens of Mæcenas. This palace was burnt to the ground in the great fire of Rome, whereupon Nero commenced a new palace known by the name of *Domus Aurea,* which embraced the whole of the Palatine, the Velia, the valley of the Colosseum and the heights of the Thermæ of Titus, extended near the Esquiline gate, and was cut through not only by the Via Sacra but also by other streets. The whole building, however, was not finished at the time of Nero's death; and Vespasian confined the imperial palace to the Palatine, converting the other parts of the Domus Aurea into public or private buildings. The palace itself was not finished till the time of Domitian, who adorned it with numerous works of art. The emperor Septimius Severus added on the S. side of the Palatine a building called the Septizonium, which was proably intended as an Atrium. Among the numerous private palaces at Rome the following were some of the most important. 2. *Domus Ciceronis,* probably on the N.E. edge of the Palatine, was built by M. Livius Drusus, and purchased by Cicero of one of the Crassi. It was destroyed by Clodius after the banishment of Cicero, but was subsequently rebuilt at the public expense. 3. *D.*

Pompeii, the palace of Pompey, was situated in the Carinæ near the temple of Tellus. It was afterwards the residence of M. Antonius. 4. *D. Scauri* also on the Palatine, celebrated for its magnificence, subsequently belonged to Clodius. 5. *D. Lateranorum*, on the E. confines of the Cælius, was a palace originally belonging to the distinguished family of the Plautii Laterani; but after the execution of Plautius Lateranus under Nero, it became imperial property. It was given by Septimius Severus to his friend, Lateranus, and was subsequently the palace of Constantine, who adorned it with great magnificence. The modern palace of the Lateran occupies its site.

XVII. Sepulchral Monuments. 1. The *Mausoleum Augusti*, was situated in the Campus Martius and was built by Augustus as the burial-place of the imperial family. It was surrounded with an extensive garden or park, and was considered one of the most magnificent buildings of his reign; but there are only some insignificant ruins of it still extant. 2. *Mausoleum Hadriani*, was commenced by Hadrian in the gardens of Domitia on the right bank of the Tiber, and was connected with the city by the Pons Ælius; it was finished and dedicated by Antoninus Pius, A.D. 140. Here were buried Hadrian, Antoninus Pius, L. Verus, Commodus, and probably also Septimius Severus, Geta, and Caracalla. This building, stripped of its ornaments, still forms the fortress of modern Rome (the castle of S. Angelo). 3. *Sepulcrum Scipionum*, the burial-place of the Scipios, was situated, left of the Via Appia, near the Porta Capena. Most of the tombs of the distinguished Roman families during the Republican period lay on the Via Appia. 4. *Sepulcrum Cæciliæ Metellæ*, erected to the memory of

Cæcilia Metella, the daughter of Metellus Creticus, not far from the Circus Maxentii. This imposing monument is still extant and known by the name of Capo di Bove. 5. *Sepulcrum Cestii*, situated S. of the Aventine, near the Porta Ostiensis, being partly within and partly without the walls of Aurelian. This monument, which is still extant, is in the form of a pyramid, and was built in the time of Augustus for a certain C. Cestius.

XVIII. Columns. Columns (*Columnæ*) were frequently erected at Rome to commemorate persons and events. 1. *Columna Mænia*, near the end of the Forum, towards the Capitol, was erected to the honour of the consul C. Mænius, who conquered the Latins and took the town of Antium, 338 B.C. 2. *Col. Rostrata*, also in the Forum, erected in honour of the consul C. Duilius, to commemorate his victory over the Carthaginian fleet, 260 B.C. The name of Rostrata was given to it from its being adorned with the beaks of the conquered ships. The inscription upon this column, written in obsolete Latin, is still preserved. 3. *Col. Trajani*, in the Forum, in which the ashes of the emperor Trajan were deposited. This column is still extant, and is one of the most interesting monuments of ancient Rome. It is, including the pedestal, 117 feet high. The top was originally crowned with the statue of the emperor; it is now surmounted by that of the apostle Peter. A spiral bas-relief is folded round the pillar, which represents the emperor's wars against Decebalus and the Dacians, and is one of the most valuable authorities for archæological inquiries. 4. *Col. Antonini Pii*, erected in honour of Antoninus Pius after his death, consisted of a column of red granite on a pediment of white marble, and was situated in the Campus Martius, near the temple dedicated to this emperor. 5. *Col. M. Aurelii Antonini*, generally called the Antonine Column, erected to the memory of the emperor M. Aurelius, also in the Campus Martius, and still extant. It is an imitation of the Column of Trajan, and contains bas-reliefs representing the wars of M. Aurelius against the Marcomanni.

SALAMIS

An island lying between the western coast of Attica and the eastern coast of Megaris, and forming the southern boundary of the bay of Eleusis. It is separated from the coasts both of Attica and of Megaris by only a narrow channel. Its form is that of an irregular semicircle towards the W., with many small indentations along the coast. Its greatest length, from N. to S., is about 10 miles, and its width, in its broadest part, from E. to W., is a little more. Its length is correctly given by Strabo as from 70 to 80 stadia (about 20 miles).

The old city of Salamis, the residence of the Telamonian Ajax, stood upon the southern side of the island towards Ægina.

When Salamis became an Athenian deme, a new city was built at the head of a bay upon the eastern side of the island, and opposite the Attic coast. In the time of Pausanias this city also had fallen into decay (Paus. I 35, 36). There remained, however, a ruined agora and a temple of Ajax, containing a statue of the hero in ebony; also a temple of Artemis, the trophy erected in honour of the victory gained over the Persians, and a temple of Kychreus, son of Poseidon and legendary king of Salamis. Pausanias has not mentioned the statue of Solon, which was erected in the agora, with one hand covered by his mantle.

In Salamis there was a promontory Skiradion, containing a temple of the god of war, erected by Solon, because he there defeated the Megarians.

Budoron was the name of the western promontory of Salamis, and distant only 3 miles from Nisæa, the port of Megara. On this peninsula there was a fortress of the same name. In the attempt which the Peloponnesians made in 429 B.C. to surprise Peiræeus, they first sailed from Nisæa to the promontory of Budoron, and surprised the fortress; but after overrunning the island, they retreated without venturing to attack Peiræeus.

Salamis is chiefly memorable on account of the great battle fought off its coast, in which the Persian fleet of Xerxes was defeated by the Greeks, 480 B.C. The battle took place in the strait between the eastern part of the island and the coast of Attica. The Grecian fleet was drawn up in the small bay in front of the town of Salamis, and the Persian fleet opposite to them off the coast of Attica. The battle was witnessed by Xerxes, who had erected for himself a lofty throne on one of the projecting slopes of Mt. Ægaleos on the Attic coast.

SPARTA

The capital of Laconia, and the chief city of Peloponnesus. It was also called Lacedæmon, which was the original name of the country. Sparta stood at the upper end of the middle vale of the Eurotas, and upon the right bank of the river. The foundations of an earlier town of Sparta, dating from the Mycenæan age, on the left bank of the Eurotas have been discovered. It was a city of roughly the same dimensions as the Dorian Sparta of later times. In the threefold division of Peloponnesus among the descendants of Heracles, following the Dorian invasion, Lacedæmon fell to the share of Eurysthenes and Procles, the twin sons of Aristodemos. From the ninth century the double kingdom of Sparta was formed by the union of four pre-Dorian settlements with the city of Sparta itself, and gradually the Spartan supremacy was established over the whole Peloponnesus.

The city of Sparta was built upon a low range of hills, and upon an adjoining plain stretching S.E. to the river. These hills are offshoots of Mt. Taÿgetos, and rise almost immediately above the river.

Ten stadia S. of the point where the Œnos flows into the Eurotas, the latter river is divided into two arms by a small island overgrown with the oleander, where the foundations of an ancient bridge are visible. This is the most important point in the topography of the site of Sparta. Opposite to this bridge the range of hills rises upon which the ancient city stood; while a hollow way leads through them into the plain towards Knakion, a village, now named Magoula, situated about half-way between the mediæval town of Mistra and the island of the Eurotas. Upon emerging from this hollow into the plain, there rises on the left hand a hill, the S.W. side of which is occupied by the theatre. The centre of the building was excavated out of the hill; but the two wings of the cavea were entirely artificial, being built of enormous masses of quadrangular stones. The extremities of the two wings are about 430 feet from one another, and the diameter or length of the orchestra is about 170 feet. There are traces of a wall around this hill, which also embraces a considerable part of the adjoining plain to the E.

This hill is the largest of all the Spartan heights, and is distinguished by the wall which surrounds it, and by containing traces of foundations of some ancient buildings. From it two smaller hills project towards the Eurotas, parallel to one another, and these may be regarded as portions of the larger hill. Upon the more southerly of the two there are considerable remains of a circular brick building. West of this building is a valley in the form of a horseshoe, enclosed by walls of earth, and apparently a stadium, to which its length nearly corresponds.

To the N. of the hollow way leading from the bridge of the Eurotas to Knakion there is a small insulated hill, with a flat summit, but higher and more precipitous than the larger hill to the S. of this way.

The site of Sparta differs from that of almost all Grecian cities. Protected by lofty mountains, the Spartans were not obliged, like the other Greeks, to live within the walls of a city, but continued to dwell in the midst of their plantations and gardens.

It was this rural freedom and comfort which formed the chief charm and beauty of Sparta.

It must not, however, be supposed that Sparta was destitute of handsome public buildings. The temples of the gods were built with great magnificence, and the spoils of the Persian wars were employed in the erection of a beautiful stoa in the Agora, with figures of Persians in white marble upon the columns, among which Pausanias admired the statues of Mardonius and Artemisia.

Sparta continued unfortified throughout the whole period of autonomous Greek history. When Demetrius Poliorketes made an attempt upon Sparta in 296 B.C., some temporary fortifications were thrown up; and the same was done when Pyrrhus attacked the city in 272 B.C. But Sparta was first regularly fortified by a wall and ditch by the tyrant Nabis in 195 B.C., though even this wall did not surround the whole city. We learn from Polybius (IX 21) that the walls were 48 stadia (about 5½ miles) in circumference.

The four pre-Dorian settlements which coalesced with Sparta were Pitane, Limnæ, Mesoa, and Kynosura. They were united by a common sacrifice to Artemis. Pitane was at the ford of the Eurotas, and consequently in the N. part of the city. It was the favourite and fashionable place of residence at Sparta. We are also told that Pitane was near the temple and stronghold of Issorion. Limnæ was situated upon the Eurotas, having derived its name from the marshy ground which once existed there; and as the Dromos occupied a great part of the lower level towards the southern extremity, it is probable that Limnæ occupied the northern. It is probable that Mesoa was in the S.E. part of the city, and Kynosura in the S.W.

In the midst of these separate quarters stood the Acropolis and the Agora, where the Dorian invaders first planted themselves.

The chief building on the Acropolis was the temple of Athena Chalkioikos, the tutelary goddess of the city. It was said to have been begun by Tyndareus, but was long afterwards completed by Gitiadas. He caused the whole building to be covered with plates of bronze or brass, whence the temple was called the Brazen House, and the goddess received the surname of Chalkioikos. On the bronze plates there were represented in relief the labours of Heracles, the exploits of the Dioscuri, Hephæstus releasing his mother from her chains, the Nymphs arming Perseus for his expedition against Medusa, the birth of Athena, and Amphitrite and Poseidon. Gitiadas also made a brazen statue of the goddess. The Brazen House stood in a sacred enclosure, surrounded by a stoa or colonnade, and containing several sanctuaries. There was a separate temple of Athena Ergane. Near the southern stoa was a temple of Zeus Kosmetas, and before it the tomb of Tyndareus; the western stoa contained two eagles, bearing two victories, dedicated by Lysander in commemoration of his victories over the Athenians. To the left of the Brazen House was a temple of the Muses; behind it a temple of Ares Areia, with very ancient wooden statues; and to its right a very ancient statue of Zeus Hypatos, by Learchos of Rhegium, parts of which were fastened together with nails. Near the altar of the Brazen House stood two statues of Pausanias, and also statues of Aphrodite Ambologēra (delaying old age), and of the brothers Sleep and Death.

The Agora was a spacious place, surrounded with

colonnades, from which the streets issued to the different quarters of the city. Here were the public buildings of the magistrates—the council-house of the Gerousia or senate, and the offices of the Ephors, and the various magistrates, the Nomophylaces, and the Bidiæi The most splendid building was the Persian stoa, which had been frequently repaired and enlarged, and was still perfect when Pausanias visited the city. The Agora contained statues of Julius Cæsar and Augustus: in the latter was a brazen statue of the prophet Agias. There was a place called the Chorus, marked off from the rest of the Agora, because the Spartan youths here danced in honour of Apollo at the festival of the Gymnopædia. This place was adorned with statues of the Pythian deities, Apollo, Artemis, and Leto; and near it were temples of Earth, of Zeus Agoraios, of Athena Agoraia, of Apollo, of Poseidon Asphaleios, and of Hera. In the Agora was a colossal statue representing the people of Sparta, and a temple of the Mœræ or Fates, near which was the tomb of Orestes. Near the tomb of Orestes was the statue of King Polydoros, whose effigy was used as the seal of the state. Here, also, was a Hermes Agoræos bearing Dionysus as a child, and the old Ephoreia, where the Ephors originally administered justice, in which were the tombs of Epimenides the Cretan and of Aphareus the Æolian king.

The Agora was near the Acropolis. Lycurgus, it is said, when attacked by his opponents, fled for refuge from the Agora to the Acropolis; but was overtaken by a fiery youth, who struck out one of his eyes. At the spot where he was wounded, Lycurgus founded a temple of Optiletis or Ophthalmitis, which must have stood immediately above the Agora. Plutarch says that it lay within the *temenos* of the Brazen House; and Pausanias mentions it, in descending from the Acropolis, on the way to the so-called Alpion, beyond which was a temple of Ammon, and probably also a temple of Artemis Knagia. The Agora may be placed in the great hollow E. of the Acropolis. Its position is most clearly marked by Pausanias, who, going westwards from the Agora, arrived immediately at the theatre, after passing only the tomb of Brasidas.

The principal street, leading out of the Agora, was named Aphetais. It ran towards the S. wall, through the most level part of the city, and was bordered by a succession of remarkable monuments. First came the house of King Polydoros, named Booneta, because the state purchased it from his widow for some oxen. Next came the office of the Bidiæi, who originally had the inspection of the racecourse; and opposite was the temple of Athena Keleutheia, with a statue of the goddess dedicated by Odysseus. Lower down the Aphetais occurred the *heroa* of Iops, Amphiaraos, and Lelex—the sanctuary of Poseidon Tainarios, a statue of Athena, dedicated by the Tarentini—the place called Hellenion, so called because the Greeks are said to have held counsel there either before the Persian or the Trojan wars, the tomb of Talthybios, an altar of Apollo Akreitas, a statue of Apollo Maleates, and close to the city walls the temple of Dictynna, and the royal sepulchres of the Eurypontidæ. Pausanias then returns to the Hellenion, probably to the other side of the Aphetais, where he mentions a sanctuary of Arsinoë, the sister of the wives of Castor and Pollux; then a temple of Artemis near the so-called Phrouria, which were perhaps the temporary fortifications thrown up before the completion of the city walls; next the tombs of the Iamidæ, the Eleian prophets—sanctuaries of Maro and Alpheios, who fell at Thermopylæ, the temple of Zeus Tropaios, built by the Dorians after conquering the Achæan inhabitants of Laconia, and especially the Amyclæi—the temple of the Mother of the Gods, and the *heroa* of Hippolytus and Aulon. The Aphetais upon quitting the city joined the great Hyacinthian road which led to the Amyclæon, the sanctuary of Apollo.

The next most important street leading from the Agora ran in a south-easterly direction. It is usually called Scias. Near the Scias was a round structure, containing statues of the Olympian Zeus and Aphrodite; next came the tombs of Cynortas, Castor, Idas, and Lynceus, and a temple of Kore Soteira (Persephone). The other buildings along this street or in this direction, if there was no street, were the temple of Apollo Karneios—a statue of Apollo Aphetaios—a quadrangular place surrounded with colonnades, where small-wares were anciently sold—an altar sacred to Zeus, Athena, and the Dioscuri, all surnamed Amboulioi ('Delayers of Death'). Opposite was the place called Colona and the temple of Dionysus Colonatas. Near the Colona was the temple of Zeus Euanemos. On a neighbouring hill was the temple of the Argive Hera, and the temple of Hera Hypercheiria ('of the protecting hand'), containing an ancient wooden statue of Aphrodite Hera.

After describing the streets leading from the Agora to the S. and S.E., Pausanias next mentions a third street, running westward from the Agora. It led past the theatre to the royal sepulchres of the Agiadæ. In front of the theatre were the tombs of Pausanias and Leonidas.

After proceeding to the tomb of Tænaros, and the sanctuaries of Poseidon Hippokurios and the Æginetan Artemis, Pausanias returns to the Lesche, a public debating place, near which was the temple of Artemis Issoria, also called Limnaia. Pausanias next mentions the temples of Thetis, of Demeter Chthonia ('Protectress of the Fields'), of Serapis, and of the Olympian Zeus. He then reached the Dromos, which was used in his day as a place for running. It extended along the stream southwards, and contained gymnasia. The Roman amphitheatre and the stadium were included in the Dromos. In the Dromos was a statue of Heracles, near which, but outside the Dromos, was the house of Menelaus. Proceeding from the Dromos occurred the temples of the Dioscuri, of the Graces, of Eileithyia, of Apollo Karneios, and of Artemis Hegemone; at the beginning of the Dromos there were statues of the Dioscuri Aphetarii; and a little farther the *heroum* of Alcon and the temple of Poseidon Domatites.

South of the Dromos was a broader level, which was called Platanistas, from the plane-trees with which it was thickly planted. It is described as a round island, formed by streams of running water, and was entered by two bridges, on each of which there was a statue of Heracles at one end and of Lycurgus at the other. The *heroum* of Cynisca, the first female who conquered in the chariot-race in the Olympic games, stood close to the Plataniston, which was bordered upon one side by a colonnade. Behind this colonnade there were several heroic monuments, among which were those of Alcimos, Enæphoros, of Dorceus, with the fountain Dorceia, and of Sebros. Near the latter was the sepulchre of the poet Alcman; this was followed by the sanctuary of Helena and that of Heracles, with the monument of Œonos. The temple of Heracles was close to the city walls. Since the poet Alcman, whose tomb was in this district, is described as a citizen of Mesoa, it is probable that this was the position of Mesoa, the name of which might indicate a tract lying between two rivers.

After reaching the S.E. extremity of the city, Pausanias returns to the Dromos. Here he mentions two ways: the one to the right leading to a temple of Athena Axiopoinos ('the Avenger'), and the other to the left to another temple of Athena, founded by Theras, near which was a temple of Hipposthenes, and an ancient wooden statue of Enyalios in fetters. He afterwards returns to the theatre, and mentions the different monuments in its neighbourhood; among which were a temple of Poseidon Genethlios; a temple of Asclepios, near the Booneta; on a height not far distant, an ancient temple of Aphrodite Armed, upon an upper story of which was a second temple of Aphrodite Morpho; in its neighbourhood was a temple of Hilaeira and Phœbe, containing their statues, and an egg suspended from the roof, said to have been that of Leda. Pausanias next mentions a house, named Chiton, in which was woven the robe for the Amyclæan Apollo. Near the Chiton was the house of Phormion, who hospitably entertained the Dioscuri when they entered the city as strangers.

In the N. of the city there are on the right bank of the Eurotas, some 200 yards below the ancient bridge, the remains of a huge altar, possibly the Altar of Lycurgus. Some 750 yards farther down are the remains of the Limnæon or Sanctuary of Artemis Orthia. The Limnæon consisted of a small temple of the second century B.C., erected on the foundations of an earlier temple of the sixth century. The extremity of the temple in the S.E., is framed by a Roman amphitheatre, 177 feet in diameter. The temple of Artemis Orthia was the common place of meeting for the four villages of Pitane. Mesoa, Kynosura, and Limnæ. The ritualistic scourgings and feats of endurance of the Spartan youth took place here, and festivals were held in honour of the goddess. These ceremonies were continued into Roman times, and it was to enable spectators to witness them that the amphitheatre was built.

SYRACUSE

The most powerful and important of all the Greek cities in Sicily, situated on the E. coast of the island, about midway between Catana and Cape Pachynus. With the exception of Naxos, Syracuse was the most ancient of the Greek colonies in Sicily. It was a Corinthian colony and was founded in 734 B.C.

Syracuse was built on a table-land or tabular hill, forming the prolongation of a ridge which branches off from the more elevated table-land of the interior, and projects quite down to the sea, between the bay known as the Great Harbour of Syracuse and the more extensive bay which stretches on the N. as far as the peninsula of Thapsus or Magnisi. The broad end of the kind of promontory thus formed, which abuts upon the sea for a distance of about 2½ miles, may be considered as the base of a triangular plateau which extends for above 4 miles into the interior, having its apex formed by the point now called Mongibellisi, which was occupied by the ancient fort of Euryalus. This communicates by a narrow ridge with the table-land of the interior, but is still a marked point of separation, and was the highest point of the ancient city, from whence the table-land slopes very gradually to the sea. Though of small elevation, this plateau is bounded on all sides by precipitous banks or cliffs, varying in height, but only accessible at a few points. It may be considered as naturally divided into two portions by a slight valley or depression running across it from N. to S., about a mile from the sea: of these the upper or triangular portion was known as Epipolæ, the eastern portion adjoining the sea bore the name of Achradina, which thus forms in some degree a distinct and separate plateau, though belonging, in fact, to the same mass with Epipolæ.

The S.E. angle of the plateau is separated from the Great Harbour by a small tract of low and level ground, opposite to which lies the island of Ortygia, a low islet about a mile in length, extending across the mouth of the Great Harbour, and originally divided by only a narrow strait from the mainland, whilst its southern extremity was separated from the nearest point of the headland of Plemmyrium by an interval of about 1,200 yards, forming the entrance into the Great Harbour. This last was a spacious bay, of above 5 miles in circumference; thus forming a very nearly land-locked basin of a somewhat oval form, which afforded a secure shelter to shipping in all weather. But between the island of Ortygia and the mainland to the N. of it, was a deep bight or inlet, forming what was called the Lesser Port or Portus Laccius, which, though very inferior to the other, was still equal to the ordinary requirements of ancient commerce.

S. of the Great Harbour again rose the peninsular promontory of Plemmyrium, forming a table-land bounded, like that on the N. of the bay, by precipitous escarpments and cliffs, though of no great elevation. This table-land was prolonged by another plateau at a somewhat lower level, bounding the southern side of the Great Harbour, and extending from thence towards the interior. On its N.E. angle and opposite to the heights of Epipolæ, stood the temple of Jupiter Olympius, or the Olympieum, overlooking the low marshy tract which intervenes between the two table-lands, and through which the river Anapus finds its way to the sea. The beautiful stream of the Cyane rises in a source about 1½ mile to the N. of the Olympieum, and joins its waters with those of the Anapus almost immediately below the temple. From the foot of the hill crowned by the latter extends a broad tract of very low marshy ground, extending along the inner side of the Great Harbour to the walls of the city itself. This marshy tract, which is above a mile in breadth, extends towards the interior for a considerable distance, till it is met by the precipitous escarpments of the great table-land of the interior. The proximity of these marshes must always have been prejudicial to the healthiness of the situation. But in every other respect the situation was admirable; and the prosperity of Syracuse was doubtless owing in a great degree to natural as well as political causes. It was, moreover, celebrated for the mildness and serenity of its climate, it being generally asserted that there was no day on which the sun was not visible at Syracuse.

The topographical description of Syracuse as it

existed in the days of its greatness cannot better be introduced than in the words of Cicero. 'You have often heard [says he] that Syracuse is the largest of all Greek cities, and the most beautiful of all cities. And it is so indeed. For it is both strong by its natural situation and striking to behold, from whatever side it is approached, whether by land or sea. It has two ports, as it were, enclosed within the buildings of the city itself, so as to combine with it from every point of view, which have different and separate entrances, but are united and conjoined together at the opposite extremity. The junction of these separates from the mainland the part of the town which is called the Island, but this is reunited to the continent by a bridge across the narrow strait which divides them. So great is the city that it may be said to consist of four cities, all of them of very large size; one of which is that which I have already mentioned, the Island, which is surrounded by the two ports, while it projects towards the mouth and entrance of each of them. In it is the palace of King Hiero, which is now the customary residence of our prætors. It contains, also, several sacred edifices, but two in particular, which far surpass the others, one a temple of Diana, the other of Minerva, which before the arrival of Verres was most highly adorned. At the extremity of this island is a fountain of fresh water, which bears the name of Arethusa, of incredible magnitude, and full of fish; this would be wholly overflowed and covered by the waves were it not separated from the sea by a strongly-built barrier of stone. The second city at Syracuse is that which is called Achradina, which contains a Forum of very large size, beautiful porticoes, a most highly ornamented Prytaneum, a spacious Curia, and a magnificent temple of Jupiter

Olympius; not to speak of the other parts of the city, which are occupied by private buildings, being divided by one broad street through its whole length, and many cross streets. The third city is that which is called Tycha, because it contained a very ancient Temple of Fortune; in this is a very spacious gymnasium, as well as many sacred edifices, and it is the quarter of the town which is the most thickly inhabited. The fourth city is that which, because it was the last built, is named Neapolis: at the top of which is a theatre of vast size; besides this it contains two splendid temples, one of Ceres, the other of Libera, and a statue of Apollo, which is known by the name of Temenites, of great beauty and very large size, which Verres would not have hesitated to carry off if he had been able to remove it' (Cic. *Verr.* IV 52, 53).

Cicero here distinctly describes the four quarters of Syracuse, which were commonly compared to four separate cities. In later times, also, we find Syracuse alluded to as 'the quadruple city'. Others, however, enumerated five quarters, as Strabo tells us that it was formerly composed of five cities, probably because the heights of Epipolæ towards the castle of Euryalus were at one time inhabited, and were reckoned as a fifth town.

1. *Ortygia*, more commonly known simply as 'the Island', was the original seat of the colony, and continued throughout the flourishing period of the city to be as it were the citadel or Acropolis of Syracuse, though, unlike most citadels, it lay lower than the rest of the city, its strength as a fortress being derived from its insular position. It is about a mile in length, by less than half a mile in breadth, and of small elevation, though composed wholly of rock, and rising perceptibly in the centre.

There is no doubt that it was originally an island, naturally separated from the mainland, though in the time of Thucydides it was united with it: probably, however, this was merely effected by an artificial mole or causeway, for the purpose of facilitating the communication with 'the outer city', as that on the mainland was then called. At a later period it was again severed from the land, probably by the elder Dionysius, when he constructed his great docks in the two ports. It was, however, undoubtedly always connected with the mainland by a bridge, or series of bridges, as it is at the present day. The citadel or castle, constructed by Dionysius, stood within the island, but fronting the mainland, and adjoining the docks or *navalia* in the Lesser Port. Its front towards the mainland, which appears to have been fortified, was known as the Pentapyla; and this seems to have looked directly upon the Agora or Forum, which we know to have been situated on the mainland.

Ortygia was considered from an early time as consecrated to Artemis or Diana, whence Pindar terms it 'the couch of Artemis', and 'the sister of Delos'. Hence one of the principal edifices in the island was a temple of Diana. Some remains of this are supposed to be still extant in the N.E. corner of the modern city, where two columns, with a portion of their architrave, of the Doric order, are built into the walls of a private house. Much more considerable remains are extant of the temple of Minerva. This was one of the most magnificent in Sicily. Its doors, composed of gold and ivory, and conspicuous for their beautiful workmanship, were celebrated throughout the Grecian world: while the interior was adorned with numerous paintings, among which a series representing one of the battles of Agathocles was especially celebrated. No other ancient remains are now extant in the island of Ortygia; but the celebrated fountain of Arethusa is still visible, as described by Cicero, near the southern extremity of the island, on its western shore.

At the extreme point of the island, and outside the ancient walls, was situated a temple of the Olympian Juno. Of the other edifices in the island the most remarkable were the Hexecontaclinus, built, or at least finished, by Agathocles; the public granaries, a building of so massive and lofty a construction as to serve the purposes of a fortress, and the palace of King Hiero. No trace now remains of the ancient walls or works on this side of the island, which have been wholly covered and concealed by the modern fortifications. The remains of a tower are, however, visible on a shoal or rock near the N. angle of the modern city, which are probably those of one of the towers built by Agathocles to guard the entrance of the Lesser Harbour, or Portus Laccius.

2. *Achradina*, or 'the outer city', as it is termed by Thucydides, was the most important and extensive of the quarters of Syracuse. It consisted of two portions, comprising the eastern part of the great triangular plateau, which extended from the angle of Epipolæ to the sea, as well as the lower and more level space which extends from the foot of this table-land to the Great Harbour, and borders on the marshes of Lysimeleia. This level plain, which is immediately opposite to the island of Ortygia, has a rocky soil, of the same limestone with the table-land above, of which it is as it were a lower step. Hence the city, as soon as it extended itself beyond the limits of the island, spread at once over this

area; but not content with this, the inhabitants occupied the part of the table-land above it nearest the sea, which is partly separated by a cross valley or depression from the upper part of the plateau, or the heights of Epipolæ. Hence this part of the city was of considerable natural strength, and seems to have been early fortified by a wall.

Of the buildings noticed by Cicero as still adorning Achradina in his day there are scarcely any vestiges; but the greater part of them were certainly situated in the lower quarter, nearest to the island and the two ports. The Forum or Agora was apparently directly opposite to the Pentapyla or fortified entrance of the island; it was surrounded with porticoes by the elder Dionysius. The Temple of Jupiter Olympius also adjoined the Agora. The Prytaneum, which was most richly adorned, and among its chief ornaments possessed a celebrated statue of Sappho, was probably also situated in the neighbourhood of the Agora; as was certainly the Timoleonteum, or monument erected to the memory of Timoleon. The splendid sepulchral monument which had been erected by the younger Dionysius in memory of his father, but was destroyed after his own expulsion, seems to have stood in front of the Pentapyla, opposite the entrance of the citadel. The only other ruins now visible in this quarter of the city are some remains of Roman baths of little importance. But beneath the surface of the soil there exist extensive catacombs, constituting a complete necropolis. There exist, also, at two points on the slope of the hill of Achradina, extensive quarries hewn in the rocks.

Traces of the ancient walls of Achradina, crowning the low cliffs which bound it towards the sea, may be found from distance to distance along the whole line extending from the quarries of the Cappuccini round to the little bay or cove of Sta Panagia at the N.W. angle of the plateau.

3. *Tycha,* so called, as we are told by Cicero, from its containing an ancient and celebrated Temple of Fortune, was situated on the plateau or table-land W. of Achradina, and adjoining the northern face of the cliffs looking towards Megara. Tycha probably grew up after the great wall erected by Dionysius along the northern edge of the plateau had completely secured it from attack. Its position is clearly shown by the statement of Livy, that Marcellus, after he had forced the Hexapylum and scaled the heights, established his camp *between* Tycha and Neapolis, with the view of carrying on his assaults upon Achradina. It is evident therefore that the two quarters were not continuous, but that a considerable extent of the table-land W. of Achradina was still unoccupied.

4. *Neapolis,* or the New City, was, as its name implied, the last quarter of Syracuse which was inhabited, though the New Town seems to have eventually grown up into one of the most splendid portions of the city. In the time of Cicero, Neapolis had spread itself over the whole of the southern slope of the table-land, which here forms a kind of second step or underfall, rising above the low grounds beneath, though still separated from the heights of Temenitis by a second line of cliff or abrupt declivity. The name of Temenitis for the district on the height seems to have been lost, or merged in that of Neapolis, which was gradually applied to the whole of this quarter of the city. But the name was retained by the adjoining gate, which was called the Temenitid Gate, and seems

to have been one of the principal entrances to the city.

Of the buildings described by Cicero as existing in Neapolis, the only one still extant is the theatre, which he justly extols for its large size. It is not less than 440 feet in diameter, and appears to have had 60 rows of seats, so that it could have accommodated no less than 24,000 persons.

Near the theatre have been discovered the remains of another monument, an altar raised on steps and a platform not less than 640 feet in length by 60 in breadth. A little lower down are the remains of an amphitheatre, a structure which undoubtedly belongs to the Roman colony. No traces have been discovered of the temples of Ceres and Libera or Proserpine on the height above.

5. *Epipolæ* was the name originally given to the upper part of the table-land which slopes gradually from its highest point towards the sea. Its form is that of a tolerably regular triangle, having its vertex at Euryalus, and its base formed by the western wall of Achradina. The name is always used by Thucydides in this sense, as including the whole upper part of the plateau, and was doubtless so employed as long as the space was uninhabited; but as the suburbs of Tycha and Temenitis gradually spread themselves over a considerable part of the heights, the name of Epipolæ came to be applied in a more restricted sense to that portion only which was nearest to the vertex of the triangle. No ancient buildings remain within the walls; but the line of these may be distinctly traced along the top of the cliffs which bound the table-land both towards the N. and the S.; in many places two or three courses of the masonry remain; but the most

important ruins are those at the angle or vertex of the triangle, where a spot now named Mongibellisi is still crowned by the ruins of the ancient castle or fort of Euryalus. The ruins in question afford one of the best examples extant of an ancient fortress or castle, designed at once to serve as a species of citadel and to secure the approach to Epipolæ from this quarter.

The main entrance to the city was by a double gate, flanked on both sides by walls and towers, with a smaller postern or sally-port a little to the right of it. The fortress itself was an irregular quadrangle, projecting about 200 yards beyond the approach to the gate, and fortified by strong towers of solid masonry with a deep ditch cut in the rock in front of it, to which a number of subterraneous passages gave access from within. These passages, communicating with the fort above by narrow openings and stairs, were evidently designed to facilitate the sallies of the besieged without exposing the fortress itself to peril.

THEBES

Thebes (Greek, Thebai), the chief city in Bœotia, was situated in the southern plain of the country, which is divided from the northern by the ridge of Onchestos. According to the generally received tradition, Thebes was founded by Cadmus, the leader of a Phœnician colony, who called the city Cadmeia, a name which was later confined to the citadel. It was governed in legendary times by the Labdacidæ and became, 60 years after the fall of Troy, the capital of Bœotia. Certainly, in the seventh century, Thebes was the head of the Bœotian Federation, and in active rivalry with Orchomenos. In the Persian wars, Thebes was allied with Persia out of hatred for Athens, and shared in the defeat of Platæa (479). Later the Athenians were defeated by the Thebans at Coroneia (447). The Theban supremacy in Greece followed the battle of Leuctra (371) in which Epaminondas defeated the Spartans, ending the Spartan hegemony, but the power of Thebes did not long survive the death of Epaminondas (362).

Thebes stood on one of the hills of Mt. Teumessos, which divides S. Bœotia into two distinct parts, the northern being the plain of Thebes and the southern the valley of the Asopos. As Bœotia lies between two seas, the founders of Thebes chose a spot in the centre of the country, where water was very plentiful, and where the nature of the ground was admirably adapted for defence. The hill upon which the town stands rises about 150 feet above the plain, and lies about 2 miles northward of the highest part of the ridge. It is bounded on the E.

and W. by two small rivers, distant from each other about 6 or 7 stadia (nearly 1 mile), which run in such deep ravines as to form a natural defence on either side of the city. These rivers, which rise a little S. of the city, and flow northward into the plain of Thebes, are the celebrated streams of Ismenos and Dirce. Between them flows a smaller stream, called Strophia, which divided the city into two parts, the western division containing the Cadmeia and the southern the hill Ismenion and the Ampheion. Both the Ismenios and Dirce, though so celebrated in antiquity, are nothing but torrents, which are only full of water in the winter after heavy rains. The Ismenos is the eastern and the Dirce the western stream. Though the position of Thebes and of its celebrated streams is certain, almost every point connected with its topography is more or less doubtful.

The most interesting point in Theban topography is the position of the celebrated seven Theban gates. They are alluded to by Homer (*Od.* XI 263) and Hesiod (*Op.* 161); and their names are given by seven different authors. The position of three of the gates can be fixed from the description of Pausanias alone (Paus. IX *passim*). These are the Electræ, Prœtides, and Neitæ. From Pausanias it is evident that the Gate Electræ was in the S. of the city, between the hill Ismenion and the Cadmeia. The Gate Prœtides was on the N.E. side of the city, since it led to Chalcis. The Gate Neitæ was on the N.W. side of the city, since it led to Onchestos and Delphi. The names of these three gates are the same in five of the seven writers. Of the other four gates, the Homoloides is also the same. Of these four gates, taken in the order of Æschylus, the fourth gate was probably situated on the W. side of the city, and was called Crenææ, because it was near one of the fountains of Dirce, now called *Paraporti*. Near the fountain was a hill, called by the Greeks *Onkos*, whence Athena derived the name Onka. Nonnus, who calls this gate Onkæa, describes it as situated towards the W.

The fifth gate was called Ogygian, from Ogyges, the most ancient king of Thebes, in whose time the deluge is said to have taken place. There is no part of Thebes so exposed to inundation as the N. of the city, where the torrent Strophia descends into the plain. Here we may probably place the Ogygian gate, which Æschylus called the Northern, from its position.

The exact position of the sixth gate, called Homoloides, and of the seventh, designated by its number in Æschylus and Euripides, but by the name of Hypsistæ in the other writers, is doubtful.

The city was divided into two parts by the torrent Strophia; the western half between the Strophia and the Dirce was the Cadmeia, while the eastern half between the Strophia and the Ismenos was the lower city said to have been added by Amphion and Zethos. The Cadmeia is again divided by a slight depression near the fountain of Dirce and the Crenæan gate into two hills, of which the larger and the higher one to the S. was the acropolis proper, while the northern hill formed the agora of the acropolis. The eastern half of the city was also divided between the Strophia and the Ismenos into two parts, of which the southern consisted of the hill Ismenion, and the northern of several minor eminences, known under the general name of Ampheion. Æschylus describes the tomb of Amphion as standing near the northern gate.

Hence Thebes consisted of four parts, two belonging to the acropolis, and two to the lower city, the former being the acropolis proper and the agora of the acropolis, and the latter being the hill Ismenion and the Ampheion.

About one-third of a mile from the Gate Prœtides where the road to Chalcis crosses the Ismenos, is the present fountain of Saint Theodore, identified with the ancient Œdipodeia where Œdipus purified himself.

Pausanias, leaving Potniæ, entered Thebes on the S. by the Gate Electræ, before which he noticed the Polyandrion, or tomb of the Thebans who fell fighting against Alexander. Upon entering the city through the Gate Electræ, he noticed the hill Ismenion, sacred to Apollo, named from the river Ismenos flowing by it. Upon the hill was a temple of Apollo, containing several monuments enumerated by Pausanias. Above the Ismenion, Pausanias noticed the fountain of the Ismenos, sacred to Ares, and guarded by a dragon.

Next Pausanias, beginning again from the Gate Electræ, turns to the left and enters the Cadmeia. He does not mention the acropolis by name, but it is evident from the list of the monuments which he gives that he was in the Cadmeia. He enumerates the house of Amphitryon, containing the bed-chamber of Alcmena, said to have been the work of Trophonios and Agamedes; a monument of the children of Heracles by Megara; the stone called Sophronister; the temple of Heracles; and, near it, a gymnasium and stadium, both bearing the name of this god; and above the Sophronister an altar of Apollo Spodios.

Pausanias next came to the depression between the acropolis and the agora of the Cadmeia where he noticed an altar and statue of Athena, bearing the Phœnician surname of Onga, or Onka, according to other authorities, and said to have been dedicated by Cadmus.

In the agora of the Cadmeia the house of Cadmus is said to have stood; and in this place were shown ruins of the bedchamber of Harmonia and Semele; statues of Dionysus, of Pronomos, the celebrated musician, and of Epaminondas; a temple of Ammon; the place where Teiresias observed the flight of birds; a temple of Fortune; three wooden statues of Aphrodite, with the surnames of Urania, Pandemos, and Apostrophia; and a temple of Demeter Thesmophoros.

Crossing the torrent Strophia, Pausanias saw near the Gate Prœtides the theatre with the temple of Dionysus. In this part of the city, the following monuments are mentioned by Pausanias: ruins of the house of Lycos and a monument of Semele; monuments of the children of Amphion; a temple of Artemis Eukleia, and, near it, statues of Apollo Boëdromios and of Hermes Agoraios; the funeral pile of the children of Amphion, distant half a stadium from their tombs; two statues of Athena Zosteria; and the monument of Zethos and Amphion, being a mound of earth.

THERMOPYLÆ (or simply PYLÆ)

That is, the *Hot Gates* or the *Gates*, a celebrated narrow pass, leading from Thessaly into Locris, and the only road by which an enemy can penetrate from northern into southern Greece. It lay between Mt. Œta and an inaccessible morass, forming the edge of the Maliac gulf. In the time of Herodotus the river Spercheios flowed into the sea in an easterly direction at the town of Anticyra, considerably W. of the pass. Twenty stadia (2¼ miles) E. of the Spercheios was another river, called Dyras, and again, 20 stadia farther, a third river, named Melas, 5 stadia from which was the city Trachis. Between the mountains where Trachis stood and the sea the plain is widest. Still farther E. was the Asopos, issuing from a rocky gorge, and E. again was a small stream, named Phœnix, flowing into the Asopos. From the Phœnix to Thermopylæ the distance, Herodotus says, is 15 stadia (1¾ miles). Near the united streams of the Phœnix and the Asopos, Mt. Œta approached so close to the morass of the gulf as to leave space for only a single carriage. In the immediate vicinity of the pass was the town of Anthela, celebrated for the temples of Amphictyon and of the Amphictyonic Demeter, containing seats for the members of the Amphictyonic council, who held here their autumnal meetings. At Anthela Mt. Œta recedes a little from the sea, leaving a plain a little more than half a mile in breadth, but again contracts near Alpenœ, the first town of the Locrians, where the space is again only sufficient for a single carriage. At this pass were some hot springs, which were consecrated to Heracles, and were called by the natives *Chytroi* or the Pans, on account of the cells here prepared for the bathers. Across this pass the Phocians had in ancient times built a wall to defend their country against the attacks of the Thessalians, and had let loose the hot waters, so as to render the pass impracticable (Herod. VII 20, 176). It appears that the proper Thermopylæ was the narrow pass near the Locrian town of Alpenœ; but the name was also applied in general to the whole passage from the mouth of the Asopos to Alpenœ. Taking the term in this acceptation, Thermopylæ consisted of the two narrow openings, with a plain between them rather more than a mile in length and about half a mile in breadth. Issuing from the pass are foundations of a Hellenic wall, doubtless the remains of fortifications; and to the left is a tumulus and the foundations of a circular monument. Upwards of a mile farther is a deep ravine, in which the torrents descending from Mt. Callidromon, are collected into one bed, and which affords the easiest and most direct passage to the summit of the mountain. This is probably the mountain path by which the Persians, under Hydarnes, descended in the rear of Leonidas. This path, as well as the mountain over which it leads, is called Anopæa by Herodotus, who does not use the name of Callidromon. He describes the path as beginning at the gorge of the Asopos, passing over the crest of the mountain, and terminating near Alpenœ and the rock called Melampygos, and the seats of the Cercopes, where the road is narrowest. The history of the defence of Thermopylæ by Leonidas (480 B.C.) is too well known to require to be related here. The wall of the Phocians, which Leonidas repaired, was probably built a little eastward of the hot springs. When the Spartan king learnt that Hydarnes was descending in his rear, he advanced beyond the wall into the widest part of the pass, resolved to sell his life as dearly as possible. Upon the arrival of Hydarnes, the Greeks retired behind the wall, and took up their position upon a hill in the pass, where a stone lion was afterwards erected in honour of Leonidas.

INDEX

TO THE

CLASSICAL ATLAS

INDEX

TO THE

CLASSICAL ATLAS

EVERYMAN'S LIBRARY

By ERNEST RHYS

VICTOR HUGO said a Library was 'an act of faith,' and another writer spoke of one so beautiful, so perfect, so harmonious in all its parts, that he who made it was smitten with a passion. In that faith Everyman's Library was planned out originally on a large scale; and the idea was to make it conform as far as possible to a perfect scheme. However, perfection is a thing to be aimed at and not to be achieved in this difficult world; and since the first volumes appeared there have been many interruptions, chief among them Wars, during which even the City of Books feels the great commotion. But the series always gets back into its old stride.

One of the practical expedients in the original plan was to divide the volumes into separate sections, as Biography, Fiction, History, Belles-lettres, Poetry, Philosophy, Romance, and so forth; with a shelf for Young People. The largest slice of this huge provision of nearly a thousand volumes is, as a matter of course, given to the tyrranous demands of fiction. But in carrying out the scheme, publishers and editors contrived to keep in mind that books, like men and women, have their elective affinities. The present volume, for instance, will be found to have its companion books, both in the same class and not less significantly in other sections. With that idea too, novels like Walter Scott's *Ivanhoe* and *Fortunes of Nigel*, Lytton's *Harold*, and Dickens's *Tale of Two Cities*, have been used as pioneers of history and treated as a sort of holiday history books. For in our day history is tending to grow more documentary and less literary; and 'the historian who is a stylist,' as one of our contributors, the late Thomas Seccombe, said, 'will soon be regarded as a kind of Phoenix.'

As for history, Everyman's Library has been eclectic enough to choose its historians from every school in turn, including Gibbon, Grote, Finlay, Macaulay, Motley, and Prescott, while among earlier books may be found the Venerable Bede and the Anglo-Saxon Chronicle. On the classic shelf too, there is a Livy in an admirable translation by Canon Roberts, and Caesar, Tacitus, Thucydides, and Herodotus are not forgotten.

'You only, O Books,' said Richard de Bury, 'are liberal and independent; you give to all who ask.' The variety of authors old and new, the wisdom and the wit at the disposal of Everyman in his own Library, may even, at times, seem all but embarrassing. In the Essays, for instance, he may turn to Dick Steele in *The Spectator* and learn how Cleomira dances, when the elegance of her motion is unimaginable and 'her eyes are chastised with the simplicity and innocence of her thoughts.' Or he may take *A Century of Essays*, as a key to a whole roomful of the English Essayists, from Bacon to Addison, Elia to Augustine Birrell. These are the golden gossips of literature, the writers who learnt the delightful art of talking on paper. Or again, the reader who has the right spirit and looks on all literature as a great adventure may dive back into the classics, and in Plato's *Phaedrus* read how every soul is divided into three parts (like Caesar's Gaul). The poets next, and he may turn to the finest critic of Victorian times, Matthew Arnold, as their showman and find in his essay on Maurice de Guerin a clue to the 'magical power of poetry,' as in Shakespeare, with his

> daffodils
> That come before the swallow dares, and take
> The winds of March with beauty.

Hazlitt's *Table Talk* may help us again to discover the relationship of author to author, which is another form of the Friendship of Books. His incomparable essay, 'On Going a Journey,' is a capital prelude to Coleridge's *Biographia Literaria*; and so throughout the long labyrinth of the Library shelves one can follow the magic clue in prose or verse that leads to the hidden treasury. In that way a reader becomes his own critic and Doctor of Letters, and may turn to the Byron review in Macaulay's *Essays* as a prelude to the three volumes of Byron's own poems, remembering that the poet whom Europe loved more than England did was, as Macaulay said, 'the beginning, the middle and the end of all his own poetry.' This brings us to the provoking reflection that it is the obvious authors and the books most easy to reprint which have been the signal successes out of the many hundreds in the series, for Everyman is distinctly proverbial in his tastes. He likes best of all an old author who has worn well or a comparatively new author who has gained something like newspaper notoriety. In attempting to lead him on from the good books that are known to those that are less known, the publishers may have at times been even too adventurous. But the elect reader is or ought to be a party to this conspiracy of books and bookmen. He can make it possible, by his help and his co-operative zest, to add still more authors, old and new. 'Infinite riches in a little room,' as the saying is, will be the reward of every citizen who helps year by year to build the City of Books. With such a belief in its possibilities the old Chief (J. M. Dent)

threw himself into the enterprise. With the zeal of a tru
book-lover, he thought that books might be alive and pro
ductive as dragons' teeth, which, being 'sown up and down
the land, might chance to spring up armed men.' That is a
great idea, and it means a fighting campaign in which every
new reader who buys a volume, counts as a recruit.

> To him all books which lay
> Their sure foundation in the heart of man . . .
> From Homer the great Thunderer, to the voice
> That roars along the bed of Jewish song . . .
> Shall speak as Powers for ever to be hallowed!